Charles Kerry

A History of the Municipal Church of St. Lawrence, Reading

Charles Kerry

A History of the Municipal Church of St. Lawrence, Reading

ISBN/EAN: 9783337004118

Printed in Europe, USA, Canada, Australia, Japan

Cover: Foto ©ninafisch / pixelio.de

More available books at **www.hansebooks.com**

Municipal Church

OF

St. Lawrence,

Reading.

Ballantyne Press
BALLANTYNE, HANSON AND CO., EDINBURGH
CHANDOS STREET, LONDON

THE CHURCH.

A

History

OF THE

Municipal Church

OF

ST. LAWRENCE,

Reading.

BY

Rev. Charles Kerry,

Curate.

PUBLISHED BY THE AUTHOR,

FORBURY ROAD, READING, AND LITTLE EATON, DERBY.

1883.

TO THE

WORSHIPFUL THE MAYOR

AND THE

ALDERMEN AND BURGESSES OF READING,

THIS ACCOUNT OF THEIR

ANCIENT MUNICIPAL CHURCH

is Respectfully Dedicated

BY THEIR OBEDIENT SERVANT

The Author.

Preface.

The archives of St. Lawrence's Church, in Reading, are amongst the oldest and most interesting in England. They commence in 1410, and are tolerably complete down to the present time.

The earlier details are so graphic, that they afford not only a wonderful insight into the history and changes of the fabric, the exquisite nature of its furniture and decorations—so valuable to the ecclesiologist and art student—but also illustrate to a great extent the parochial life of the fifteenth and following centuries.

It is quite beyond the Author's means to publish the documents *in extenso*, but he has endeavoured to illustrate, by hundreds of literal extracts, the various points of interest connected with the Church, and the manners and customs of the people; so that the present work will be found to contain all that is really interesting in the records, not only to the antiquary, but to the general reader.

In many respects this work may be considered a typical history of every parish church in England—everywhere the ancient centre of parochial life; and it is on this account chiefly that the Author has felt justified and encouraged in his responsible undertaking.

The writer desires to express his warmest thanks to the
Vicar and Churchwardens for the loan of Church documents; to J. Challenor Smith, Esq., of the Probate Registry,
for his courtesy and assistance during his researches at
Somerset House ; to Arthur Billing, Esq., for the interesting description of the mural paintings discovered by him
in the chancels in 1848 ; and to his valued friend, Llewellyn
Jewett, Esq., F.S.A., &c., the editor of the " Reliquary,"
for the pictorial illustrations of the tumbrel.

CHARLES KERRY.

June 24, 1883.

CORRIGENDA ET ADDENDA.

p. 5, line 18, *for* "have," *read* "has."

,, 13. ,, 25, *for* "springing," *read* "springings."

,, 28, ,, 20, under 1638, *add*—

"A canopy was erected over the altar this year, at a cost of 4*l.* 16*s.* 6*d.* It is not probable that this survived the visit of the Earl of Essex's lambs in 1643."

,, 61, ,, 7, *for* "291 lbs.," *read* "261 lbs."

,, 99, ,, 19, *for* "ied." *read* "vied."

,, 157, ,, 30, *for* "Xading," *read* "Xading."

,, 158, ,, 11, *for* "Xeding," *read* "Xeding."

,, 221, ,, 28, *for* "PHANNEL," *read* "PHANUEL."

,, 232, ,, 11, *should be*

"Honey and fish with *us* he ate."

,, 232, ,, 39, *for* "bleds and," *read* "bledsand," *i.e.,* bloody or bleeding.

logical Society for 1881-2, p. 45, writes: "Some relics of an early date were found in the Plummery Ditch (on the *north side* of this headland). They consist of bones of a large ox or bison, and osseous remains of an ox domesticated by the Romans. Bones also of a horse, dog, and a *fragment of a human skull, and pottery of a rude character,* and some pieces of glass form part of the collection." (Now in the Reading Museum.) These remains prove incontestably that the *eastern extremity* of the headland was occupied by prehistoric races, ages before the Roman

The writer desires to express his warmest thanks to the Vicar and Churchwardens for the loan of Church documents; to J. Challenor Smith, Esq., of the Probate Registry, for his courtesy and assistance during his researches at Somerset House ; to Arthur Billing, Esq., for the interesting description of the mural paintings discovered by him

Early History.

THE Parish of Saint Lawrence, Reading, occupies the angle formed by the Thames and the Kennett. The gravel bank on which the older portion of the town is built, here terminates abruptly in a narrow headland, protected originally on the north and east by marshy swamps and deep water-courses, and on the south by the Kennett.

A spot so well defended would naturally commend itself to an aboriginal people ; and here, if anywhere, we might expect to find indications of a primitive occupation ; but the surface of the hill has been so much disturbed in mediæval and modern times, that research in this direction would not produce much satisfactory evidence. There can be no doubt, however, that the numerous remains found in the Kennett in the vicinity of the new bridge at the Reading Gasworks in 1881, many of which consisted of prehistoric implements formed of the bones of animals, were swept down there from the margin of the headland by the force of the river floods, and so must be regarded with special interest as illustrating the very early occupation of this elevation many ages before any portion of modern Reading came into being. Dr. Stevens, in his account of these discoveries in the Transactions of the Berks Archæological Society for 1881-2, p. 45, writes : " Some relics of an early date were found in the Plummery Ditch (on the *north side* of this headland). They consist of bones of a large ox or bison, and osseous remains of an ox domesticated by the Romans. Bones also of a horse, dog, and a *fragment of a human skull, and pottery of a rude character,* and some pieces of glass form part of the collection." (Now in the Reading Museum.) These remains prove incontestably that the *eastern extremity* of the headland was occupied by prehistoric races, ages before the Roman

B

invasion; that it was inhabited during the Roman-British period, and, subsequently, in Anglo-Saxon times. A portion of this high ground, now a public garden, is termed the "Forbury;" a name obviously derived from the A.S. "Forburh," a vestibule : that is, a portion of ground *before*, or in front of the "*burg*," or "*bury*." A vestibule is a court or porch *through which* a building or habitation is *approached*. The early Saxon burgh, then, must have been seated at the *eastern* extremity of the headland, because the Forbury could never have formed a vestibule to the present town on its western side, since there never was any approach to it through that quarter.

The way to the Saxon bury was *through* the Forbury, and hence the name. The position of the once circular Danish intrenchment in the Forbury, now completely effaced, is very significant as to the locality of the original Saxon Burgh. It was formed just where such an earthwork, under a good military leader, would have been placed so as to command the Burgh on the promontory if intact, or to prevent its reoccupation if destroyed. Had the Saxon vill been on the *western* side of the Forbury, no invader would have intrenched himself in a position like this, where his chance of escape would have been cut away by any formidable descent from the town-quarter.

About half of the fosse was remaining until the formation of the Forbury Gardens, about the year 1858. The extremities of the arc extended from the western half of the Abbey gateway to a point opposite the old bay-windowed house used by the Messrs. Fuller and May. According to Mr. Coates' Map, dated 1802, the arc was as nearly a semicircle as possible ; the line of the *front* of the buildings from the Assize Courts to the old house before mentioned, forming the chord of the segment. This ditch or fosse was in some parts at least six or seven feet in depth, and about four or five yards in width. The southern half was obviously filled in at the construction of the Abbey gateway, and other original buildings to the west of it. When intact, the intrenchment was at least ninety yards in diameter.

The history of this Danish incursion is thus given by Roger de Hoveden (*temp.* Hen. II.) :—" Anno 871. The Danes, marching into Wessex, came to Reading, situated on the south side of the river Thames, in the county of Berks. On the third day after their arrival, two of their leaders, with a part of their army, went on a foraging party, the remainder, in the meantime, being employed in throwing up an intrenchment between the Thames and the Kennett on the right side of the town of Reading. These (the foragers) were met by Ethelwulf, Earl of Berks, at a place called Englefield, that is, 'The Field of the English.' Here both parties fought with the utmost animosity, till one of the Danish generals being killed, and their army being either routed or destroyed, the Saxons obtained a complete victory. Four days after this battle, King Ethelred and his brother Elfred having collected their forces, marched to Reading, killing and destroying all before them as far as the gates of the fortification ('arcis'). At length the Danes, sallying out from all the gates (ports), attacked the victorious army, when after a long and bloody battle the Danes obtained the victory."

It is probable that the mound in the Forbury, close by this old earthwork, was originally a "tumulus," though it may have been modified in later times : if not of prehistoric origin, it may cover the remains of the slaughtered Danes interred after the struggle *on this spot* in the year 871, when they overcame the Saxons, flushed with victory on their return from Englefield. By this defeat, the Danes became masters of the field, and nothing can be conceived more natural than that they should bury their dead after their wonted manner. They died the death of heroes, and as such it was fitting the high mound should be raised over them. Curiously enough, this mound is on the verge of the Saxon cemetery, though this is not of uncommon occurrence : thus there is a fine barrow in the old churchyard at Taplow, Bucks ; and there are tumuli contiguous to the churchyards at Morley, Derbyshire, and Puttenham, co. Surrey. The old church was undoubtedly of no great antiquity at the time of its removal by Henry I., for the burg then clustering round it had been burnt by the Danes only 115 years before, and the original Saxon sanctuary (probably a humble structure of wood) undoubtedly perished in that conflagration.

If Leland and Camden had only adhered to the words of the original historian of this transaction, it would have prevented much misconception in later times with regard to the early topography of the town. There was no castle in Reading, properly so called, before the time of King Stephen, and this was destroyed about two or three years after its erection by King Henry II. It would appear from the valuable evidence mentioned by Coates, p. 145, to have stood on the site of the old gaol in Castle Street ; but this evidence, so weighty, he seems inclined to set aside.

Site of the Original Church.

In Anglo-Saxon times, parish churches and parish church-yards were inseparable ; and this arose from the almost natural desire of Christians to be interred, if not within, at least as near the walls of their sanctuaries as possible. This privilege of interment within the towns and cities of England was procured by St. Cuthbert, Abp. of Canterbury, who died A.D. 758 (Weever, Fun¹. Mon¹ˢ., p. 8). From this time, therefore, it may be affirmed that there was no parish church in this country without its adjacent cemetery, and no Christian graveyard without its church.

The original burial-ground of St. Lawrence's parish before A.D. 1557, lay on the north side of the Abbey, as appears from an entry of that date in the churchwardens' accounts, and far away from the present parish church. As this arrangement was a deviation from the universal custom, there must have been some special cause.

The Abbey Church, to which the *parish* burial-ground was contiguous, was *never* the parish church, and as the parishioners from the remotest times had no other place for general interment, we must look back to a period *anterior* to the foundation of the Abbey for the solution of the difficulty. It must be this :—

That the old parish church of St. Lawrence, before the foundation of the Abbey, stood *within* or *near* this ancient *parish* cemetery—stood, in fact, in the heart of the old Saxon Burgh ; for the situation of these early graveyards was regulated entirely by the position of the church, and not *vice versâ*. One thing is very certain, that if the parishioners of St. Lawrence had not possessed the right of interment there *before* the foundation of the Abbey by Henry I., they would not so easily have obtained that right afterwards, because the precincts of the Abbey were extra-parochial.

The old parish church was without doubt demolished by Henry I. in A.D. 1121, to make room for the magnificent church of his new monastic foundation, most probably built on its site. The old Saxon church would be used in common by the inhabitants of the Burgh, and the members of the Convent of Leveva. In the adjoining churchyard then, situated as it was near the centre of the Saxon Burgh, lie the remains of the first Christian population of Reading, and, it may be, of the prehistoric population too ; for the sites of heathen temples were frequently selected for the erection of Christian churches, and the bodies of the faithful were deposited near the ashes of their pagan ancestors. (The churchyard of Ribchester, co. Lancaster, occupies the site of a Roman Temple dedicated to Minerva.)

It is not improbable that the Saxon church was dedicated to St. Matthew, because of the fair formerly held in the Forbury on St. Matthew's Day. Many of our old fairs have grown out of the dedication festivals of the churches where they are held, and are even now frequently coincident with these commemorations.

The Saxon vill, with its humble church and convent, have long since passed away, and the stately monastic foundation which supplanted them is now a crumbling ruin—a perishing fragment of its former grandeur ; whilst the parish church of St. Lawrence, the single representative of these ancient associations, and the hereditary successor of the church of the Saxon Burg, still survives. That she may long continue to inherit the venerable prestige which time has conferred upon her, is the earnest hope of one whose chiefest privilege is to minister within her walls.

Domesday Survey.

The earliest survey of Reading is in Domesday Book, completed A.D. 1086.

The account is divided into three distinct portions :—

1. The survey of the Hundred of Reading.
2. The survey of the Burgh or Bury ; and
3. The survey of the Church and its lands.

In the absence of direct evidence, it seems probable that the Hundred of Reading was co-extensive with the parishes of St. Lawrence, St. Mary, and St. Giles.

The Hundred.

(TRANSLATION.)

"THE KING HOLDS READING IN DEMESNE. KING EDWARD (THE CONFESSOR) HELD IT. IN READING HUNDRED. THEN, AND NOW, IT DEFENDS ITSELF FOR FORTY-THREE HIDES. THE ARABLE LAND IS FORTY CARUCATES. ONE IS IN DEMESNE. FIFTY-FIVE VILLEINS, AND THIRTY BORDARS, WITH FIFTY-FIVE PLOUGHS. THERE ARE FOUR MILLS OF EIGHTY-FIVE SHILLINGS, AND THREE FISHERIES OF FOURTEEN SHILLINGS AND SIXPENCE, AND A HUNDRED AND FIFTY-FIVE ACRES OF MEADOW. THE WOODS ARE SUFFICIENT FOR ONE HUNDRED PIGS. OF PASTURE, TO THE VALUE OF SIXTEEN SHILL. AND SIX PENCE. IN THE TIME OF KING EDWARD AND AFTERWARDS, IT WAS WORTH FORTY POUNDS, NOW FORTY-EIGHT POUNDS."

The Bury or Burgh.

"THE KING HAS IN THE BURY ("*habet in Burgo*") OF READING, TWENTY-EIGHT HOUSES ("*hagas*," or *homesteads*), PAYING FOUR POUNDS FOUR SHILL. FOR ALL CUSTOMS. NEVERTHELESS, HE WHO NOW HOLDS IT PAYS A HUNDRED SHILL. HENRY DE FERRARS HAS A HOUSE THERE, AND HALF A VIRGATE (*twelve acres and a half*) OF LAND, IN WHICH ARE FOUR ACRES OF MEADOW WORTH SIX SHILL. GODRIC THE SHERIFF HELD THIS

LAND FOR THE PURPOSE OF HARBOURAGE ("*ad hospicium*"). HENRY NOW HOLDS THE SAME. REINBALD, THE SON OF PETER THE BISHOP, HELD ONE HOUSE THERE, WHICH HE HAS ANNEXED TO HIS MANOR OF EARLEY. IT IS NOW IN THE HANDS OF THE KING, AND IS WORTH SIXTEEN SHILL. PER ANNUM."

Here we have a picture of Saxon Reading. There were only thirty homesteads within the Burgh, two of which were clearly of the better class. It was then a mere hamlet of wooden houses of one story, and covered with straw and reeds. The next item is very interesting :—

"Henry de Ferrars holds a homestead and twelve and a half acres in the Burgh, in which are four acres of meadow of the value of six shillings. Godric the sheriff held this land *for harbourage*. This expression, '*ad hospitium*,' is very remarkable, and in the absence of direct evidence, I am much disposed to believe that it was the plot of ground now called the 'Forbury,' which was not then so circumscribed on its western and southern sides as at present; and the hospitality or harbourage was the accommodation it afforded for the encampment of the itinerant tradesmen and others who frequented the festivals or fairs of those days."

The Church and its Lands.

"HE, THE ABBOT (*i.e.*, *of Battle in Sussex*), HOLDS A CHURCH IN READING WITH EIGHT HIDES THERE APPERTAINING. LEVEVA, THE ABBESS, HELD IT OF KING EDWARD. THEN, IT DEFENDED ITSELF FOR EIGHT, NOW, FOR SEVEN HIDES OF LAND, AND SEVEN CARACUTES IN THE LORDSHIP. THERE ARE NINE LABOURERS (*villani*), AND EIGHT FARMERS (*bordarii*), WITH FIVE PLOUGHS. THERE ARE TWO MILLS OF ELEVEN SHILL[s], AND TWO FISHERIES AND A HALF OF FIVE SHILL[s]. IN READING ARE TWENTY-NINE RUINOUS COTTAGES, OF 28*s.* 8*d.*, AND TWELVE ACRES OF MEADOW. WOODS FOR FIVE PIGS. THE CHURCH PRODUCES THREE POUNDS. IN THE TIME OF KING EDWARD IT WAS VALUED AT 9*l.*, AFTERWARDS AT 8*l.*, AND NOW AT 11*l.*"

The church was originally held by Leveva, the abbess of the Saxon convent which was burnt by the Danes at a second incursion in 1006, and which does not appear to have recovered from that disaster. In the year 1076 the

Conqueror founded the Abbey of Battle in Sussex, and
between this date and the year 1085 the endowments of
the old Reading convent, including the church and its
lands, were granted to the monks of Battle, having been in
lay hands since the visit of the Danes. ' Sciatis quod tres
abbatiæ in Regno Angliæ peccatis suis exigentibus olim
destructæ sunt Radingia scilicet atque Chelseya et Leomin-
stria *quas manus laica diu possedit earumque terras et pos-
sessiones alienando distraxit.*" (Foundation Charter, Hen. I.
Dugdale, iv. 40.)

On the foundation of Reading Abbey, this estate was
withdrawn from the monks of Battle and given to the new
convent at Reading; certain lands at Apeldreham, with
the farm of Boseham, the wood of Bocfalde and Betle-
sparrioc, with Yringesmed being given to Battle in exchange. (*Vid. Cayley and Ellis' Dugdale*, iii. 233—" Alia
Carta eiusdem Regis pro excambio de Rading.")

The estate near Reading, called Battle Farm, may probably serve to identify some of these old church lands,
which amounted to about 1,540 acres at the Domesday
survey.

In 1120 the eastern part of the Forbury appears to have
been cleared of every obstacle by Henry I. for the foundation of the Abbey ; even the old church of the Burgh was
swept away, *and re-erected just outside the projected boundary of the new monastery*. Parker, in his introduction to
the " Study of Gothic Architecture," p. 29, gives an interesting parallel :—

" The Conqueror, having taken possession of about a
quarter of the old city of Lincoln to build a castle upon,
and Bishop Remigius having purchased nearly another
quarter *to build a cathedral and monastery*, the Saxon inhabitants were driven down the hill on which the old city
stands, and took possession of some swampy land at the
foot of the hill, which they drained and redeemed from
the fens or marshes, of which nearly all the low country
then consisted. On this new land they built several
churches."

The church of Reading Abbey appears to have been
completed in the year 1163, when it was consecrated by
St. Thomas a Becket.

"Et was endlebe hundred зer & sixti & two
 Of grace that Sein Tomas was erchebissop tho
 The next зer therafter as it wold be
 Endlebe hundred зer of grace & sixti & thre
 He halwede as the King him bed, the Church of Redinge
 That berst ifounded was, thoru Henri the other Kinge."

(Rob. of Gloucester, Hearne, 469.)

The Norman Church

consisted of a simple nave with a tower at its western end,
and probably an apsidal sacrarium at the other, and, as the
original boundary wall of the Abbey crossed the site of the
present church from north to south, about the position of
the Blagrave Memorial, it was obviously not more than half
the length of the present structure.

The wall at the south-west corner of the nave for about
27 feet in length, and from 6 to 12 feet in height, is about
five feet in thickness, and is unquestionably a remnant of
this first sanctuary.   It has no distinctive character, but as
it is capped by a Norman window in a wall of reduced
thickness, all this superstructure must be of later date than
the lower work ; and as the contiguous wall containing the
doorway of A.D. 1196 is of precisely the same thickness
as this upper masonry, I have no doubt they are coeval,
and the little Norman window was reinserted then, at its
original level.   It is clearly *one of a series* long since
destroyed, and is especially interesting.

The original tower was brought into its present form in
1458.   During its restoration in 1882 several fragments of
Norman work were brought to light, showing that it was
either modified or reconstructed in 1458 with the materials
of the earlier tower.   The fragments found in 1882, and
preserved in the ringing chamber, are—

1. A scolloped capital, showing a plain chambered abacus
   (c. 1120).
2. Another capital, very like those on the south doorway
   of the nave (c. 1196).
3. A piece of chevron moulding of largish proportions
   (c. 1120).
4. A piece of perpendicular moulding (c. 1430).

(All these formed the reverse side of old ashler stones in
the angle turrets.)

There is another in-built fragment of Norman moulding
in the north wall of the bell-chamber, on a level with the
bell frames, forming the side of a " putlog" hole (c. 1120).

The presence of the second capital above mentioned, shows

that something was done to the tower in 1196, when the church was so much enlarged. A similar inference may be made from the moulding of 1430.

As the stones composing the piers and arches of the tower, as well as the voissoirs of the great west window, are of a different material to the rest, they seem to point rather to a modification of the Norman tower in 1458 than to an entire reconstruction at that time ; and it is not unlikely that the massive piers of the tower arches may contain the original Norman masonry beneath the covering or adaptations of 1458. Indeed, it is probable that the north and south walls of the tower to a considerable height remain as they were first constructed in 1120. They are more than five feet in thickness.

So rapidly did the town increase after the foundation of the Abbey, and so great were the claims on conventual hospitality, that it was found necessary to erect an outer hospitium for the relief of the poor, and to enlarge the church for the accommodation of increasing worshippers. Both of these great works appear to have been carried out by the good Abbot Hugh about the same time, and, as soon as completed, the church was assigned to the new hospicium, or, as it was called, "The Hospital of St. John the Baptist," in the seventh year of the pontificate of Hubert Walter, Bishop of Salisbury, A.D. 1196.

In this year, or about this time, the Norman church was enlarged to its present dimensions. Of the work of this period there remains—

1. The south doorway of the nave.
2. The piscina in the south wall.
3. The jamb of a window discovered above Blagrave's monument, with shaft and capital like those of (No. 4).
4. The three lancets in the chancel.
5. The arcade between the chancel and the chapel of St. John the Baptist (perhaps a little later).
6. The two lancets blocked at the formation of the east window of the north chapel.
7. (Probably) the low blocked arch in the wall of the north aisle.

All these in their several positions show the *extent* of the additions made at this time.

There is a long list of subscribers on the roll of 1440–1, to the "work of the church" ("opus ecclesiæ") ; but as the sum of 8*l*. 13*s*. 5*d*. appears to have been expended this year on the tenements belonging to the church, and the aforesaid subscriptions amounted only to 9*l*. 16*s*. 5½*d*., it was probable that this was the purpose to which those contributions were applied, and that nothing material was then done to the fabric. In this account a few old terms occur which may be interesting :—We have " eves borde," " borde nale," " window nale," " lath nale," hertlath, suplath, crests, " zabul," twysts, " dawbyng," and " pynnyng."

A Complete List of the Subscribers to the "Work of the Church" in 1440.

Dñs Hen. Coup vicar, iij^s iiij^d
Pætr' Dalamare, iij^s iij^d
Joñes Kirkeby, vj^s viij^d
Robt^9 Morys, vj^s viij^d
Witts Bryssele, iij^s iiij^d
Joñes Deyr, xx^d
Witts Boteler, xij^d
Witts Hunt, vj^s viij^d
Robt^9 Kayns, vj^s viij^d
Witts Stapper, xx^d
Thoñ Swayn, ij^s (M.P. for Reading, 1426, died in 1441).
Denys Coke, ij^d
Joh^ane Benton, ij^d
Joh' Aleward, tyler, viij^d
Riĉus Turnour, vj^s viij^d
Joñes Wyse, iij^s iiij^d
David^9 Gower, iij^s iiij^d
Hen. Robf, xij^d
Ricus Hawkeley, xij^d
Witts Bartheran, iiij^s
Henric^9 Boteler, iiij^d
Thom^ns Laurence, viij^d (clᵉic^9 poch dce ecctie).
Joñes Plumer, tyler, xij^d
Robt^9 Budd, viij^d
Witts pvecote, x^d
Joñes Chaundeler, xx^d
Hen' Ffurberoe, xij^d

Joñes Brown, smyth, i^d
Joñes Barthelot, iiij^d
Witts Rede, iiij^d
Joñes Morys, iiij^d
Emmota nup relict Joñis Plumer, ij^d
Joñes Kale, iiij^d
Joñes Netter, iiij^d
Hugo fchemyner, iiij^d
Joñes Taylour, xij^d
Riĉus Monmouth, ij^d
Witts Ludlowe, vi^d
Joñes Benham, xij^d
Witts Drover, xij^d
Witts Dyer, xij^d
Joñes Mercham, vj^s viij^d
Joñes Benet, iiij^d
Robt^9 Brynger, viij^d
Joñes Pasteler, viij^d
Heñ Hurtlond, iiij^d
Riĉus Veston, xij^d
Thom^ns Hakker, xx^d
Thom^ns Culvhouse, xij^d
Joñes Garden, xij^d
Edward' Dyer, iij^s iiij^d
Thom Coleshill, iiij^d
Joñes Reynolds, ij^d
Joñes Stevyns, iiij^d
Joñes atte Hatch, viij^d
Thom Hampton, iiij^d

Jol̃es Canon, ij⁴
Jol̃es Barton, taillour, iiij⁴
Jol̃es Bothenall, iiij⁴
Wil̃s Hyne, xij⁴
Agn' Gowler, iiij⁴
Robt⁹ Pasteler, viij¹
Johes Merk, ij⁴
Niclius Mountford, xij⁴
Radus Younge, ijˢ
Ric' Ffarle, xx⁴
Jol̃es Vanner, vij⁴
Reginald Crokesley, iv⁴
Jol̃es Athelard, vi⁴
Ricus Stovyle, ij⁴
Margeria Baker, xx⁴

Thom²s Fferrour, ij⁴
Jol̃es Colyns, vi⁴
Jol̃es Buck, viij⁴
Jol̃es atte Hethe, viij¹
Ffelicia Weldere, ij⁴
Thom²s Luff, vi⁴
Rog̃ Coke, xij⁴
Jol̃es Bernard, xx⁴
Jol̃es Hale, xii⁴
Ricus Coup, vi⁴
Jol̃es Heryng, viij⁴
Johes Est, iiij⁴
Wil̃s Wever, iiij⁴
Smᵃ ix l̃i xvjˢ v⁴ ob.

In 1458 the churchwardens' roll gives the names of those who contributed to the " Emendation of the campanile ;" but unfortunately the roll has been so much injured by damp, that almost the entire face of the skin has perished, and with it of course the record. There are only twenty-six names legible. In this year the original bell tower was brought into its present form.

At this time the arches between the nave and north aisle, erected in 1196 by Abbot Hugh, were probably reconstructed. The springing of the arches from the responds at the east and west ends of the arcade between the nave and aisle give the original height of the capitals.

The greenish-tinted stone was now first introduced, and it may enable us to detect the alterations of this period. We find it in the tower arches, the newel at the south-east corner, the voissoirs of the great west window, the nave arches, the *sides* of the niches in the spandrels, and the windows of the north aisle. Hence we may infer that the lancets of 1196, formerly in the north aisle, were now supplanted by the present windows. A corresponding series were also inserted in the south wall, the easternmost window excepted ; *teste*, the old engravings of the church, especially one by " Shury and Son." Another, if it may be relied upon, shows one window on each side of the nave doorway, exactly like those in the north aisle ; and another, the second from the east end of this wall, of a still later character.

The last alteration took place about the year 1521,

though something was begun as early as 1518, as appears
by the following entry in the church books :—

> " Item, gyven by dyûce psons toward the repacõn of the
> church gatherid eûy Sonday after new yer⁸ day unto
> Sonday aft^r Michelmas day which amounteth to the
> sm̃ of (as apperith by a boke of their names) xxi^li ij^s j^d.

> " It. payd to Myller the Joyno^r in pte of paymēt
> iiij^li vi^s viij^d for makyng of the pclose in the new
> chapell, xxvi^s viij^d.

> " It. payd to Harry Horthorne for tymbre workman-
> shypp, and for bowrdyng of men as apperith by
> his bill⁸, vij^li iiij^d."

A new vestry seems to have been constructed this year,
containing a separate altar.

> " Anno 1520-1. It. paid for a hose cloth gyven to the
> oûseer of My lord Cardynall⁸ werks to licence
> Chayney the mason to cū from thens, iiij^s iiij^d
> (from Hampton Court).

> > " It. paid to John Knyght for coûyng of the rode
> > lofte and the imag⁸ xiiij^d.

> > " It. paid for charg⁸ in Ridyng for Chayney the
> > Mason, iij^s iiij^d.

> > " It. paid to Harry Cobbe in pte of vj^s for takyng
> > downe of the bracis of the beamys & for
> > settyng vpp of vj new corsis, iij^s.

> > " It. paid to White the belfounder for arrerag⁸ of
> > the glasse for *the new wyndows in the quere* in
> > full payment for the same wyndows, xiij^s iiij^d.

> " Anno 1521-2. It. payd for the tymber & sawyng of
> viij Corvetts for the *new arches*, viij^d.

> > " It. payd to my laborar⁸ for besynes done yn the
> > chyrch when the new arches were mayd,
> > iiij^s xi^d."

From this we learn the exact date of the present four-
centred arches between the nave and aisle. The previous
ones of 1458 were not considered sufficiently lofty, so the
columns were now raised and the arches stilted : the inter-
vening niches were covered with crowns (perhaps in the
place of loftier canopies), and new bases adorned with
cherubs and shields attached to the whole. The devices on
these shields, proceeding from east to west, are as follow :—

1. A shield bearing a gridiron for St. Lawrence.
2. Two chevrons between three roses. Probably intended

for " Wickham ;" argt. 2 chev. sa., between 3 roses
gules, seeded or, barbed vert.

3. A shield bearing a rebus, consisting of a tun impressed
with the letter " B," intended no doubt for Baynton
(B-in-Tun, or, B-on-Tun). Richard Baynton was
one of the officiating clergy in 1524. " It. to S^r
Ric. Baynton for mendyng the grett organs at ij
tymes iiij^s." The same year *his chamber* was repaired
at an outlay of 1*l*. 2*s*. 2*d*.

4. A shield with a chevron between 3 tuns.

5. A shield bearing 3 chevrons between 3 bezants, or
torteaux.

There is another shield behind this in the north aisle,
with a rose in the centre. The remaining shields in the
north aisle are without devices.

The old chancel arch was coeval with the lancets at the
east end, c. 1196, and was about *five feet narrower than the
present one*, erected under Mr. Ferrey about 1848. At that
time Mr. Billing discovered the stairs to the rood loft in the
south pier. The steps were then removed, and the hole
was filled with rubble and grouting to form a stronger
abutment for the new chancel arch.

The old views of the church exhibit two dormer windows
in the south side of the nave roof ; one near the tower, and
another over the south doorway inclining to the east. The
former of these was of no very recent date :—

" Anno 1521. It. payd to Henry Horethorne for the
wyndow yn the south syde of the chyrch next
the stepyll besyds y^t he have gyven, vij^s viij^d.
" It. payd for half a b$_3$ of tyle pynes occupyed ou
the wyndow, ij^d ob."

There were similar windows inserted in the north and
south sides of the chancel roof, and three more over the
north aisle looking northwards.

For repairs of the chancel see under *Vicars :*—" JOHN
SMITH."

The writer has received a most interesting communication
from Mr. Arthur Billing, architect and surveyor, 185,
Tooley Street, London Bridge, relating to some discoveries
made at the restoration of the two chancels about forty years
ago. The notes were taken at that time :—

" Immediately beneath the triplet windows in the east
wall of the chancel were discovered the remains of three

'Aumbries' or 'Lockers,' in one of which was a portion of wood and iron work remaining, evidently showing that they were once closed by doors, and were probably used for keeping the sacred vessels and other articles of that description. These had been completely hidden by the large wooden altar screen of the Georgian era. Upon the south side of the chancel, at the eastern end, was found a large portion of a piscina, but the bowl altogether gone. There had also been sedilia, but these had been entirely taken out, and the place filled up with brickwork.

"On the south side of St. John's Chapel, in the portion of wall forming the respond to the eastern arch of the arcade separating the chancel from the chapel, was also discovered a piscina nearly perfect, with the exception of a part of the bowl being broken. This, together with the piscina, the aumbries, and the sedilia in the chancel, have all been entirely filled up.

"P.S.—Several portions of the rood screen were found under the nave floor, near the chancel arch.

"I have a sketch and plan of the slabs with their legends lying in the chancel and in the north chapel."

The Tower.

The stately tower of St. Lawrence's is one of the finest specimens of ecclesiastical architecture in the county, and is justly considered the chiefest ornament of the town. From whatever point it may be viewed, its exquisite proportions cannot fail to strike the observer. The parishioners and townsmen have shown their appreciation of the treasure, by restoring it to its pristine beauty. The structure is divided into three stages or stories, defined by exterior string courses : the lowest is open to the body of the church, the second forms the ringing chamber, and the uppermost contains one of the most musical rings of bells in the south of England. Octagonal buttresses occupying the angles terminate in lofty embattled pinnacles crowned with spirelets, which rise to an elevation of 111 feet, or 23 feet above the top of the battlements.

The uppermost windows are a careful reproduction of the old ones existing in 1881 ; and, although they are somewhat incongruous in their character, it was thought better thus to preserve the architectural history of the building, than to resort to a more correct type, but of no local authority.

The *original* south window was probably first destroyed for the admission of the great bell Harry, in 1498. At its first recasting in 1567, it was lowered, and readmitted through this opening :

"Anno 1567. For xlij foote of boorde for y[e] south window in the steple where the bell was taken out and in, and one hondreth & a half of nayles, 11*s*. vj*d*."

It is probable that the tracery just removed, of which the present is a copy, was of this period.

The canopied niches on either side the tower doorway were formerly occupied by statues of St. Lawrence and St. Vincent. These figures are now preserved in the Vicarage garden, but are in a sadly mutilated condition. The effigy of St. Lawrence shows the remains of a fringed purse on the left side, but the sustaining hand and arm are broken off. He is habited in alb, tunicle, and dalmatic, the orfrays of which exhibit a grape and vineleaf pattern, with an undulating stem. The statue of St. Vincent is habited in a similar costume, but is less perfect. The original heads of both effigies have been destroyed. The backs of the figures are bevelled, to adapt them to the recesses they once occupied. Mrs. Jamieson says : " St. Vincent is usually grouped with St. Lawrence: the Spanish legend makes them brothers, but I find no authority for this relationship in the French and Italian Martyrologies."

Mr. Coates, in his " History of Reading," writes : " On each side of the door are two niches for images, with two escutcheons of arms in stone now greatly defaced ; on one were the arms of Reading Abbey, and on the other the arms of William Aiscoth, or Ayscough (a chevron between three asses), impaled with the arms of the See of Salisbury, of which he was Bishop from 1438 to 1450." These arms are given by Capt. Symonds in his " Notes" taken April 3, 1644, the arms of the Abbey being then on the south side of the doorway. In 1806 the whole of the stonework of the tower was coated with Roman cement, and the old carvings reproduced in the same plastic material, the two escutcheons above mentioned included.

Owing to objections having been made by an influential tradesman, the arms of the See of Salisbury (the Blessed Virgin and Child) have not been reproduced. This is much

C

to be regretted, for in every honest restoration original types should be carefully followed.

Ancient edifices are not exponents of modern thought: we restore them in their integrity as relics of the past; as monuments of a bygone age. In stamping them with our own impress, we falsify history and the history of art, and proclaim our own incompetence to deal with the precious heirlooms our generous forefathers have bequeathed to their children.

On the south-west pinnacle of the tower is the following inscription :—

> " THIS TOWER
> WAS NEW ROOFED
> AUGUST 1864,
> W. H. W. STAVELEY
> J. T. MORRIS
> CHURCHWARDENS."

In 1806, as before stated, the decayed ashler work of the tower was injudiciously repaired with Roman cement—even the face of the window tracery and of all the mouldings of the windows and doorways had been hewn away to be re-produced in stucco ; it was very creditably done, too, for the period.

In 1881-2 the tower and west end of the aisle were thoroughly restored, all the pinnacles reinstated, the one at the south-west angle *rebuilt*, the window tracery and doorways renewed, and all the decayed stonework replaced, under the care of Joseph Morris, Esq., architect, by Mr. Higgs, builder and contractor, at a cost of about £2,000.

Knowles' Transept.

This adjunct, resembling a transept, was erected on the south side of the church about midway between the south door and the west end of the nave, by Sir Francis Knollys the elder, in 1637,* " For the peculiar use of himself and his posteritie, as well for their seates there, as for their burial-place underneath. And to that end and purpose, the Lord Bishop of the diocese in his own person, according to the ecclesiastical lawes of this realme, consecrated the same to be united and holden as a parte and member of the said church for ever." (*Coates.*)

* " On the outside of the aisle was this inscription, ' Sr. F. K. 1633.' "—(Coates.)

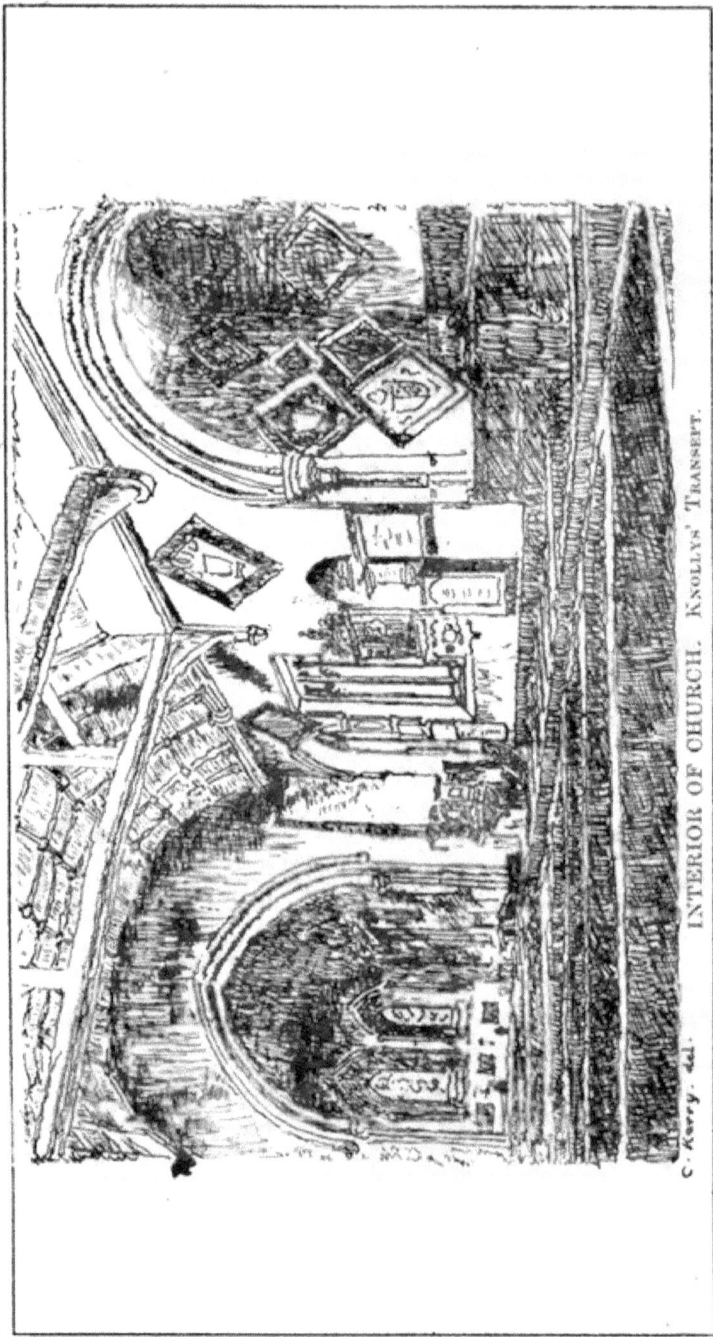

C. Kerry, del.

INTERIOR OF CHURCH. KNOLLYS' TRANSEPT.

According to an old engraving, it had on its west side a flat-headed window of three lights overlooking the roof of the piazza. On the south side was a large pointed window of three lights, with a flat-headed doorway beneath, and a small square-headed window above. Its southern limit was coterminous with the front of the piazza. The following achievements, given by Mr. Coates, formerly adorned its walls :—

" 1. Quarterly 1st, and 4th, a cross moline voided throughout, between twelve cross crosslets or (*Knollys*) ; 2nd, and 3rd, Gules, on a chevron arg^{t}, three roses proper (*Cave*).

" 2. 1st (*Knollys*). 2nd sable, on a bend, cotised, azure, three lioncels passant guardant of the second. 3rd, Gules a lion rampant or. 4th, Azure, a fesse, betw. three fleur-de-lis or. 5th, Chequy, or and azure. 6th Sable, a frette or.

" 3. 1st Azure, a chevron gu. betw : three ravens sable. 2nd Gu : a talbot passant, or : A chief ermine. 3rd Sa. a chev : az : between three escallops or. 4th Argent, on a cross sa : a leopard's face, or (*Bridges*), impaling Knollys.

" 4. Or, five crescents azure, impaling (*Knollys*).

" 5. (*Knollys*) ; with the crest, an elephant arg^{t}.

" 6. 1st, and 4th, (*Knollys*). 2nd, Gu : on a chev. arg^{t} three roses proper. 3rd, party per pale ermine and gu : three talbots heads counterchanged. Over all an escutcheon of pretence—1st, and 4th, sa. a chev : ermine betw. three fishes haurient, argent. 2nd and 3rd, az : a fesse chequy or and sable betw. three eagles displayed of the second.

" 7. (*Knollys*), bearing an escutcheon of pretence, party per pale ermine and gu : three talbots heads, counterchanged. On each side of the shield are two small escutcheons—1st (*Knollys*), impaling—sable, a saltire engrailed or. 2nd (*Knollys*), impaling—azure on a fesse sable, three escalops or.

" 8. (*Knollys*), quartering the talbots, counterchanged as before ; and bearing an escutcheon of pretence, the same as No : 6."

The preceding were in Knollys' chapel. Mr. Coates mentions other escutcheons, which may be inserted here :—
" Over the staircase leading to the north gallery, hangs this

achievement; 1st (*Blagrave*); 2nd Gules, a lion couchant,
or on a chief arg¹, three crescents of the first.   (*Deane.*)
2nd Barry of six, or and az : on a fesse gu : three mullets
of the second.   (*Merrick.*)

On the south side of the church is this achievement :—
1st or, a chief indented sable, a lion passant guardant of
the same for *Loggins.*   2nd, party per pale, or, and sable,
four griffins heads erased, counterchanged.   3rd, arg¹, a
fesse, vert, between three maunches of the same for
Staverton.   4th, arg¹, a plain cross sable, in the first quarter,
a fleur-de-lis of the second."

The remains of the Knollys' family were to have been
removed at the demolition of the structure, but it was
never done, and the outer pavement now covers the graves
of numerous members of this family.

Blagrave's Piazza.

This structure consisted of a covered walk, extending
from the south-west tower buttress or staircase to the west
wall of Knollys' transept.   The south front exhibited six
arches, each of which was capped by a double ogee-shaped
gable.   The west front presented a single arch (round like
the rest), with engaged flat columns, or rather pilasters, on
either side.   In the gable above was a stone tablet with the
following inscription :—

IOHANNES BLAGRAVIVS
GENEROSUS, MATHESIOSQUE
ENCOMIIS CELEBERRIMUS,
LIBRAS C. AD AMBULACRUM
HOC EXTRUENDUM DEDIT, QUOD
OPUS MAJOR BURGENSESQUE (PIÆ
BENEFICII HUJUS INTER CÆTERA
MEMORIÆ ERGO) PERFICIENDUM
CURARUNT,
FEB. I, 1619.
REPARATUM & ADORNATUM
ANNO 1680.

The easternmost compartment of this portico adjoining
the Knollys chapel, had been converted into a cell for
delinquents, and a playful story is told of a former churchwarden (not a member of the "Blue Ribbon Army") having
been compelled to spend an evening there to recruit his

THE TUMBRIL.

p. 21.

shattered powers before the morrow's dawn. It was thence-forth spoken of as the "Churchwarden's Pew."

Beneath this piazza, too, and within the memory of many, stood the "stocks," an old-fashioned instrument of parochial discipline, seen in almost every village and town in England fifty years ago.

In the churchwardens' accounts for 1638, mention is made of a "*Tumbrel*," deposited, no doubt, under the piazza with the stocks, and perhaps the pillory too; for this last instrument was in existence a few years ago, when it was sold with some rubbish which had been deposited in the chamber beneath the old town-hall.

The "tumbrel," or "cucking stool," was specially de-signed for the correction of scolds, brawlers, and women of unlawful condition. Of this instrument there were two kinds: one consisted of a long plank balanced on an axis carried by two wheels. To one end of the plank was attached a chair, in which the offender was secured; the other was grasped by the officials of *justice* (?) (too often by those whose private piques rendered them merciless administrators), and then bowled to the water's edge, where, by a see-saw-like action, the poor culprit was alternately elevated and immersed.

Mr. Burn, in his "History of Henley-on-Thames," observes: "Another form of cucking stool was a post set up in the water, upon which was a transverse beam turning on a swivel, with a chair at one end of it, and the other end fastened with lock and chain to a short post in the ground. To this *fixed* machine Gay refers in his lines on Sparabilla, who thinks of committing suicide:—

> I'll speed me to the pond, where the high stool
> On the long plank hangs o'er the muddy pool,
> That stood the dread of every scolding quean:
> Yet—sure a lover should not die so mean."

Halliwell writes : " The tumbrel was originally used for the punishment of offences against the assize, but was afterwards used for scolds and prostitutes, and continued in vogue in some places till the middle of the last century. The sitting in the chair with the head and feet bare, was also used as a penance, unaccompanied with the ducking, and the form of the stool contributed to increase the degradation."

Roof.

In 1410, the church, or a portion of it, was re-roofed with timber from " Erley," and the oldest roll of the churchwardens' accounts contains the names of 150 contributors to the work.   One of the largest subscribers was John Kent, whose brass commemorating himself and his wife Joan, was removed from the chancel floor to the south wall last year for its better preservation.   He died about 1415.   Some of the largest contributors were John Hence, 4s. 4d.; William Baker, 4s. 4d.; John Tinte, 4s. 4d.; Rob. Peyntour, 4s.; John Bennett, 6s. 8d. ; Gilbert Dyer, 17d. ; John Lathum, 4s. ; Robert Keynes, 8s. 8d. ; John Swalolyf, 2s. ; Philip Rich, 6s. ; John Mereham, 13s. ; Walter Baron, 4s. 4d.; Nicholas Barbour, 8s. 8d.; John Persy, 14s.; Will. Smyzt, 4s. ; Ric. Pale, 4s. 4d.; Ric. Gos, 3s. 4d.; Hen. Couper, 4s. 4d.; Rob. Rythe, 22d.; Thomas Chandler, 6s.; John Kent, 13s.; Will. Peris, 4s. 4d.; Will. Boteler, 13s.; Joh. Ydefisch, 4s.; Nich. Copland, 2s. 4d.; Ric. Casse, 8s. 8d. ; John Whyte, 8s. 8d.; John Bladier, 4s. 4d. ; Joh. Wodemancote, 4s. 2d.; William Derby, glover (Wm. Derby was M.P. for Reading, 5 Ric. II. 1382) ; Nic. Spiser, 4s. 4d. ; John Cras, 4s. 4d.; Ric. Glover, 4s. 4d.; Will. Carpenter, 4s. 4d.; Steph. Everard, 4s. 4d. ; Rob. Baker, 4s. 4d.; Barthol. Clisth, 4s. 4d. ; Rob. Beche, 4s. 4d.; Rob. atte Lee, 4s. 4d. ; Joh. Tylere, 2s. ; John Cras gave for a Tyler for one day, 3d., &c. &c.

It is probable that much of the nave roof is of this date.

The roof of the north aisle was repaired with boards in 1524-5.   The chancel roof was ceiled with panel work, or else repaired, the same year, and made resplendent with gold and colours.

The roof at the east end of the nave, from above Blagrave's monument to the chancel arch, at the beginning of this century, was elliptical and of panel work, with roses and other ornaments at each intersection of the groining.   This portion, showing the extent of the ancient rood loft, was removed at the restoration of the nave in 1867. A dormer window was inserted in the " selyng" of the rood loft in 1436, by John Hale, who received 28s. 4d. for his labours.

The Church "Reconciled."

Anno 33-4 Hen. VIII. (1542-3).

" Payd to the Suffregan in money for reconsyleyng the churche, xl°."

This entry implies a desecration of the fabric by blood-shedding, or some other profanation.

The culprits are clearly indicated :—

" Itm. Rec. of Robt. Watlyngton to pay the Suffregan for reconsylyng the churche, xx°.

" Itm. Rec. of Mark Awsepp towards the same, x°.

" Itm. Rec. of Robt. Letsh^am towards the same, iij°. iiij^d."

    " Sm^a xxxiij°. iiij^d."

Mark Awsepp, *the sexton*, was discharged from his office on Lady Day the same year, and one Richard —— appointed in his place.

" It. to mark his dī yeres wayges endyd at thannūciation of o^r ladie last iiij°. vj^d." " It. to the *newe* sexton for a q^art waiges endyd at Michelmas last past xiij°. iiij^d."

The next accounts, beginning at Michaelmas the same year, place Robert Watlington at the *head* of the *interment* list :—

" Rec. for the grave of Robt. Watlyngton & coůyng, vij°. iiij^d." " Rec. for the knyll & tolying at the monethe mynde of Robt. Watlyngton, xvj^d."

This is significant, and seems to point to a serious fray, in which Watlington, obviously the aggressor, from the extent of his fine, received very serious, if not mortal, injuries.

The Font.

The charge for the Font Taper occurs yearly in the church accounts from their commencement to the Reformation.

1503-4. "It. payed for lettyng hyer the coũyng of the font, ob." (a halfpenny).

1508. "It. payed for a padlok to the font, iij^d."

1510. "It. payed for ij. b₃ (bushels) of colys at the halowyng of the vante, ij^d."

1521-2. "Rec. for led of the old font sold, vij^s."

"It. payd for bordyng of the olde seatts where the old font stode, & for makeỹg of a seate at the west doore, xviij^d."

"It. payd for makeỹg of the coũ for the ffonte, xij^d."

1522. It. to Chenye the mason for makeyng the fronte, xxxi^s. viij^d."

„ "It. payd to the plũmar for makeỹg the font and mendyng of the stepull, ix^s. x^d."

"Chenye" appears to have been employed at Cardinal Wolsey's new works at Hampton Court. His services were procured for St. Lawrence's by an effective honorarium :—

1520. "It. paid for a Hose cloth gyven to the oũseer of my lord Cardynalls werks to licence Chayney the mason to cũ fro thens, iiij^s. iiij^d."

"It. paid for chargis in Ridyng for Chaney the mason, iij^s. iiij^d."

1526. "It. for new burneshyng the Crysmatorye, vj^d."

1576. "Expenses in masons worke about removing of the font & paving, xvj^s. viij^d."

1639. "It. p^d to John Milkesop for a brasse cock for the font, 4^s. o^d."

(For the ancient position of the fonts, see article "Seats," anno 1538.)

Unfortunately, the old font of 1521-2 has been submitted to the "drag," and its venerable aspect greatly injured during the present century; but it is the identical font made by Master Cheyney, and the font to which the parents and sponsors of Archbishop Laud brought him in his infancy for Holy Baptism. A few traces of original colouring may still be seen on the bowl and shaft.

H. A. Collins. del.

p. 24.

THE FONT.

Altars.

No less than twelve altars bearing distinct names are mentioned in the churchwardens' accounts, but it is hardly probable that so many existed in the church at the same time. An imperfect inventory of 1523 gives the names of five, but it omits the "High" altar and that of " Jesus," so there must have been at least seven at that period.

Six altars were sold in 1549, one of which was St. Clement's, and the Lady altar is not in the list, so that at the Reformation there would seem to have been EIGHT, unless the altar of the B. Virgin had been re-dedicated, which is not at all probable ; indeed, the "Lady Mass" is mentioned as late as 1546, so that that altar must then have been in existence.

> "M^d. that in the yere of our lorde 1557 & the iij^d & iiijth yer^s of the reignes of our Soüaigne lord & ladye Phillipp & Marye by the g^ace of God Kyng & Quene of Englond, &c., the Second Day of May beyng Sonday, Wiłłm ffynche Suffrigan vnto the Bisshopp of Bathe & Welles hath hallowed the church yarde of the pishe of Saynt Laurence in Redyng. And also the same day & yere hath hallowed in the seid pishe fyve awters of stone that is to witte the High Awter of Saynt Laurence ; in the chauncell next called St. Johns Chauncell one awter called Saynte Johns Alter: in the body of the churche the myddell alter ther called Jħus Alter : in the South syde ther one Alter called our ladye Awter of the Nativitie: and in the north side ther one Awter called Saynt Thomas Awter."

In the accounts ending Michaelmas, 1559, we have

> "Itm. for takinge downe the awlters & laying the stones, v^s."
> " To Loryman (the clerk) for carryeng out the rub-bysh, x^d."

A description of these old altars will be interesting, as serving to show the attachment and devotion of our fore-fathers to the service of God, and what great sacrifices they must have made to make the place of His Name glorious.

1. The High Altar.

This is first named in the roll of 1433.

Anno 1499. "It. payd for scowryng of þᵉ iiij candylstyks at þᵉ hy auᵗ xijᵈ. (the two great standards and the two candlesticks on the altar).

Anno 1503. "It. payed for whipcord to draw þᵉ blak cloth at sakⁿ)ȳg of masse iᵈ."

(It was a custom in the old English church to draw a vail before the altar during the consecration of the elements in accordance with the words: "Eye hath not seen, nor ear heard, nor have entered into the heart of man to conceive the things which God hath prepared for them that love Him.")

1508. "Itm. payed for a carpyntⁿ)s lyne to draw the black sarsenet before the sacramẽt at the Hy Aulter, iᵈ."

1510. "Itm. payed for a small lyne to hange the kanape oŭ the Hy auter."

1513. "Payd to Robt. Hawtrell for removyng of the front of the Hygh Auᵗ, & setting upp of the same in Seynt Johns Chaⁿncell, &c. xiiijˢ."

A *new* altar appears to have been erected in 1514.

"It. payd to a Suffrygan for Halowyng of the High Awᵗ, Seynt Johns awᵗ & a supaltare, viˢ viijᵈ."

" It. payd to John Knyzt for makyng crossis to the Hygh Awtar & oþⁿ) sⁿ)vice, viijᵈ" (probably the five crosses at the centre and angles of the slab or mensa.)

In 1526 the story of the Transfiguration was painted on the wall above it, at a cost of 6*l*. 13*s*. 4*d*. (See under " Mural Paintings.")

" It. to Robt. Pasteler for making a skaffold & enlargeyng the High Awᵗ iijˢ iiijᵈ."

Anno 1528. "It. for enlargying the Awᵗ clothes for the hygh Awᵗ wᵗ all manⁿ) of stuff therto belongyng & workmanshypp as by a byll appereth, xxiiˢ ixᵈ."

A beam of brass passed over the chancel, from which lights were suspended before the sacrament.

Anno 1537. "Payd for skowryng the beam hangyng before the sac^ament, viij^d."

There were figures of the twelve Apostles, probably in niches in the reredos.

Anno 1518. "It. paid for wasshyng & dressyng of the Halpas w^t the xii Appostels xiij^s. iiij^d. ("Haut-pas"—the highest level of the flooring in the sacrarium—the altar place).

Anno 1546–7. "Payd to a paynter for wrytyng of the cloth at the High Awt^r ij^s. iiij^d. (probably some covering for the defaced east wall).

In 1547 many things were sold : among the rest, a coffer, termed a "coffyn," belonging to the High Altar, purchased by Mr. Bureton (Walter Barton's nephew).

In 1549 the High Altar was purchased for 6s. 8d. by Mr. Bell.

There was a cupboard or almery standing at each end for books and utensils, probably concealed by projecting curtains.

The old stone aumbries, piscina, and *place* of sedilia were discovered and filled up with rubble, &c., at the restoration of the chancel in 1848.

At the commencement of Queen Mary's reign there was a return to the old order and ritual :—

Anno 1552–3. "Paid for making of the high Awt^r & paving in the churche, xij^s."

There are plain indications in the accounts of this period of searching official inquiries with regard to the disposal of the goods of the church in the previous reign.

On the accession of Elizabeth the *régime* was again changed, as may be seen above at the commencement of this article.

Anno 1560. "Itm. for a seate of ye comvnyon table and the boord and nayles and the workmanshipp, xiiij^d."

"Itm. for dressynge the high alter and the wall beneth and the bourdes where the altar stoode, ij^s. viij^d.

1568. "Itm. to Martyn Woodnett for makinge of the
    fframe for the comunion table xxii^d."

"Itm. to Edward Paynter for colloringe of ye
    same, iii^d."

The following entry would seem to show that the ecclesiastical pendulum had swung to the other extreme :—

1569. "It. to the joynar for makyng the comunion table
    and benches with a doore, iiij^s.

This is an early instance of an arrangement which pre-
vailed in the later Puritanical era, when the altar was
dragged from its normal position and placed in the middle
of the chancel, the communicants being seated round it
during the administration of the sacrament.

The next entry shows a return to the old position—
perhaps under Laudean influence.

1634. "Paied to the jynor for making the new and mend-
    ing the oulde winscotte *above the communion
    table*, 1*l.* 1*s.* 0*d.*"

"Paid for the communion table, 14*s.*"

1638. (Inventory) :—

"Item, one velvet cover for the Ciōn Table
    with silke fringe of the gift of Mrs. Saunders,
    price 8*l.*"

"One velvet quisheon and a booke of Comōn
    Prayer gilt for the Comōn Table of the gift
    of James Read & Mr. Henry, 3*l.*"

Mr. Coates, writing in 1802, says :—"The altar-piece is
a plain handsome frontispiece of oak, containing in the two
centre panels, in gold letters, on a black ground, the two
tables of the Law ; and in the side panels, the Lord's Prayer
and the Apostles' Creed. In the pediment, which is circular,
is the tetragrammaton or word Jehovah, in Hebrew characters, with this text of Scripture : 'The law was given by
Moses, but grace and truth came by Jesus Christ.' Below
this : 'Glory to God in the highest, and on earth peace,
goodwill towards men.'"

This Georgian screen was removed in 1848. Its place is
now occupied by a reredos of stone, marble, and tile-work.

The Altar and Mass of Jesus.

Henry Kelsall, clothier, of Reading, who died in 1493,
states in his will that he was the "fyrst mynder, susteyner,

and mayntener of the devocyon of the Masse of Jĥu, kept
and songen in the parisshe chirch of Saynte Lawrence in
Reding."

Ten persons, called the "Brethren of the Mass of
Jesus," formed the guild or brotherhood at that time : these
were—

Richard Cleche, Draper.
John Baxtster, Tanner.
John Langham, " Iremonger."
Stephen Dunster, Draper.
Rauff Myllington, " Clothyer."
William Tru, "Yoman."
John Whylcokks, Chandler and ffisshemonger.
William Scochon, Draper.
Richard Smyth, Gent.
John Twytt. (See "Will of Kelsall.")

Anno 1505-6. " It. payed to Maister Cleche for old det
     du to Jĥu masse."

This chauntry was refounded in 1506 by a licence granted
by Hen. VII. to the inhabitants for that purpose.

It apears from the will of John Pownsar, 1522, that at that
time a certain number of sisters were associated with this
guild, and that they each contributed 6s. 8d. per annum
to the funds.

Anno 1545. " Rec. of the Wardens of the Jĥis masse for
     a teñt in th m̅ ̔ ̔ cat place next to the well for
     iiij yeres endid at thaunūciaĉon A° xxxvj^to at
     x^s by the yere.

" Rec. of the same Wardens for the same tent for An°
     xxxi in the yere that Mr Cawode was warden
     and by hym rec. of John Poynt as apperithe
     uppon thaccompte of the seid Cawode, vj^s viij^d.

"Rec. of the same Wardens for the same teñt for A°
     xxxii paid by Mr Turnor to Mr Justice then
     byng warden as apperithe uppon his accompte
     x^s.

                    Sm̅^a lvj^s viij^d."

" Ordinaunce 1547.—M^d the xviij^th day of Ap^rl the
first yere of the regne of our Soŭaigne lord Kyng Edward
the vj^th before Wiĥm Bureton then Mayo^r of the Borough
of Redyng, Richard Justice & Wiĥm Edmunde late Mayo^rs
ther, John Maynforth, Clerk, vicar of the pisshe of Saynt
laurence in Redyng aforseid John Sawnders & Edward

Butler Wardens of the seid pisshe churche, Nicholas Niclas,
John Bell, Robt Blake, John Bukland, Thom^{a}s Sayntmore,
Raphe Gladwyn, Gilbt. Johnson & dyùce others inhitants
of the seid pisshe assembled together for maynten^{a}unce of
the charge of the Clerks & Mynesters of the quyer ther,
And other good orders ther to be had & contynowed, it
is ordered & enacted by the pties above named in man'
& fo^{r}me followyng :—

Jhc Masse—That is to witt, the masse of Jhu in the seid
churche to be charged & to pay the sexten his wagis yerely
iiij^{ll}, to the same Sexten for tollyng to Jhc Masse, to our
lady Masse ij^s viij^d. For kepyng of the Clock & scowryng
the Cansticks & Desks iiij^s ij^d—ij prests Chambres & the
Clarks ch^{a}mbre.

"*Or lady Masse*—It. that our lady masse to be charged
& to pay John Barkers wage a syngyngman xl^s.

"*The Churche.*—It. the Churche wardens to be charged
w^t the Clarke wage xx^s : w^t Dixson's wage a syngyngman
liij^s iiij^d : Darlyngtons wage xx^s in money, & hous x^s : and
the vndersexton xiij^s iiij^d.

"*Ordinaunce.*—And oũ that, it is ordered & enacted that
all women of the seid pisshe whos husbonds nowe be, or
heretofore have bene bretherne of the Masse of the Jhc
shall from hensforth sitt & have the highest seats or pewes
next unto the Mayo^{r}s wifs seate towarde the pulpitt."

In the accounts for 2 & 3 Phil. & Mary, A.D. 1555, is a
record of the loss of 80*l*. sustained by the Jesus Chantry.

"One Richard Turn^9 late of Redyng, Mercer, disceassed
solde unto the bretherne of the Masse of Jhc founded in
the seid pisshe certayn lande lying in the pisshe of
Kyngsclere in the countie of South, to the yeerley value
of iiij^{li} : ffor the whiche he received & had of the seid
bretherne the sm̃ of lxxx^{li} in full and entier payment for
the same, And desyred that the possession therof myght
be stayed for a tyme for c^{9}tayne consideracõns Albeit immediately aft̃ the money by hym so received he became
ten^{a}nt vnto the seid bretherne, And paied to them to the
vse of the seid Masse, the seid rent of iiij^{li} yerely duryng
his lyfe (And dyed) so that the seid bretherne then had none
other possession, whervppon one John Turn^9 son & heire
vnto the seid Richard, into the seid londe entred And the
same doth w^{t}holde & kepe, so that as yet the seid bretherne
ar w^{t}out ther money & also ther londe." (*Ch. Wards. Accts.*)

"By the return of the Commissioners appointed to

survey colleges and chantries, anno 1 Ed. VI., it appeared that this chantry was worth by the yere in lands and tenements 14*l*. 7*s*. 1*d*.: reparations communibus annis 5*l*. 17*s*. 1*d*. and so remaineth to Richard Adeane, incumbent of 39 yeres, and mete to serve cure and having besides a share of a free chapel in Wallingford 8*l*. 10*s*. Goods remaining there 70*s*. over and besides one chalice weighing 20 ounces."

" Belonging to this chantry was a stipendiary priest founded by Thomas Justice, clerk, and John Clampard, who for the sum of 400 marks, paid to the master and wardens of the guyld of St. Catharine's appertaining to Haberdashers' Hall in London, have bounden the same to pay yerely at iiij termes out of their said hall, to maintain a priest perpetuaily to sing in the said church 7*l*. ; whereof to the mayor for his cost in riding to London for the same, 6*s*. 8*d*., and so remaineth to William Webbe, clerk, of the age of 52 yeres, decrepit, and not able to serve any cure, nor having beside this any living, 6*l*. 13*s*. 4*d*. Goods remaining there 112*s*. 4*d*., chalice, none.

" Rents given to the use of the poore, and to maintain one yerely obit in the pishe church there by one Henry Kelsall, by his last will, anno 1493 per annum 20 shill. ; whereof in relief of the poor 10*s*. and so for the obit 10*s*. The number of houseling people in the said parish be a thousand." (Coates' " Reading.")

From the original Pension Roll of Philip & Mary (Addit. MSS. 8102, Brit. Mus.) we have the following :—

Penc'
{
" Willmi Webbe nup celebrañ in poch Sci Laurens in Reading p. ā. Cˢ.

Rici, A Deane incumbeñ nup cant' voc "Ihs Chañty" in poch Sci Laurenc ibm—viˡˡ."
}

The tenements belonging to this chantry, with those belonging to Jesus chantry in St. Giles's Church, and to Colney's chantry in St. Mary's, were all granted to the mayor and corporation by Queen Elizabeth in her charter.

The altar of this chantry was situated in the nave against the north pier of the chancel arch.

Anno 1502. "It. payed for byndyng & new couyng of the grete antyphoner, & for makyng of &

puttyng in of the ffeste of the visytaͨõ t*nsfy-guraͨõn of Jhu."

Anno 1508. "It. payed to John Cokks for mending of the gret p̓ksong boke of Jhu Masse, xxᵈ."

"It. for mendyng of Jhc cope and for sowyng on of the aulͭ cloth þᵉ neþ̓ frontell of Jhũ autͭ xᵈ.

1512–3. John Pownser, warden.

1513–18. Nicholas Hyde, warden.

1517. "It. a cope paned wᵗ blew velwett & black, & orfrey of grene saten-a-brydgis of the gifte of the x brethern, enbrod̓yd wᵗ the name of Ihc." (Invent.)

1527. "It. for a lok to the long cofer in *Ihc pew*, vijᵈ."

1534. "Payd for ij clamps of Iren for the stepp afore Ihs awͭ iiijᵈ."

1537. "Rec. for tollyng at the ͭment for the Brethren of Ihs masse iiijᵈ." (a common entry).

1541. "It. payd for glewyng an Image upon the long desk befor Ihs awͭ iᵈ.

"It. payd for paveyng afore Ihs awͭ xᵈ.

1542. "Rec. of the wardens of Ihs masse toward the repacoñs of the churche bokes xvˢ."

1549. "Recᵈ of Mʳ. Bukland for Ihc alͭ & Saynt Thomas' alͭ iiijˢ."

1572. "Itm. paied for workmanshypp and stufe to the seats where the chyldren doo sytt where Ihesus Altar was, iijˢ."

See also Wills of Henry Kelsall, John Pownsar, and Walter Barton.

The brass of Walter Barton has been recently placed on the spot formerly occupied by the "table" or reredos of this altar for its better preservation.

Incumbents of Jesus Chantrey.

1509. July 9. Edward Colyer, M.A., was instituted, being presented by Thomas Carpenter, mayor, and Walter Barton, and Robert Benet, the real patrons. He died the same year.

1510. April 20. John Richmond, instituted by the same persons.

1517, Jan. 26. John Richmond, instituted on the resignation of John Richmond, his predecessor, to which he was presented by William Watts, mayor, and Thomas Everard, and John Vansby, wardens of the church of St. Lawrence, the patrons. He died in 1519, and was buried in St. John's chancel, as appears from the church accounts. (See "Inventory," 1517.)

1521. April 17. William Wright, instituted on the death of John Richmond, being presented by William Gyfford, mayor of the borough; William Knyght and Richard Turner being churchwardens. He died in 1527.

Richard a Deane was the last incumbent of the Jesus Chantry. Queen Mary assigned him a yearly pension of 6*l.*

1537. "Payd for horse hire for Sr Ric. Dean, iiij^d."

1547. "Paid to Sr Richard Deane for wag^s allowed hym by the pisshe, x^s.

1549. "Paid and lent to Richard a Deane by th'assent of the pisshe iiij^{li}.

„   "Paid to Sir Ric. a Deane for his yer^s wag^s, xx^s."

Note.—The great bell given by Henry Kelsall was termed "The bell of Ihũ," in honour of this chauntry, which he first founded.

In the same way the fourth was called "Our Lady Bell," and was probably used for the "Angelus" as well as for the offices performed at the Lady Altar. The Lady Bell was usually rung at the death of children, as though the Virgin mother had sympathy with parents in their bereavement. The men sat facing the Jesus Altar on the north side of the nave, and the women sat opposite the altar of the Blessed Virgin on the south side; a coincidence probably intentional.

Our Lady Altar of the Nativity, and the Lady Mass.

This altar was at the east end of the nave on the south side of the chancel arch.

It was probably one of the earliest of the chauntry altars. The writer has not hitherto been able to find any trace of lands or tenements belonging to this chauntry, so that its revenues must have been derived from bequests and voluntary offerings. It is first mentioned in the roll of 1436:

D

"Et de dono Juliane Roche j linth' & j Keûcheff p altare Bte Marie."

There was also an image of the Virgin probably standing near this altar.

> 1441-2. "A new bench or settle was placed before the Image of the B. Mary at a cost of 8ᵈ.
> 1506. "It. payd for mending of one of the grete candlestikks before oʳ Lady vjᵈ."

Her figure was probably supported by a bracket in the wall above or near the Lady Altar, so that the two large candlesticks which stood near the altar might be said to stand " before our Lady."

Anno 1512-13. The wardens of the two masses were first charged with an annual payment of 33ˢ. 4ᵈ. each towards the sexton's wages. It was paid from this time until the Reformation.

> "It. rec. of William Edmonds warden of oʳ lady masse towards the wagˢ of the seid sexten for a yere endid at the seid ffest, xxxiijˢ. iiijᵈ."

This is the first time the "Lady *Mass*" is mentioned in the accounts.

> 1513-4. "John Barfote, warden.
> 1533. "Rec. of the wardens of oʳ lady masse towards the repacõns of the churche bokes, xvˢ."
> "Rec. & borowed of oʳ ladyes box towards the repacõns of the ij chᵒuncells vjˡⁱ ijˢ iiijᵈ.
> "Whereof is payd to the hands of *Richard Turner* in parte of payment of vjˡⁱ ijˢ. iiijᵈ. boroed of oʳ ladyes box this yere, xxijˢ. iiijᵈ."
> 1543. "Rec. & borowed of the wardens of oʳ lady towards the makyng of the newe Canstiks for rode light & for makyng of Clock x mᵃrcs."
> 1545-6. "Mᵈ that Robt Blake owithe for the hire of Sercletts in full payment of xxiiijˢ. dewe to our· lady Masse & Assigned to be paied to the Churche wardens, iiijˢ."
> „   "Paid Nicholas (Niclas) the *warden* of oʳ lady Masse owing to the seid Masse, x mᵃrcs."

There is a most interesting relic of this altar inserted in the north wall of the church, consisting of a panel of white marble, formerly a part of the reredos, and bearing a repre-

VISIT OF THE MAGI.

H.A. Collins - del.

p. 34, 35.

sentation in high relief of the visit of the Magi to the infant
Saviour. The Virgin mother is sitting up in her bed bearing
the Holy Child in her arms, her head reclining on a pillow
placed lozenge-wise against the tester. Her open mantle
is secured by a cord passing across the breast and forming
a triangle, the lower point ending in a tassel a little above
the waist. The aged Joseph with his staff is seated in a
chair at the foot of the couch. One of the royal visitors
(all three are crowned), in a stooping attitude is presenting
his offering to Christ; his two companions stand in the
background, habited in the cassock of the artist's own time
—a smaller female figure stands near the head of the Virgin.
Faint traces of gold and rich colouring are still visible.
Every artistic feature points to the end of Richard the
Second's reign, c. 1400, as the period of its execution. The
iconoclasts of the Reformation have destroyed all the heads
with most of the canopy work above. This very interesting
fragment was discovered in the vicinity of the pulpit, and
judiciously inserted in the wall at the last restoration.

(See end of chapter on the Jesus Altar for "Lady Bell.")

"𝕿𝖍𝖊 𝕺𝖗𝖓𝖆𝖒𝖊𝖓𝖙𝖘 𝖇𝖊𝖑𝖔𝖓𝖌𝖞𝖓𝖌 𝖙𝖔 𝕺𝖚𝖗 𝖑𝖆𝖉𝖞𝖊𝖘 𝕬𝖜𝖑𝖙𝖊𝖗 𝖜𝖎𝖙𝖍𝖞𝖓 𝖙𝖍𝖊 𝖈𝖍𝖚𝖗𝖈𝖍 𝖔𝖋 𝕾𝖆𝖎𝖓𝖙𝖊 𝕷𝖆𝖜𝖗𝖊𝖓𝖈𝖊." (A.D. 1524–5.)

"ffyrste a vestemente of Russet veluet & whytt damask
payned & enbroderyd.

It. a vestement of grene damask enbrod'ᵈyd wᵗ kaᵗyn
whells. (See under St. John's Chapel, anno 1436.)

It. a vestement of whytt Brydge satten wᵗ a crosse of
grene.

It. a vestmᵉte of grene bawdkyn wᵗ a crosse of Blew
enbrod'ᵈyd.

It. an awlᵗ cloth of blew brydgeˢ satten enbrod'ᵈyd wᵗ the
ymage of the trynyte and ffloweres wᵗ ij cᵗteyns of
blew serssenet belongyng to the same.

It. an awlᵗ cloth of Russett veluet enbrod'ᵈyd wᵗ filoʳˢ
wᵗ ij cᵗteyns of Russet & whyt serssenet to the same.

It. an awlᵗ cloth of bawdkyn & blake veluet enbrod'ᵈyd
wᵗ garters and a nother cloth to the same payned of
blew & oreng sarssnet w'owt Cᵗteyns.

It. ij rede awlᵗ clothes paynted wᵗ ij cᵗteyns to the
same.

It. an awlᵗ cloth of lynnen wᵗ ij cᵗteyns to the same,
wᵗ rede crosse for lente.

D 2

It. ij al̃l clothes on diap & a nother playn & ij other al̃l clothes wth a canvas coůyng.

It. ij towels of playn clothe one of them diap.

It. a prynteyd masboke, in the second leffe ' Dn̄ica p^rma Aduēt.'

It. a peyre of cruett^s of pewder.

It. iij paxes.

It. a Corpas m^)ked w^t saynt Anteny Crosse cōteynyng a yerde w^t a casse of cloth of gold & tawnye veluet enbrod^)yd w^t thes lr̃:s 𝕽 & 𝕾. (*Probably the gift of 𝕽ichard 𝕾mith.*)

It. a Corpas m^)ked w^t an 𝕵 in whyte sylke cōteynyng a yerde w^t a casse of dornex to the same.

It. a nother Corpas m^)ked w^t this ̄tre 𝕵𝕳 in blake sylke & a casse of dornex (very ffebyll).

It. a candlestik with ij roses.

It. ij greatt standard^s & ij small kanstyks of laten.

It. vij seyrclett^s yn iiij basketts, in the wardens kepeyng.

It. a vestment of purple velvet.

It. a vestiment of Rede velvet and a white . . . .

It. a vestiment of white Damask w^t a velvet crosse w^t flowres, rede flo^rs.

It. a white wth a grene crosse.

It. a vestment of crimesyn velvet.

It. a white vestiment of fustien for lent.

It. a rownd box gilt abowt.

Itm. a pcessionall pchement, & j ympn^) p^rnted. (*hymner printed*)."

(See Will of Thomas Platts.)

The Altar of St. John the Baptist.

This was situated at the east end of the north chancel aisle, still called St. John's Chapel. This part of the church was separated from the chancel proper by a screen or parclose. It was sometimes called the "Vicar's Chancel," to distinguish it from the other then termed "The Church Chancel."

The references to this chapel in the old accounts are frequent and interesting, and from them we may form an accurate estimate of its former condition.

Anno 1436. "Paid to Thomas Hawe for 2 lbs. of wax, purchased for the *lights of St. Catharine* in the chapel of St. John."

There may have been an altar dedicated to St. Catherine at this time. If so, it must have been removed soon afterwards, because there is no later reference to it in the accounts. This idea is strengthened by the fact that there was a vestment—*i.e.* a chasuble, *embroidered with Catherine wheels*, which in 1524 belonged to the Lady Altar.* The Lights of St. Catherine are first mentioned in the roll of 1433.

"About the fifteenth century, some reasonable doubts having been cast not only on the authenticity of her legend, but on her very existence, vain attempts were made to banish her from the calendar : her festival, after being one of the most solemn in the Church, was by several prelates of France and Germany suppressed altogether, and by others left free from all religious obligations. In England, St. Catharine was especially popular. About the year 1119, Geoffry, a learned Norman, was invited from the University of Paris to superintend the direction of the schools of the Abbey of Dunstable, where he composed a play, entitled ' St. Catherine,' and caused it to be acted by his scholars. This was, perhaps, the first spectacle of the kind ever attempted, and the first trace of theatrical representation that ever appeared in England." (Mrs Jameson.)

Opposite the south-west angle of the tower of St. Lawrence's stood an old hostelry under the invocation of this saint, known as the "Catherine Wheel." It was taken down in 1882, and its site is now occupied by the newly erected premises of the Messrs. Gregory, Love, and Clarke. This inn was probably of mediæval origin.

1505. " It. rec. of the gyft of John Greke toward a payre of grete candylstykkes in Seynt Johns chauncell, iij^s iiij^d.
"John Pownser to the same candylstikks, iij^s iiij^d. Richard Eve to the same, viij^d."
"John Cokks to the same, iiij^d. Ric. Ffrankleyn to the same, viij^d."
" It. payed for a payre of gret candylstykkes in Seynt Johns chau"cell weying $\frac{xx}{v}$ & iii^{ll} (103 lbs.) p'c le li, vi^d. sm̃ lj^s vi^d."

In 1513 the front of the High Altar was transferred to the altar in this chapel.

* See "Altar of St. Blaise." See also "Monuments."

"It. payd to a laborer for iiij dayes at Removyng of the hygh awter & Seynt Johns awt̃ xvj^d.

1514. "It. payed to a laborer for iij dayes & di. at the besynes in brekyng of the awter in Seynt Johns chauncell, xiiij^d.

"It. payed to Croll & hys s꙳uⁿnts for iij dayes work in makyng of the awter in Seynt Johns chauncell & op̃꙳ werks þer iiiˢ iiij^d."

It was consecrated the same year (*vide* High Altar).

1515. "It. payd for makyng of the dore in to the quere out of Saynt Johns chaunsell, xiij^d."

In 1519, Sʳ John Richmond was buried here. He was one of the Incumbents of the Jesus chauntry.

1523. "It. to an Alabast̃ man for makeying clene the table at Saynt John's Awlt̃, & *other* ymages, xvj^d."

In the Inventory of the Altars of 1524–5, we have :—

" 𝕿𝖍𝖊 𝕺𝖗𝖓𝖆𝖒𝖊𝖓𝖙𝖘 𝖇𝖊𝖑𝖔𝖓𝖌𝖞𝖓𝖌 𝖙𝖔 𝕾𝖆𝖞𝖓𝖙𝖊 𝕵𝖔𝖍𝖓'𝖘 𝕬𝖜𝖑𝖙𝖊𝖗 𝖜𝖎𝖙𝖍𝖎𝖓 𝖙𝖍𝖊 𝖘𝖆𝖒𝖊 𝕮𝖍𝖚𝖗𝖈𝖍.

"In p'mis an awlt̃ cloth payned, of red and blew brydge satten.

"It. an awlt̃ cloth of Blak veluct & bawdkyn enbrod̃꙳yd wᵗ gart̃es & c'teyns to the same.

"It. a nother cloth payned of blew & oreng collo͏ʳ s꙳ssenet.

"It. an awlt̃ cloth of Russet veluct & whyte satten.

"It. a stayned cloth wᵗ the ymage of oʳ ladye thervppon.

"It. ij grete standards of latten wᵗ ij small kanstyk꙳ of latten."

1537–8. "Payd for makeyng a hangyng of rede bawdkyn at Seynt Johns Awt̃ & the curtens before th'appostles at the high Awt̃, vj^d."

At the sale of church goods, in 1549, this altar, with a cope chest, was purchased by Mr. Grey for 6s. 8d.

1562. "*Sale of olde Tymber.*"

"Item of Willm Dudlesoll (C. W.) for the borders of the roode lofte and a trymmar that stoode uppon S. Johns Awlter, xˢ."

1568. " Itm. for makinge the partycion betwene the chaun-
sells & mendinge ye seats in St Johns chauncell, iiij^s."
" Itm. for mendinge of the east wyndowe in S. Johns
Chaunsell & the wyndowe by the organs in y^e
same chañcell, xvj^d." (See " Organ.")

The old stalls or desks, undoubtedly the very same provided by Henry Kelsall in 1493, were removed out of this
chapel into the choir at the restoration, under Mr. Ferrey,
in 1848. (The east ends of three of these stalls only are of
fifteenth century work.)

This chapel was probably constructed for the Brethren
and Sisters of the Hospital of St. John the Baptist, founded
by Abbot Hugh, in 1196.

A good piscina, but with a broken bowl, was discovered
in the respond of the arches in the south-east corner of this
chapel, in 1848.

(See Will of Thomas Platts, 1522. Also under article
" Seats.")

The Altar of St. Blaise.

There is only one reference to this altar in the church
records :—

Anno 1433. " Et in panno cepiti emp' ad summ altare
& altare Sancti Blasii, ij^s."

This saint keeps his place in the English reformed
calendar. He was considered the special patron and pro-
tector of woolcombers and woolstaplers. The dedication
of an altar to him in the municipal church indicates the
existence of the woollen manufacture in the town at this
early period.

" In simple figures and devotional pictures he is represented as an old man with a white beard, attired as a bishop
with the planeta and mitre, holding in one hand a crosier,
and in the other an iron comb such as is used by woolcombers, the instrument of his torture : this is his peculiar
attribute." (Mrs. Jamieson.)

If the altar of St. Thomas was not substituted for the
altar of St. Blaise in 1502, then the latter was probably
removed about 1520, when so much was done to the interior
of the church. Its old altar cloth with the embroidered
figure of St. Blaise was assigned to the altar of St. Thomas.

St. Thomas' Altar.

This stood on the north side of the entrance to St. John's Chancel, and in a line with the Altars of Jesus and the B. Virgin. It is not mentioned in the church records before 1502.

> "It. payed for *makyng of Scÿte Thom's Awter*, Seynt Georg⁸ Awter for settyng of Seynt George in to the loft, viij⁸ viij."

It seems probable that the loft here mentioned was an extension of the rood loft over the north aisle; the altar and image of St. George being *on* the gallery, and the altar of St. Thomas, and perhaps two others, *beneath* it. This apostle was considered the patron saint of *"carpenters,"* builders, and architects.

> ("*Thomas*" "*Carpenter*," a parishioner, was Mayor of Reading in 1504–6–8–9. His wife's mother was interred in the church in 1498–9, and he in 1519–20. *He may have been the founder.* His widow "*Mres*" Carpenter was buried in the church in 1534.)

> Anno 1508. "It. payed to Willm Stamford for mending & setting on of a lyon upon a grete candylstyk before Seynt Thomas Aulᵗ iijᵈ."

> (The lion was probably one of three—couchant, on which the base of the standard rested.)

> 1541. "Payd for the desk before Sayn Thomas Awᵗ viij⁸ xi."

In 1549 this altar was purchased by Mr. John Buckland (mayor) with the Jesus Altar for 4s. It was replaced in the reign of Queen Mary :—

> 1558 "Itm. for paynting the table oū S. Thom⁸s awlter v⁸."

" The Ornaments belongyng to Saynte Thomas Awlter within the same Church. (1524.)

In pˡmis a vestemēte of grene damask wᵗ a Crose of blew veluete.

It. a vestmēte of whyte brydg⁸ satten wᵗ a crose of grene brydg⁸ satten.

It. a vestmēte of crymson sylk wᵗ grypp⁸ & a small crose of whyte.

It. a vestmēte of rede silk with a small crosse.

It. a white fusstian for lent.

It. a blew awlᵗ cloth enbrodᵈyd wᵗ the ymag of sent Clemēte & awngellˢ in the ffronte.

It. an awlᵗ cloth of crayne colloʳ veluete & whyte satten & ij cʳteyns of sᵈssenete of the same colloˢ.

It. an awlᵗ cloth of blak veluete & bawdkyn payned enbrodᵈyd wᵗ garters & ij cʳteyns of blew and orenge colloʳ sᵈssenete.

It. an awlᵗ cloth of blak veluete & blew satten wᵗowt cʳteyns wᵗ a crucifix.

It. an awlᵗ cloth wᵗ the ymage of Saynte blasse.

It. an awlᵗ cloth of lynnen wᵗ Rede Crosses for lente wᵗ cʳteyns.

It. an aulᵗ cloth of cᵈsenet playn blak & oreng.

It. a corporas mᵈlked wᵗ a ffloʳ of blak sylke & a case of Rede tyssew.

It. a corporas of blak velvet wᵗ a kercher.

It. a nother of blew bawdkyn wᵗ a kercher.

It. a pax of copp enamelled wᵗ a crucifix.

It. ij grete standards of latten wᵗ ij small kanstyks of latten.

It. a masboke prynted begynyng in the second leff ' stat memoria.'

It. ij altᵗ cloths of diap old & a . . . ."

The Sepulchre Altar.

This appears to have been situated on the north side of the choir beneath the middle arch of the arcade (see below, " 1513"). It was appointed for the deposition of the consecrated elements of the Eucharist from the evening of Good Friday until the morning of Easter Day; during which time it was watched by a quasi-guard, after the manner of our Lord's sepulchre. The sacrament was then removed with loud Alleluias and much rejoicing to its accustomed place on the High Altar.

The church books contain many references to this mediæval ceremony.

Anno 1498. "In pᵈmis payed for wakyng of the sepulcr viijᵈ."—Similar entries occur yearly until the Reformation.

1507.* "It. paied to Sybel Derling for nayles for the sepulcre & for rosyn to the *resurreccyon pley* ij^d. ob."

1512. "It. payed to Water Barton to the new Sepulcur iiij^{li}. xiij^s.x^d."—This was a very considerable sum at that period, and it must have been an object of unusual magnificence.

Anno 1513. "It. payd to Harry Horthorne for settyng upp of the frame aboute the sepulcre & for closyng of the dore in Seynt Johns chauncell to the quyre, vj^d." (See end of this article "*Henry Hawthorne.*")

(A new door was opened in 1515.)

1513-4. "It. payd to Harry Horthorne for ij pecis to hang the sepulcre cloth on, ij^d."

1513-4. "It. payd for ale at Removyng of the sepulcre to the carpenters iij^d. ob."

1516. "It. paid for makying of the lofte for the sepulcre light li^s. ij^d."

" The Ornaments belongyng to the sepulcre Awlter in the same Church. (1524.)

In p^{l}mis a vestemēte of Crymson veluet w^t a crose of rych tyssew.

It. a vestemēte of Russet satten w^t a crose of cloth of gold.

It. a vestemēte of whyt brydg^s satten w^t a Crose of grene brydg^s satten.

It. an awlt cloth of Crymson & tawny veluet enbrod'yd w^t fílo^{rs} of gold : & for the *nether* pte of the same, Crymson saten & cloth of bawdekyn—for the sepulcr awter. (*Inv.* 1517.)

It. an awlt cloth of crymson satten & blew bawdkyn w^t ij C^{r}teyns to the same of grene.

It. iij^o C^{r}teyns of Russete & blew s ssenete w^t an awlt cloth of whytte & grene.

It. ij small Kanstykks of latten."

1538-9. "Paid for makeyng the beam lights ou the sepulcre ayenst east' xxj^d."

1544-5 "Paid for sylk poynts for the Sepulcre ij^d."

* This entry may relate to the performance of a Mystery on "Corpus Christi" day.

In 1549 the whole seems to have been swept away.
"Rec^d of Mr. Bell for the sepulcre & the
frame for taps thereto annexid xx^s."

Among the inquiries in 1554 after the goods alienated
sold and stolen in the time of Edward VI. we have—

"Item for the valence about the sepulcre to know who
hath it in kepyng."

This is repeated. "It. to enquire for the valence &
ffrenge about the sepulcre."

1561. "Item receyved of Mathew Reynoldes and Water
Sawyer for the sepulcre they bought, xx^s viij^d."

In 1562, "The fframe where the sepulcher Lighte dyd
stand" was taken down by Willyam Marten and his man
together with the rood loft and the way to the same.

"Sayle of olde Tymber."

"In p⁹mis of Master Butler for ye loft *over* the chancell
x^s"—evidently the loft "where the sepulcher Lighte dyd
stand." (Edward Butler's brass is now on the south wall of
the sacrarium.)

Note.—"Henry Hawthorn" was a Reading carpenter, and
obviously a man of some note in his time. He first occurs
in 1501 as one of the churchwardens of St. Lawrence's. In
1508 he presented a ladder of "xx rongs" to the church.
It once belonged to John Turner, a turner in the High
Street. In 1510 he prepared the wainscot for the ceiling
and the decorations of the altar by the Mayor's seat. In
1513 a gallon of ale was given to him and his men for
raising a "coffer" into the steeple. In 1516 he repaired the
seats on the north side of the church.

Anno 1518. "It. payd to Harry Horthorne for tymbre
werkmanshipp & for bowrdyng of men as
apperith by his bills, vij^{li} iiij^d."

Very much must have been done to the roof or fittings
of the church at this time.

In 1519 he relaid the gutter between the two chancels.

He died in 1522 and was buried in the church.

"Rec. for the grave of Henry Horthorn vi^s viij^d—couyng
the same viij^d."

His widow died in 1527, and in the same year William
Coon or Cone, Hawthorn's associate, who executed the
carving in 1518, was laid to his rest.

This Henry left a son Henry, who followed his father's

occupation. He first occurs as the maker of a railing for the belfry in 1528, and in 1530 he was employed for ten days in mending the bells at 6d. " by the day."

He is mentioned no more in the records of St. Lawrence. In the fine collection of MSS. at Loseley House near Guildford, belonging to Wm. More Molyneux, Esq., there is an account of the removal of certain tents or wooden lodgings from Oatlands to be re-erected at Chobham, anno 38 Hen. VIII. by *Henri Harthorn*. Under the heading of "*Carpenters*" the time of his service is reckoned to be 28 days 40 hours; and again under the heading of "*Sawyers*," we have

"D. to Henry Hothorne in prest on a Reconyng for his owne wadges and other carpenters nott yett payd for Chobbã. Reconyng vj^{li}."

This document formerly belonged to Sir Thomas Cawarden, Master of the Revels at that time.

Curiously enough, either himself or another of his *name* and *calling* crops up at Seale near Farnham, where in the C.W. accounts for 1598—" For a boorde and mending the pulpett one daies worke." The name does not occur in Seale Registers before the 27th of Jan. 1593, when he married " Joan Brombye" of that place. He settled there and had issue, William, bap. 1594, Eliz., bap. 1596, Mary, bap. 1599, Thomas, 1603, John, bap. 1606, Robert, bap. 1613. The children of William, John and Robert appear in these Registers.)

St. George's Altar

was constructed at the same time as the altar of St. Thomas (q.v.) anno 1501–2, and apparently on the loft above it.

(There is a remarkably early instance of this arrangement at Compton Church, Surrey, where the eastern half of the chancel is divided into two stories by an original Norman gallery of stone with cross groinings beneath. The vault is of one span, and its western arch or face is richly decorated. The old Norman rail of *oak* traversing the front of this gallery is in wonderful preservation. The altar was visible from the nave.)

Anno 1503–4. "It. payed for ij yerds & an di of wyer to þ^e auter in Seynt Georg^s loft, & for dressyng of the same aut^r iij^d. ob."

As the loft was repaired at the same time as the altar
of St. Thomas was constructed, it may be concluded that
the gallery *above* St. Thomas' altar was that which is here
called St. George's loft; indeed, there was no other to
which such a term could be applied, for besides the rood
loft and this, there were only the ringing floor in the
tower, and a loft for the sepulchre light. It was approached
by a staircase in the north wall, the upper doorway of
which is still visible near the entrance to St. John's Chancel.

Besides the altar, this loft contained a famous image of
St. George on horseback, probably triumphing over the
terrible dragon. This was coeval with the gallery and the
altar.

The church records for 1534 present some interesting
details relating to this image.

" **Charge of**   { Ffirst, payd for iiij^{or} Caffes (calves)
Saynt George.   { skynes & ij° horsse skynes iiij^{s} vj^{d}."
         (Evidently for the horse's coat.)

" Payd for makeyng the loft that Saynt George standeth
    apon vi^{d}" (*a small dais*).

" Payd for ij° plonks for the same loft viij^{d}."

" Payd for iiij^{or} pesses of clowt-lether ij^{s} ij^{d}."

" Payd for makeyng the yron that the hors resteth
    apon vj^{d}."

" Payd to John Paynter for his labo^{r} xlv^{s}."

" Payd for roses, bells gyrdle, swerd, & dager iij^{s} iiij^{d}."

" Payd for settying on the bells & roses iij^{d}."

" Payd for naylls necessarie therto x^{d} ob."

    Note.—The George and Dragon Hotel in this
    parish, commonly called " The George," is mentioned
    in the church accounts for 1523–4 :—

      " Rec. for the knyll of a straung^{r} that dyed at the
        George xij^{d}."

      " Rec. for the manes grave that dyed at the George
        & for couyng of the same vij^{s}. iiij^{d}."

Mr. Justice's Altar.

Thomas Justice was appointed vicar of St. Lawrence's,
Sept. 18, 1502. He resigned Dec. 20, 1518. Mr. Coates
states that he and John Clampard gave 400 marks to the
wardens of the guild of St. Catharine, Haberdashers' Hall,
London, in order that they should pay the yearly sum of
7*l.* to provide a priest to sing perpetually in the said church

of St. Lawrence. Mr. Coates assigns this endowment to the *Jesus Chauntry*. But as there were only two chauntry priests surviving in Q. Mary's days, one of whom, *Richard a Deane* is expressly named as the incumbent of the Jesus Chauntry, and as Mr. Coates associates William Webb with *Mr. Justice's* foundation at the same time, the two chantries were evidently distinct.

He was probably the son of William Justice, the elder, of Reading, who represented the town in Parliament in 1509–10, and served the office of Mayor in 1513. In his will, dated 18 Feb. 1520, at Somerset House (Reg. Mainwaring, fo. 6), is the following :—" I bequeath to *Thomas* Justice my son *preest* C ounces of plate most necessary to him wᵗ a blake gowne," &c. He bequeathed to the church of Myre, where he was born, 10*l.*, that the priest there might pray for his soul and the souls of his parents. He desired that his body might be buried in St. Mary's, Reading, before the Altar of Jesus.

> Anno 1520-1. "It. vppon m̃. Thomᵃs Justice for the grave of Mʳᵉˢ Smyth his moder vjˢ viijᵈ—covering vjᵈ." The sum was paid the year following.
>
> 1531. "Payd for makyng the foldyng hatche by *Mr. Justice Awter* viijᵈ."
>
> Anno 1552-3. "In the custodie of Thomᵃs Byggs a fair Table for an awᵗ of the gift of Mʳ Thomᵃs Justice late vicar ther."
> (See Index.)

The Vestry Altar.

There is no clue in the church accounts to the position of the ancient vestry. It seems to have been a wooden chamber constructed within the church; its flat covering forming a sort of small gallery.

> 1518. "It. for making of an auter in the vestrie, vjᵈ."
>
> 1525. "It. to the glasyer for mendyng the wyndow in the ' halpac' oũ the vestre, xvjᵈ."
>
> 1562. "Itm. payd to Willyam Marten and his man for setting up of the borders of the lofte ouer the vestry, xvjᵈ." (These were the carved borders of the old rood loft purchased by W. Duddelsoll, the C.W., and presented by him for this purpose.)

St. Nicholas Altar.

1538–9. "Payd for ij tap͛s made for Saynt Nichūs Awt͛, vj^{d}."

The chamber of a priest or chaplain called "Sir Nicholas" was repaired by the churchwardens in 1534.

1537–8. "Rec. for a surples of Sr Nicholas sold, iij^{s}.

Whether this was a temporary altar, erected on the occasion of some boys' festival, or whether it was an old one with a new name, under the auspices of "Sir Nicholas," it is impossible to say, for this is the only reference to it in the church accounts.

The Trinity Altar.

"The Ornaments belongyng to the trynyte awlter within th͛t same Church." (Anno 1524.)

In p^{i}mis a vestemente of cloth of sylu͛, w^{t} a Crosse of cloth of gold.

It. a vestemēte of Blak veluet w^{t} a Crosse of grene cloth of gold.

It. a vestemēte of grene brydge^{s} satten w^{t} a Crosse of cloth of gold.

It. a vestemēte of grene bordalexaund͛ w^{t} a crosse of yellow dornex.

It. a Corpras mayd of a Crysom w^{t} a case of cloth of golde & grene veluete.

It. a corpras cōteynyng a yerd m͛kyd w^{t} this lr̄e **M** in golde w^{t} a case of Rych Bawdkyn.

It. a pax of Copp & enamylled w^{t} the pytye of o^{r} ladye.*

It. a payr of Cruetts of pewd͛.

Itm. ij small Kanstyks of latten.

Itm. ij Awlt͛ Clothes of lynnen playn.

Itm. A wrytten maseboke couyd w^{t} crymson veluete in the second leff begynyng '*inimici rugiēt*', w^{t} a pyn of sylu͛ for the Regesters."

Anno 1549. "Rec. of Mr Grey for the Trinitie Alt͛ of m͛ble w^{t} the Trynyte, x^{s} viij^{d}."

There is no reference to this altar in the church accounts

* A representation of the B. Virgin mourning over the dead body of Jesus reclining on her knees.

under this name.   As the altar was of marble, it must have stood on the ground floor.

The Side Altar,

mentioned in 1510, is probably the same as the "The altar by the Mayors Seat," referred to in the same year.

It seems to have been situated immediately under the rood screen, on the south side of the church, in a chapel to west of the Lady Altar.   The piscina, visible in the bottom of one of the nave windows, probably marks its approximate position.

> 1510. "Itm. payed for hewyng & pgettyng off the syde awter, xiij^d."
> 1510–11. "It. payd to Cone for selyng & dressyng of the aw^e be Mr Mayo's set, ij^s iij^d." (See p. 43.)
> 1541. "Payd for settyng the seats agaynst the syde aw^{e}s, ij^s viij^d."

St. Clement's Altar.

St. Clement was acknowledged as the patron of smiths. On the easternmost pillar, between the nave and aisle, are the remains of a painted shield, charged with the smith's arms :—

Ermines, two horseshoes in bend arg^t on a bordure of the last, a pair of pincers, hatchet, and sword, sable.   It is very probable that his altar was in the vicinity of this pillar, and in the north aisle.   The shield is on the *north*-east side of the pillar.

> 1516. "It. paid for mendyng of the beame for Saynt Clements light, viij^d."
> 1520. "It. payd for mendyng of the cloth before Saynt Clement, iiij^d."
> 1549. "Rec. of Thomas Turner for boks & for Saynt Clements Alt^e, xvij^s."

Holy Loaf.

Anno 5 Ed. vj.   (1551.)

"At this day it was concludid & aggreid that from hens-forthe euy inhiitant of the pisshe shall bere & pay euy Sonday in the yere v^d for euy tenement as of old tyme the Holy Lofe was used to be paid and be received by the pisshe clark wekely, the seid clark to have eũy Sonday for his paynes i^d. And iiij^d residewe to be paied & delyũed eũy Sonday to the churchewardens to be employed for bred & wyne for the communyon. And if any oũplus therof shall be, of suche money so received to be to the use of the churche; and if any shall lacke, to be borne & paied by the seid churchewardens: ̃pvided allwey, that all suche psons as ar poore & not hable to pay the whole, be to haue Ayde of such others as shall be thoughte good, by the discrec̃õn of the Churchwardens."

1555. Rec. of money gathered for the holy lofe, ix^s iiij^d.

Bride=Pastes.

1557. Item for the hyer of the bryde pastes this yere, vi^s viij^d.
1561. Bryde-past. Item Receyved of John Radlye, vj^s viij^d. (last entry.)

Singing Bread.

A° 37–8 H. viij. "Paid for Syngyng brede on Palme Sonday, ij^d."

Lights.

The churchwardens' accounts abound with references to lights. They seem to have been of four kinds :—1. *Symbolic*, such as accompanied the celebration of all sacramental rites and the obsequies of the dead ; 2. *Festive*, such as were used for illuminations on the greater festivals, and especially at Christmas and Candlemas; 3. *Honorary*, or *Votive ;* of such were the lights before the Sacrament, the Rood light, and the lights of St. Catharine ;* and 4. *Ordinary*, or *Necessary*.

Symbolic.

Of this kind were the Font Taper, the Paschal Candle, and the Altar Lights. Each altar in the church was provided with two candlesticks for the re-table, and *not more:* it was the old English use. Two of these,

* See under "Altar of St. John the Baptist."

E

weighing 41 oz., were of silver, and belonged to the High
Altar, having been presented by Mr. Richard Cleche.   (Inventory.)

> 1508. " It. payd to Hew Goldsmyth for mendyng of the
> vices in the sylu candylstykks xvjᵈ."   They
> were parcel-gilt.
>
> " It. payd to the same Hew for gyldyng and sow-
> deryng of þᵉ fote of on sylu canstyk iiijᵈ."

At the Reformation sale in 1547, *six* great candlesticks
or standards were purchased by John Saunders, bellfounder,
of Reading.   Two belonged to the Lady Altar, two to
St. Thomas', and two to St. John's.   Two more are mentioned
in 1502 as standing in the chancel (see under *Paschal
Bason*).

> " It. payed for scowryng of the grete candylstikks in the
> quere vjᵈ." (see Altars).

Torches and wax lights were always used at funerals.
The tapers were provided by the churchwardens, who
charged the friends of the deceased for the amount consumed, and from the varying sums we may form some estimate of the quality of the deceased, and the nature of the
obsequies—*e.g.*, 1498—" Itm. rec. for the sepulcr of Thomas
Butler vjˢ viijᵈ.   It. rec. for wast of Torchys at the burying
of the same Thomˢ ijˢ jᵈ"—whereas the next entry, at the
burying of " Webb's wife" shows only 4*d*. for consumption
of wax.

> 1501. " It. rec. for wast of torchis at the berying of Sʳ
> John Hide vicar of Soñyng ijˢ vjᵈ."
>
> 1502-3. " It. rec. ffor the graue of lawrence Morton gen-
> tyllman xˢ."
>
> " It. rec. for wast of torchis at the same byryng xxᵈ."

After 1510 this demand for waste of torches seems to be
included in the charge for tolling the great bell.   These
funeral torches were of large size.

> 1498. " Itm. payed for ij torchys weying lxiˡⁱ pᵒc le ɫi ijᵈ.
> ob. xijˢ viijᵈ."
>
> 1502. " It. payed to Mʳ Smyth for ij torchis weying xlvijˡⁱ
> pᵒc le ɫi iiijᵈ. smˢ xvˢ iiijᵈ."
>
> 1505. " It. payed for vj torchis weying $\frac{xx}{iiij}$ & xvjˡⁱ
> (96 lbs.) pᵒc le ɫi iiijᵈ.—xxxiiˢ."

A lantern also was carried before the priest when bearing

the Eucharist to the sick in his visitations.   It is frequently mentioned.

The *Paschal Taper* for Easter was usually large and costly.

The cost of the provision of this and the font taper occurs as a yearly item.

1498. "Itm. payed for the Pascalls and the ffonte taper to Mr Smith iiij^s."

1498. "Itm. payed for makyng long^9 of Mr Smythis molde w^t a Judas to the Pascall vj^d."

1503. "It. rec. at Estur for the pascall xl^s."

1505. "It. paid to Maistres Smyth for wast of the pascall ij^s."

"It. payed for xxviij ℔ wex for a *stoke* to the pascall & to the font tapyr and for to renew the rode light p^{9}c le ℔ v^d sm^a xj^s viij^d."

1508. "It. payed the same day to Wa^9 Barton for xx^{lt} of wax for a pascall p^{9}c le ℔ v^d sm^a—viij^s iiij^d."

"It. payed to maistres Smyth for making of xiiij^{lt} wax to the same pascall vj^d."

"It. payed to the same maistres for j^{lt} of grene fflowris to the for seid pascall vj^d."

THE PASCHAL BASON.

1498. "Itm. payed for the Pascall bason and the hangyng of the same xviij^s."

"Itm. payed for vij pendaunts for ye same bason and þ^e caryage fro London iij^s."

1513. "It payd for makyng clene of the basyn *for the pascall* & the ij grete candstyks in the quere ayenst Est^9."

From the preceding entries it would appear that the Paschal candle was fixed in a bason weighted by pendants necessary to keep the candle upright, and suspended probably near the High Altar. With a Judas of wax attached, and a wreathing of green wax flowers, the laving of the candle would be considerable—hence the necessity for the bason beneath.

Festal Lights. (CHRISTMAS.)

1510. "Payed for iij^{lt} of talow candylls for to sett in þ^e churche on Crystmas Daye iij^d ob."

1524. "It. for makeyng the fframe for the aungells vppon Cristmas day iiij^d."

1525. "It. for i^lb of Sysses (*small wax tapers*) for the Aungells at Crystmas ix^d."

This would appear to indicate a constructional representation of the Nativity attended by angels, perhaps in ranks or gradations, bearing lighted tapers.

1506. "It. payed for sysis to the holy bush (*holly*) at Christmas ix^d.

"Paid Macrell for an *holy bush before the Rode* ij^d."

(CANDLEMAS DAY.)

The commemoration of the Purification of the B. V. Mary was especially a feast of lights. Barnaby Googe in his "Popish Kingdom" thus describes the ceremonies of the day :—

Then comes the day wherein the Virgin
  offered Christ unto
The Father chiefe, as Moyses law
  commaunded hir to do.
Then numbers great of Tapers large
  both men and women beare
To Church, being halowed there with pomp,
  and dredeful wordes to heare.
This done, eche man his Candell lightes
  where chiefest semeth he
Whose Taper greteste may be seene,
  and fortunat to bee
Whose Candell burneth clere and bright.
  A wondrous force and might
Doth in these candells lie, which if
  at any time they light
They sure beleve that neyther storme
  or tempest dare abide,
Nor thunder in the skies be heard
  nor any debils spide,
Nor fearfull sprites, that walk by night,
  nor hurts of frost or haile.

Alban Butler writes: "The candles are blessed previously to the use of them, because the church blesses and sancti-fies by prayer whatever is employed in the Divine service. We are to hold the candles in our hands on this day while the 'Gospel' is read or sung ; also, from the 'Elevation' to the 'Communion,'" &c. ("Lives of the Saints," Feb. 2.)

Special lights were employed in the church on this festival. A kind of chandelier, called a "trendell," was constructed for the occasion. It seems to have consisted of a wheel, or perhaps a series of wheels, of graduated size, attached horizontally to a central pole suspended from the roof, the lights being fixed on the outer margins.

A new one was made in 1502–3.

"It. payed to John Turner for makyng of the Trendyll ij^a.
It. payed for corde to the same Trendyll vj^d.
It. payed for tymber to make þ^e trendyll whele.
It. payed for colo's to þ^e same trendyll.
It. payed to Maistres Smyth for the trendyll xiij^a iiij^d.
(*evidently for lights to furnish it*).
It. payed for payntyng of the same trendyll v^d.
It. payed for a bolte & a swevyll to the trendyll vj^d.
It. payed for polys to John Turn') for þ^e trendyll ij^d."

1539–40. "Payed for the tymber trendle for *Candlemas Day* iiij^d."

The *sepulchre* was illuminated on Easter Day.

1538–9. "Payd for makeyng the beam lights oũ the sepulchre ayenst east xxi^d."

Ibonorarp or Votive

lights were those burning before the Eucharist, the Rood and other images or pictures. (See under *High Altar*, 1537, *Rood Loft*. The light of St. Catharine is mentioned in 1433.

Ordinary Lights.

1534. "Payde to Pastler for settynge the braunche apon the Rode loft," &c., xvj^d."
1536–7. "Payd for takeyng down the braunche in the qwere iiij^d."
„ "Payd to Hugh Smyth for settyng upp the same braunche agayne & for mendyng a dore to an aumbrey viij^d."
1547. At the "Reformation Sale" John Saunders, the bellfounder, purchased the following articles of latten :—
"A Braunch w^t vij cansticks."
"iiij litel cansticks."

"vj greate cansticks."

"ij lampes."

"A beame w^t x cansticks and spyndells."

"vj lynks."

"xx laten bolls that were of the rode light."

1633 (Inventory). "Item, one swinginge brasse candle-sticke wth xij braunches or socketts" (given by Richard Johnson in 1631).

1772 (Inventory). "One Brass Hanging Candlestick with sixteen branches or socketts," the gift of Mr. Richard Underwood.

"One with eleven do. the gift of Mr. Richard Johnson."

The church is now lighted with gas.

The Pulpit.

1537-8. "Payd for makeyng the *walls* about the pulpett ij^s."

1592-3. "To John Braker for ye work ouer y^t Pulpit xxij^d."

1639. "It. by a tax of the pishioners towardes the new pulpett and church reparations, 13^{li} 19^s 3^d."

"Itm. p^d goodman lime for mooving the pulpit and setting him lower 4^s 3^d."

1642. The pulpit was removed.

"It. for taking downe the old Pulpitt and making the reading place and setting upp the seats in the chancell and for new tymber & worke iij^{li} ij^s ij^d.

"It. for a hinge & a latch to the old pulpitt xiij^d.

"It. for an houre glasse & painting, and v turned banisters xiij^d."

This pulpit was sold in 1741, when the present one was erected:—

"Oct. 6. Of Mr Slade for the old Pulpit, 4*l*. 4*s*. o*d*."

From Hewett's "Hundred of Compton," p. 79, it would appear that the pulpit of 1639 was sold to the church-wardens of Aldworth, where it may still be seen, with the reading pew of corresponding style, though of somewhat more ornate workmanship. The three lower panels of the prayer desk are large, and exhibit porticos of a temple in perspective (basso-relievo). There are cherubs' heads, and

THE PULPIT, ALDWORTH.

p. 54.

PRAYER DESK, ALDWORTH.

H.A. Collins del.

p. 54.

wreaths of flowers depending from perforated scroll-like designs peculiar to the Elizabethan and Jacobean styles. The panels are divided by pilasters with caryatides. The pulpit is similarly treated, but the lower panels instead of porticos have a shield-like design with scrolled and perforated margins.

The pre-Reformation pulpit stood somewhere about the middle of the nave, and probably near one of the pillars not far from the mayor's seat (see under " Jesus Altar," anno " 1545"). The pulpit as it was in 1802 is thus described by Mr. Coates :—

" The pulpit is hexagonal, having a rich foliage of carved work running round the bottom and the compartments on each side. In each compartment is a piece of inlaid work : 1, the cross ; 2, the sacramental cup ; 3, the letters I. H. S , with a cross radiated ; 4, an open book, with the words ' Biblia Sacra ;' 5, an inlaid square with a border of scroll-work. The sounding-board is ornamented by a piece of inlaid work representing the Dove, from which flow rays terminated by stars in clusters. It is supported by two fluted pilasters of a composite order. It is said to be after the model of St. Giles-in-the-Fields."

The Rood Loft.

This was a large gallery immediately in front of the chancel arch, occupying the whole width of the nave, and extending westward as far as the great beam above Blagrave's monument. It was approached by a stone staircase in the south-east corner by the Lady Altar, where the blocked angle indicating its position still remains. The steps were removed and the hole filled up with rubble and grouting when the chancel arch was enlarged in 1848. The roof of the nave above the jubé was of a more ornate character than the western portion, and this distinction remained until very recent times. Mr. Coates writes (1802) : " From Blagrave's monument to the chancel the ceiling is elliptical, of panel work, with roses and other ornaments at each intersection." Upon the front of this gallery stood, or partly depended, the *Rood*, a carved representation (probably life-size) of the crucifixion, with the figures of SS. Mary and John standing by on the right and left of the Sufferer respectively. On the principal festivals the

"Gospel" for the day was read on the north side of this loft by the "Deacon," accompanied by acoliths with lighted tapers.

Here also the clerks sang the "Passion" on Palm Sundays.

The Rood Loft of St. Lawrence's seems to have been a goodly structure, and must have greatly enhanced the beauty and solemnity of the church. The underpart was ceiled, or perhaps groined, with oak work, and the altars beneath with their lighted tapers dimly seen through the trellis in front, must have had a striking and touching effect.

The following extracts will open many trains of thought which it would almost be impossible to follow with the pen :—

1436. "Et in fenÿ de la Selyng in le Roodloft sol' Johi Hale xxiijᵃ iiijᵈ."

1498-9. "It. payed for vj laten bolls on the *north* syde of the rode loft viijˢ." (These were sconces for tapers : see 1510.)

  ,,   "It. rec. at Alhalow tyde for the rode lyght xˢ iiijᵈ."

  ,,   "It. payed for xliijˡⁱ of Iren warke on the south end of the rode loft to stay the lyght p'c the ħ ijᵈ. smᵃ vijˢ ijᵈ."

  ,,   "It. payd for turnyd pynnys to the seid lyght vjᵈ."

  ,,   "It. payed for scowryng of the laten bolts in the seid loft iiijᵈ."

  ,,   "Itm. payed to Strawford for braggetts to fastyn the crests in þᵉ same loft vjᵈ."

(Cressets were hollow vessels employed for holding lights. The term "crests" in architecture is used for any ornamental upper finishing, so the term may refer to any ornamental border standing on the upper front edge of the Rood Loft ; but the expression "*in* the loft" seems to suggest the former interpretation.)

1488-9. "It. payed for a lyne to draw the curtens in the same loft iijᵈ."

1505. "It. payed to Macrell for tendyng of the rode lyʒt for makyng clene of the rode loft & for shottyng of the organs for a yer endyd at Mychælmas iiijˢ viijᵈ."

  ,,   "It. payed to the Clerks for syngyng of the Passion in Palme Sonday in Ale iᵈ."

1506. " It. paied for a line to draw the curtens in þᵉ rode
loft vᵈ."

  ,,   " It. paied for mending of þᵉ wyer for þᵉ clothe
before þᵉ rode vᵈ."

  ,,   " It. paid to Macrell for an holy bussh before the
rode ijᵈ."

  ,,   " It. paid to M. Smith for making of the rode
ly3t & 'for ijˡˡ of new wex to the same iijˢ
iiijᵈ ob."

1506. " It. paied to Thomᵃs Wiche smyth for makyng
of a key to the gret cofer in the rode loft, vᵈ."

  ,,   " It. paied to the same John Gege for settying
up of the wier to draw the cloþ be fore the
rode in the rode loft iijᵈ."

  ,,   " It. paied for the seling behynde the said rode vjˢ."

  ,,   " It. payed for v coples to the selyng above the
rode loft xvjˢ viijᵈ."

  ,,   " It. paied to Harry Blankstan paynt͡ for gyldyng
of the Rode Mary & John in the rode loft
xˢ iiijᵈ."

  ,,   " It. paied for setting vp the seid rode Mary &
John for removyng of th'organs & for making
yᵉ sete for þᵉ pleyer of þᵉ same organs xxᵈ."

1507. " Paied to the goodman Cone for dressyng of yᵉ
rodlow3t ijˢ."

1510–11. " It. payd for clēsyng the Imagerye of the rode
lofte at request of þᵉ pisshe ijˢ viijᵈ."

  ,,   " It. payd for Renewyng of the vj taps in the
Rode on the north syde vjˡˡ di off wax at vijᵈ
a ꝶi. A ꝶi of sysis (*small tapers*) & for the maks
of the same wax vˢ ijᵈ ob."

1513. " It. payed for a claps (*clasp*) to the cofer in the
rode loft iijᵈ."

1524. " It. for drynk in the roode loft vppon Palme
Sonday jᵈ."

1534. " Payd for makeyng the rode lights ayenst Hallon-
tyde & Cristmas xviijᵈ." (These were the
usual times for renewing these lights.)

  ,,   " It. payd for a qᵃrte of *basterd* for the passion apon
Palme Sonday iijᵈ."

     (Bastard, a kind of sweet Spanish wine, of
which there were two sorts, white and brown.
Ritson calls it a wine of Corsica. The term in

more ancient times seems to have been applied to all mixed and sweetened wines.—*Halliwell.*)

1534. "Payd for a lyne to pull upp the rode cloth j^d ob."

„ "Payd to Pastler for settyng the braunche (*a chandelier*) apon the rode loft & laying bordes there xvj^d."

1537-8. "Payd for staneyng the long Curteyns before the rode loft x^s." (Staining—*i.e.*, painting with figures or other designs.)

In the account of the sale of church goods in 1547, among the articles of brass or latten purchased by John Saunders, the bellfounder, we find "xx laten bolls that were of the rode light."

At the sale of old church timber in 1562, "the borders of the roode lofte" were purchased by William Duddlesoll, and presented by him to be set up again over the vestry.

So much wanton destruction was made of artistic work in churches at this time by the Puritanical faction that an injunction was issued by the Queen prohibiting all further demolition of Rood screens, &c., until her further pleasure therein was known. The following entry is illustrative :—

1562. "Itm. Payde vnto Gyles Jackson the xv day of November for bryngynge the orders made by the queenes maiesties comyssyoners as consernynge th'alteracyons of Rood-Loftes—for his ffee viij^d."

1562. "Itm. to Willyam Marten and his man for the takinge downe of the roode lofte & the way to the same, &c. ij^s."

It was decided by the Queen that the lofts should be removed, but that the screens beneath them should remain in every church to mark the division between the nave and chancel.

It is probable that the destruction was complete at St. Lawrence's, and that the upper and lower portions were swept away before her Majesty's pleasure became known in Reading : at any rate, a new screen was erected in 1603 by Peter Andrews and Roger Knight, the churchwardens ; for in the accounts for that year there is a marginal note in a later hand—apparently penned in no friendly humour —" They set up the skrine betweene the church and chancell."

It is not likely that this screen would survive the visitation of the fanatical soldiers of the Earl of Essex, who were quartered in the church in 1644, when they did so much mischief to the fittings and defiled the sanctuary to their heart's content. (See under *Ringing.*)

Organs.

The church possessed an organ in 1505 :—

> "It. payd for whitleder to the belys of th'organs iij^d."

In 1506, the "organs" were removed,—Mr. Coates thinks from the Rood loft, and makes his deduction from the following entry :—

> "It. paied for setting up of the seid rode Mary & John, for removing of th'organs & for making ye sete for þ^e pleyer of þ^e same organs xx^d."

In 1510, a new instrument was provided :—

> "It. payd to Backebye vppon a bargen of a peyr of org^{a}unce at the instaunce of the pisshe at ij tymes, iiij^{li}."

Of this Mr. Cleche gave vj^s viij^d, and Mr. White xx^s. It was a large instrument, and the bellows were placed apparently below the level of the floor. At Fountains' Abbey are the remains of some underground channels near the west end of the choir, which are believed to have been reservoirs or wind-ducts to the organ above.

1512. "It. rec. for bryk and mort^r left at the makyng of the vowte (vault) for the belys of the organs xxj^d.

,, "It. paied to Robt Barkbe organ maker xiij^s iiij^d.

,, "It. paied to M. White for waynscott that he bowght to the new organs xxxj^s.

,, "It. payed to Robt Turner for such stuf as he delyued to the same organs xv^s x^d.

1512. "It. payed for currying of the leder to the belys of the same organs ij^s ij^d.

,, "It. payed to Ric' Turner & John Kent for the organ maker at one tyme xxxj^s vj^d.

,, "It. payed for vj waynscotts at London xiiij^s.

,, "It. payed to Ric' Turn^r) & John Kent for the organ maker at a noþ^r) tyme l^s.

1512. "It. payed for led to ley vpon the belis of the organs vj^s viij^d.

(It seems that the old organ was retained, so now there were two instruments.)

1512. "It. payed for a shepeskyn to mend the belis of the *old* organs and for a li of glew vij^d.

„ "It. paied to a fre mason that shuld haue made the arch for the belis of the *new* organs for iiij dayes an di, by the day vj^d—ij^s iij^d.

„ "It. payed to Thom^s Nycols for makyng of the same arch and for tyling of the same viij^s.

„ "It. payed to a laborer to breke vp the wall to make the arch for iij dayes & a di by the day iiij^d sm^a xiiij^d.

1513. "It. payed to Hew Smyth for iron warke in the new organ loft x^d.

„ "It. payd for ij lokks to the same organs, one for the stopps and the oþ^r for the keyes xj^d.

„ "It. payed to Robte Barkbe organ maker for a reward v^s iiij^d.

„ "It. payed for ryding to Wyndso^r to set Mr Wod (Wood) to se the new organs, x^d.

„ "It. payed to the same M. for his costs at his comyng vij^s x^d.

„ "It. payed Ric. a Woods costs when he came to se the organs vij^d (1512).

„ "It. payed for a lok to the organ lofte dore & for iron warke to the same loft xij^d.

1513-4. "It. payd for mendyng and grownde pynnyng of the posts vnder the organs ij^d."

1514-5. Something was obviously amiss with Barkby's new organ; some faulty construction, or defect in the fulfilment of his engagement; perhaps the suit indicated by the following entry was the result of the visit of Richard a Wood, evidently the organist of St. George's at that time.

„ "It. payd for a man & a hors to London for a wryt for Barkbye iiij^s ij^d."

„ "It. payd to Willm Edmonds for makyng a tre to barkbye, j^d."

„ "It. payd for expñs to barkbye at the same tyme, vj^s. viij^d."

„ "It. payd for a pece of waynscote for mendyng of the stoppe of the same organs ij^d."

1514-5. "Sum of expenses touching Rob. Barkeby xiij^d. iiij^d."

1519-20. The pipes of Barkeky's great organ were sold to Segemond, another organ maker, who appears to have rebuilt or transposed it.

    ,,   "It. of Segemond the organ maker for the grete organs CC d^l xi^{li} (291 lbs.) of led ij^{lt}."

In the meantime "Young Slithurst" played upon the old organ. He was probably the son of Thomas Slithurst, who held two gardens in Lurkmere Lane of the churchwardens, at a yearly rent of 2s. 8d. at this time.

1520. "It. paid to Segemond the organ maker for trans-posing of the grete organs as apperithe by a bill thereof made vj^{li} xx^d."

1521. "It. payd to Segesmond by thadvyse of the pysh t^{a}nsposyng & new cast̄g ye for fronte of the org^{a}ns and settyng y^n ye new stope xiij^s. iiij^d."

1522-3. Segemond appears to have been as unfortunate with his organ as Barkeby; at any rate there appears to have been fresh litigation.

    "It. payd for a pcesse mayd agaynst Segemond, viij^s vj^d."

1524. "It. payd to Sr Ric. Baynton for mendyng the grett at ij tymes iiij^s."

1524-5. Another new organ.

    "It. payd for karyeng the new org^{a}ns from the wat̄ to the church, xv^d.

    It. to Troll for grownd pynnyng the org. ij^d.

    It. for tymber & bords to the same iij^s. ix^d.

    It. for makeyng the paysses for the organs j^d.

    It. to Ric. Bodye for workmanshypp iij^s.

    It. for brede drynk for the organ maker whylls he entewnyd the org. iiij^d."

From the inexpensive nature of these items, this must have been a small organ for the choir.

1526-7. "It. for a foldyng bord to the lytell orgons viij^d."

1529. "It. payd for mendyng the case of the *lytell organs in the ch^{e}uncell* & the bellows of the same at ij times ij^s vj^d."

1531. "It. for mendyng the stopps of the grete organs ij^d."

1533. " Rec. of the fireres in Oxford for the great organs
x^{ll}."

From subsequent entries it would seem that the great
organ was sold to them for 12*l.* 10*s.*, but that the remaining
50*s.* were never paid before the Reformation swept both
the Friars and their organ away altogether.

The organ built by Segismond and removed to Oxford
in 1533 was succeeded by another which succumbed to
Puritanical prejudice in 1578. There are no memoranda
relating to its erection, and only one touching its demolition.

On Saturday, Feb. 13, 1562, certain articles were pro-
posed for discussion in the Lower House of Convocation,
evidently by the advanced Puritan party, the 6th of which
was, " That the use of organs be removed." There were
thirteen disputers, and out of 117 votes, organs were saved
by a majority of one only !

In 1566, Bishops Grindle and Horne in their reply to
the letter of Bullinger and Gualter on the subject of further reform, wrote, that they did not approve of that
figured music, together with the use of organs, that was
continued in cathedrals, in these words : " Cantum in
templis figuratum una cum strepitu organorum retinendum
non affirmamus *imo prout decet insectamur*" (see Burnet's
" Reformation," iii. 319).

After this we shall be prepared for the following in the
old church book :—

1578. " M^d on St. Andrews day being Advent Sunday &
the last of November 1578, it was agreed That
the organes in St. Johns chauncell for that they
shoude not be forfeited into the hands of the
organ takers shoulde be taken downe and solde ;
and the tymber of them be applied to sett up
two seats higher for Mr Maior and his brethrene
aboue the seate y^t now they sitt in."

" Pd. for taking down y^c orgaines xi^d.

" Solde to Rocke 37^{li} of leade which was organ
metall, viij^s vj^d.

" Itm. xxiiij^{li} of Leade iij^s."

Pre=Reformation Organists.

1519. "Young Slithurst."
1534. "Thomas Alyn for playing at the organs for vij
wekes ixˢ."
"Thomas Skynn⁾ for playing at the organs xijˢ."
1544. "Payd to Sayntmore the clerk for playing upon
the orgayns oū & besydes the gatheryng of the
pisshe for a yere endid ut supᵃ xlˢ."

The Present Organ

was erected in 1741 by subscription, including the sum of
30l. left by Dr. De la Croix, vicar of Old Windsor, for the
support of the monthly lecture, which was applied to this
purpose. It was built by Mr. John Byfield, and received the approbation of Mr. John Stanley and other
competent judges of the time, who considered it a very
fine-toned instrument. Mr. Coates states that it cost 400l.,
and contains 1179 speaking pipes; but it has been much
enlarged since his time. In 1882 a very fine Viol de
Gamba was substituted for the old Cremona, and the
Trumpet-stop renewed by Mr. Aug. Gern, of London. It
appears to have been opened on the 27th of July, 1741,
when the local choir was augmented by the choristers from
St. George's Chapel, Windsor. A Mr. Tomson seems to
have presided at the organ on the occasion.

	£	s.	d.
1741, July 27. To Mr. Tomson, organist, and expenses for coach, & for the Windsor Boys	8	15	0
„ July 30. To Mr. Clark, organist	3	3	0
1741-2, Jan. 27. To Mr. Spencer, organist, half a year's salary	15	0	0
1742, Sept. 4. Mr. Alcock, organist	10	0	0
„ Dec. 23. To Mr. Alcock	15	0	0

Mr. Alcock was here in 1749, as appears from an original
receipt for his stipend, still preserved :—

"1749, Dec. 1. Received of Mr. Cobb, Churchwarden,
of St. Lawrence's Parish, in Reading, Berks, the
sum of Ten Pounds, being part of my half

year's Salary for playing the Organ, due September 29, 1749,

p me, John Alcock, Organist."

He afterwards became organist of Lichfield Cathedral. Dr. Alcock's compositions are well known.*

Mr. Spencer succeeded in 1750, and on his death, in 1782, Mr. Remond was elected. He was followed by Mr. Naumberger.

The late Mr. Richard Binfield was organist from 1804 to 1839, and was succeeded by his accomplished daughter, Miss Hannah Binfield, whose services and connection with the church and choir will long be remembered. On Miss Binfield's resignation, in 1880, the present talented organist, Mr. C. H. H. Sippel, A.C.O., formerly of Cambridge, was elected.

The great Musical Festivals, held at Worcester, Gloucester, and Birmingham, during the present century, were inaugurated at Reading, and the performances were held for many years in St. Lawrence's Church. The "Messiah" was performed here in 1786, and "Judas Maccabæus" in 1787 and 1789. They were discontinued about the year 1840.

In 1819 the Musical Festival was held on the 15th, 16th, and 17th of September. The following particulars are from a reprint of the original programme in the possession of Miss Binfield. The programme is headed, "Berkshire Grand Musical Festival."

Then follows a list of 170 patrons, consisting of the nobility and gentry of the town and county. To these must be added thirty gentlemen stewards, among whom may be enumerated Sir Claudius Hunter, Bart., Lieut.-Col. Vansittart, T. P. W. Benyon, Esq., R. Dimsdale, Esq., B. Simonds, Esq., Wm. Stephens, Esq., J. Wheble, Esq., &c.

The great moving spirit appears to have been Mr. Richard Binfield, upon whom the selection of the requisite talent devolved.

On the first morning, September 15, was performed the entire First Part of Haydn's "Creation," a selection from Mozart's "Requiem," and other miscellaneous pieces, by Handel, Haydn, Arne, Beethoven, &c.

---

* His "Ode to Flavia" is printed in the *Gentleman's Magazine* for Nov. 1746, p. 605.

On the second morning, the Oratorio of the " Messiah,"
with additional accompaniment, by Mozart.

On the third morning, a grand selection from Handel's
" Redemption ;" the " Dead March in Saul ;" Haydn's " Te
Deum ;" with other pieces by Guglielmi, Hasse, Pergolesi,
Kent," &c., concluding with the grand Coronation Anthem,
" Zadoc the Priest."

" PRINCIPAL VOCAL PERFORMERS.—Miss Stephens, Miss
Goodall, and Signora Corri ; Mr. Vaughan, Mr. Knyvett,
Mr. Bellamy, and Signor Ambrogetti.

" INSTRUMENTAL PERFORMERS.—*Violins.*—Mr. F. Cramer
(Leader), Mr. Marshall (Principal 2nd), Messrs. Binfield,
F. Venua, W. Griesbach, Nicks, A. Binfield, N. Binfield,
J. B. Binfield, Marshall, jun., Willcox, Greenwood, Tanner,
Berkshire, Tanner, jun., and Paine.—*Violas.*—Messrs. R.
Ashley, Richardson, Goodwin, W. B. Binfield, Shultz, and
Weippert.—*Violoncellos.*—Messrs. R. Lindley, T. Binfield,
and W. Binfield.—*Double Basses.*—Messrs. Dragonetti,
Haldon and Berry.—*Bassoons.*—Messrs. Mackintosh and
Downham.—*Trombones.*—Messrs. Mariotti and Brookman.
—*Flutes.*—Messrs. Ireland and Kates.—*Oboes.*—Messrs.
Griesbach and Sharp.—*Clarionets.*—Messrs. Stohwasser,
and Pickworth.—*Horns.*—Messrs. Charlton, Berkshire, and
Burton.—*Trumpets.*—Messrs. Schmidt, Heron, and Laden-
sack.—*Serpent.*—Mr. Middleton.—*Double Drums.*—Mr.
Jenkinson.—*Organ.*—Miss Binfield.—*Harp.*—Miss M. Bin-
field, from London.—*Conductor.*—Sir G. Smart.—The
whole under the direction of Mr. Binfield.

" The Choruses will be supported by gentlemen of St.
George's Chapel, Windsor ; His Majesty's Chapel Royal ;
St. Paul's and Oxford ; assisted by the celebrated female
choristers from Lancashire.

" Leader of the Band for the Balls, Mr. Paine, of Almack's,
so justly celebrated for arranging the quadrilles, and other
fashionable dances.—Harp for the Balls, Mr. M. Weippert.

" The whole of the Band, which will be complete, will consist of nearly a hundred performers.

" The Morning Performances will commence at eleven
o'clock ; the Evening Performances at half-past seven.—
Tickets of admission to the Morning Performances, 10s. 6d.
—The Concerts at the Town Hall, the Ball and Tea included, 10s. 6d.

" It is requested that all carriages proceeding to the Musical
Festival at St. Lawrence's Church will fall into line in the

F

Market Place, and set down at the west door in Friar Street, with the horses' heads towards the Town Hall ; and after setting down, proceed up Friar Street.—On return, the carriages to form a line in Friar Street, and to take up at the west door of St. Lawrence's Church, and drive off through the Market Place.—Ladies and gentlemen walking to the church, to enter at the south door in the Market Place. —By direction of the magistrates, carriages will not be permitted to drive thro' the entrance to the Forbury, during the performances."

Images.

Besides the Rood with SS. Mary and John, on the Rood loft, there were images of the Blessed Virgin, St. Michael, St. Clement, St. Lawrence, St. George, St. Vincent, and probably of St. Leonard. There were also smaller ones standing in the niches over the columns in the nave and aisle. Some of these statues have already been referred to under the account of the Altars—*e.g.*, those of the B. V. Mary, SS. George, Clement, and Michael.

St. Michael.

1519. " It. paid for canvas for coůyng of Saynt
         Michell iij^d.
      " It. paid for cariage of the Image from Maynard
         of London iiij^d."

St. Lawrence.

There were two images of the patron saint outside the building, one of which has already been described under the account of the *Tower :* the other was in a pentice at the east end of the chancel.

1520. " Itm. paid for bourds for makyng of the pentice
         oů the Image of Saynt Laurence and for
         settyng vpp the same Image w^{t}out the churche
         at thest end of the quere iiij^s ij^d."
1542. " Payd to Richard Joyner for mendyng of the
         Image of Saynt Laurence iiij^d."

There was an image of St. Lawrence apparently at one end of the *High Altar.*—(See *Will of Richard Bedowe.*)

There was probably an image of this saint in the niche over the easternmost pillar of the nave arcade above the shield with the gridiron.

St. Mary Magdalene.

(See Inventory of 1517 under *Vestments.*)

Her image appears to have been usually habited in a "coat" of cloth of gold, perhaps a royal mantle with sleeves, one phase of her legend representing her as of royal extraction and of the castle of Magdalon. Sometimes she was figured as the pattern of Penitence, with wasted figure, long dishevelled hair, and habited in a blue or violet robe the colour of mourning or contrition.

St. George.

This image was mounted on horseback, with arms and trappings complete.

(See under *Altars,* p. 45.)

St. Vincent.

1524. " It. to John Payne's wyff for gyldyng of pte of Saynt Vyncent Tabernacle iij^s iiij ."

We are here indirectly informed that the image of St. Vincent stood beneath a canopy.

1518-9. " It. paid for cariage of the tab^)nacles by the barge vj^s.

" It. paid Cone for settyng upp the tab^)-nacles ij^s vj^d.

" It. paid for makyng of a scafold ij^d.

" It. paid for iiij clammes of iron for the tab^)-nacles viij^d &c."

There is perhaps no single entry in the old church books from which we may form so correct an estimate of the real magnificence of the church in the olden time as the following :—

1519. " It. paid to John Payne in Ernest of xiiij^{li} xiij^s iiij^d for gilding of the ij Tab^)nacles in the quere, w^t all necessaries therto xx^s."

F 2

At this period the wages of a first-class artisan was 6*d*. a day—of a labourer 4*d*. : workmen at the present time receive ten times the amount ; reckoning therefore by this standard, the outlay in gilding these tabernacles alone was equal to about 136*l*. 10*s*. of our money.

> 1516. " It. payd to the Kyngs paynter for a reward for seying the tab⁾nacle vjˢ viij ᵈ."

The images were all removed and defaced in 1547. Here are a few particulars of the doings of the iconoclasts of that period :—

> 1547. " Rec. for c⁾tayn trifylls that were saved (*implying much wanton destruction*) at the takyng down of Imagˢ as followith, that is to witt :
> " Of Robᵗ Euard for all the Imagˢ beyng defaced xviijᵈ. Of a shomaker for c⁾tayne tab⁾nacles and other thyngˢ ijˢ viijᵈ. ! ! ! (and they cost 136*l*. for gilding only).
> " Paide to ij carpenters for takyng downe the Imagˢ and tabernacles xijᵈ.
> " Paid to Geoffry Penne & his man for emendyng of the walls wher Imagˢ stode xijᵈ."

There is a very significant entry indicative of the state of popular feeling at this time, aroused chiefly by the selfish conduct of the promoters of the Reformation and greatly augmented by the spoliation and robbery of the parish churches and the appropriation of common lands—the latter a political sop for powerful non-contents. Here it is :

> " Paid for arrerages of the money for watchyng the *bekyns* viijˢ."

There is another interesting entry immediately following, exhibiting the statecraft of the period. The church plunderers were quite aware in those days that unemployed leisure to brooding minds might prove a source of danger ; so it was enacted that every parish should provide its " Butts," where the parishioners might become proficient in archery—for the safety of the realm, of course.

> " Paid to Willm Watlyngton for that the pisshe was indetted to hym for makyng the butts xxxviˢ."

Mural Paintings.

The walls of the church were once covered with diapers and frescoes, some of which were very magnificent.

St. Christopher.

Anno 1503-4. "It. payd to Mylys payn? for payntyng of Seynt X°fer viij^s iiij^d.
"It. payed for new pgetyng (plastering) of þ^e wal wher S. X°fer is pātyd vj^d."

The legend of St. Christopher was in high favour in the Middle Ages, and the chief allegorical incident in the story was usually depicted on the walls of the churches.

He is usually represented as a man of huge stature, fording a turgid river. His staff is grasped with both hands, and on his shoulders he bears the infant Saviour, carrying in His hand a globe as Sovereign and Creator of the world. More rarely it is a cross—as its Redeemer. The giant is usually depicted with upturned face, as if in earnest conversation with the Child, but sometimes gazing intently and anxiously on the rising waters. His staff is frequently foliated. Occasionally it is an entire palm-tree with leaves and branches. In the background by the water-side is a hermit with a lantern. The fish, of course, are nearly always visible in the stream.

The following is one of the many inscriptions which usually accompanied the figure of the saint :—

Christophori sancti speciem quicumque tuetur
Illo namque die nullo languore tenetur.

Mrs. Jameson, in her "Sacred and Legendary Art." p. 265, gives the legend at length, with a copy of a fine early woodcut of this saint exhibiting all the quaint conventionalism of mediæval art, and probably as much like Miles Painter's production in St. Lawrence's as could be.

St. Leonard.

1521. "It. payed to John Payñ for payntỹg of Sent
leonard left by the wyffs onpaynted xxᵈ."

This saint is claimed by the Benedictines as a member
of their Order, and either wears the white or the black
tunic, fastened round the waist with a girdle. Sometimes
he has a crosier as abbot of the community he founded.
Occasionally he wears the dress of a deacon. He was
invoked by prisoners, or slaves, and all who pined in
captivity.

At Siena is a picture of St. Leonard kneeling and presenting fetters to the Virgin and Child. At Florence he is
portrayed in the habit of a deacon, standing by the side
of St. Lawrence throned, with St. Stephen on the other.
(Mrs. Jameson.)

The Transfiguration.

Anno 1526. "It. to the payñ for payntyng the tᵃnsfi-
guraċon oũ the hygh awÞ vjˡˡ xiijˢ iiijᵈ "

The cost was defrayed by public subscription.

" Rec. of dyũs psones towards the gyldyng & payntyng
of the tᵃnsfyguraĉon oũ the hygh auÞ as by a byll
it doth apere iiijˡˡ xiijˢ jᵈ.

" Rec. for ₓₓ_{iiij} & xˡˡ & di (90½ lbs.) of old brase sold at
jᵈ the pownde xjˢ. iiijᵈ. Smᵃ vˡˡ iiijˢ jᵈ."

A full description of the discovery of this painting in
1848 will be found at the end of this section.

The chancel roof was adorned with gold and colours, if
not with subjects and diapers.

1524. "It. to Troll for his laboʳ in seellyng & in reward
xijˢ."

   ,,   "It. layd owt for gold xxiijˢ iiijᵈ."

   ,,   "It. to the paynter for *drawyng* & *payntyng* the
enbowyng (probably a panelled waggon vaulted
ceiling like that in the north aisle) xvjˢ iiijᵈ."

   ,,   "It. for iij knotts (bosses) in the chancell vj."

   ,,   "It. for gyldyng of them ijˢ."

The nave arches were originally ornamented with red
stripes, and the niches between them with red borders.

There are also traces of colour on the font, and on the eastern face of the piers of the tower arch.

In 1547 all the paintings and frescoes were defaced :—

" Paid for iiij boketts for the werkmen to whytelyme the churche xij^d."

" Paid to Alexander Lake a mason for xxiij dayes for hym & his s'lant in white lymyng of the churche at ix^d the day xvij^s iij^d."

" Paid for coleryng of the churche porche & the churche dores xix^d."

" Paid to a paynter for writyng of the cloth at the high Awter ij^s iiij^d."

In the place of the old frescoes texts of Holy Scripture were painted on the whitewashed walls, and the objective method, so suitable for instruction, was made to yield to subjective policy.

In the following reign, anno 1556, we have—" Paid for defasyng of the wrytyngs vppon the walls ther, iiij^d." These Edwardian inscriptions were buried beneath another coat of lime, and, as far as possible, the old pictures replaced, but only again to be smeared over with dreary Elizabethan wash a few years afterwards.

In 1627 a little attempt was made to beautify the scene of cheerless desolation.

" It^m. payd to Jonathan the Paynter for payntinge the church seats and for payntinge the sprigs (of the hourglass), ffloorishing Mr Blagraves monument, as by the paynters bill appereth in pticular xv^{ll} ix^s vij^d."

The author of this work is deeply indebted to Arthur Billing, Esq., architect, 185, Tooley Street, London Bridge, for the following very interesting account of the mural paintings discovered in St. Lawrence's in 1848 :—

" The east wall of the chancel was almost entirely hidden by a large wooden altar screen of Queen Anne's or George the First's era, placed directly in front of it, the wall immediately behind being, as is universally the case, carefully coated upon the surface with successive layers of whitewash, the careful removal of which disclosed no less than five different series of paintings, one beneath the other.

" The first and second were each portions of the Creed and Ten Commandments, painted in different periods in

old English characters; the third, immediately beneath
these, consisted of the chosen sentences of Holy Writ in
the quaint spelling of the period, such as follows :—' That
at the Name of Jesus every knee shall bow,' &c. These
letters were of a more decidedly rich and flowing character
than those before described, with graceful enrichments of
leaves and sprigs, each sentence being enclosed within a
border of blue.

" Beneath these were next brought to light the remains
of a magnificent fresco of the Annunciation ; on the left,
or north side, was a full-sized figure, supposed to represent
the Archangel Gabriel, the body being covered with red
feathers, the shoulders surmounted with wings of rainbowed
plumage, and the hand carrying a long wand ; the upper
façade of a Gothic building formed the background. The
figure of the Holy Virgin kneeling at a faldstool, and the
accompanying symbolic pot of white lilies, were much
more imperfect, but could still be traced without difficulty.
Doubtless there were other paintings of a similar character
upon different portions of the wall, but they had been all
destroyed.

" The surface of the wall now just described was formed
by the filling up of a large triplet window, composed of the
several splays and small columns dividing it into three
separate portions, with its characteristic arch mouldings
extending themselves on the inside the whole width of the
east wall of the chancel. The lancet lights forming the
window were placed within a few inches of the outside of
the wall. These windows belong to the period of transi-
tion from Norman to Early English, as is distinctly shown
by the character of the mouldings and square Norman
abacus forming the upper member of the caps to the
columns : the whole of the inside mouldings and columns
were formed of chalk, and were in a good state of preservation.

" The columns were found to be covered with a bright
crimson colour : the neck mouldings to the caps and the
bases with gilding. The arch mouldings supported by
these were adorned with a beautiful triple arrangement of
gilding, crimson and blue, the larger roll moulding having
an alternate stripe of gilding and blue, the effect of which,
when first painted, must have been very striking. In addition to this, upon the several splays of the windows could
be traced a pattern, consisting of a bright crimson flowing

stalk, having the ends tipped with bright yellow flowers, harmonizing with the colours on the arch mouldings, and continuous throughout the splays, a manner of treatment which must greatly have contributed to the general effect.

" Upon the upper portion of these splays, immediately beneath the arch mouldings, were painted small figures of angels, with their hands and wings extended, and having each in their hands a small wand, but they were too mutilated to be transferred to paper. Lastly, beneath all these layers were a number of small flowers, each consisting of six leaves of a bright crimson colour on a white ground, enclosed with an oblong crimson border. This pattern was continuous throughout.

" Upon the space immediately above the triplet window was discovered a large painting of seven figures, nearly the size of life, the subject being the Transfiguration on the Mount. The centre figure represented our Saviour standing erect with the right hand uplifted, in the act of blessing. His face was exquisitely painted upon a groundwork of gilding, which extended beyond it, and formed the aureole, and the whole figure was surrounded with a vesica piscis of glory. On His right hand stood Moses, with the two Tables of the Ten Commandments in his hands. Looking upwards towards the left was Elias ; upon the same side were represented, below, the upper portions of the figures of two of the Disciples, and on the other side two more, all looking steadfastly up and in attitudes of adoration. The whole of the figures, and especially the faces, were exquisitely painted. The picture covered the whole extent of the surface above the triplet to each side of the chancel wall.*

" The east wall of St. John's Chapel·is also not without interest. Previous to its restoration it exhibited nothing but that of the usual characteristics of the Perpendicular style, having a window of large dimensions, consisting of three lights, the head of which was again divided into smaller compartments. It was evident there was much painting on the wall, but it was not possible to clear the surface sufficiently to define what it really was, on account of an incrustation of many ugly monuments ; but upon removing some of the plaster, as well as the whitewash, there appeared the remains of two small shafts of columns

---

* Sad to say, this picture was "*hacked down*," at the desire of the then Vicar, while Mr. Billing was in London.

on either side of the window, almost flush with the wall;
these, upon being traced out, gave the arch mouldings of
each, and a portion of the inner arches to two lancet
windows; the upper portion of these arches had not been
disturbed, the panelled ceiling having been added when
the larger perpendicular window was inserted. The centre
portion only had been removed, so that it was easy to make
out two small lancets or a couplet arrangement similar to
the triplet in the chancel, and of not much later date,
showing that the chancel and chapel were nearly coeval.
Upon carefully removing the whitewash on the remaining
portions of the arches, traces of painting were discovered
sufficient to decide what they once were, being similar to
those in the chancel, and composed of gilding, crimson and
blue.

"Between the arches of the windows was painted a peculiar animal of a deep crimson colour, having the head of an
eagle, and body and tail like a fox, with wings attached to
its shoulders. This, no doubt, had some mystical or sym-
bolical meaning.

" Upon the north side of this wall were remains of a large
painting of a very peculiar flowing pattern, jet black in
colour; the extreme bordure above, and at the sides, being
of a rather light crimson—the inner bordure of a light blue
colour, and that again bordured by a pattern formed of
small spaces, nearly square, with a round portion in the
centre of each. The whole appeared to form the corner-
piece of a large bordure, from the peculiar character of
which, and its position (for it was above the Perpendicular
ceiling), it must be considered nearly coeval with the windows themselves. . . . . The design is peculiarly elegant,
the scrolls intertwining and flowing together in a most
graceful manner, and each terminating with the peculiar
trefoil leaf, the symbolism of which is obvious."

Mural Inscriptions.

The face of the inner ashlers of the tower from basement
to summit reveal the Englishman's propensity to perpetuate
his memory by engraving his initials.

On the north wall of the ringing chamber we have

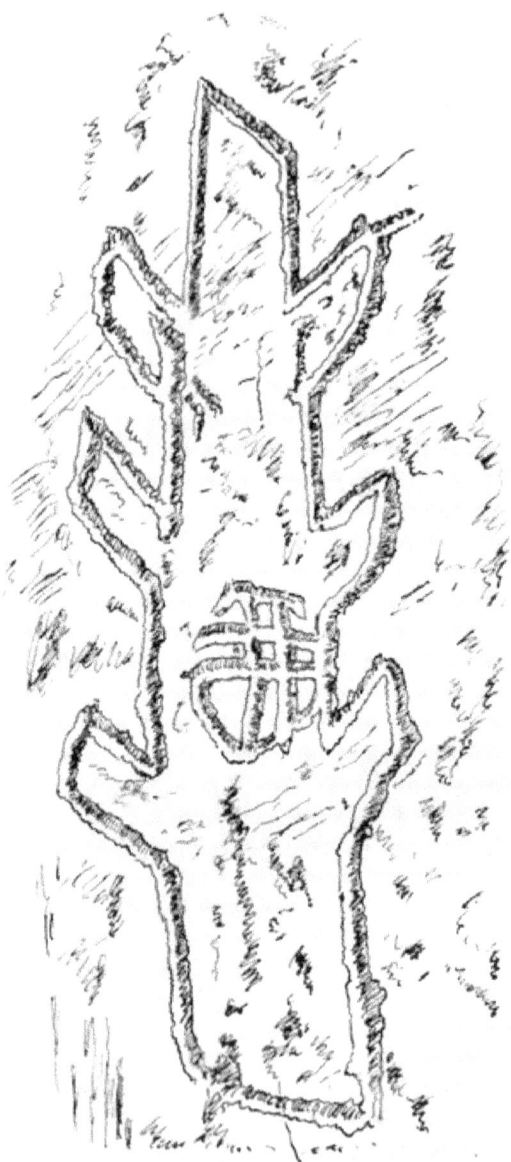

Device on North East Pier of Tower. (full size.)

p. 75.

C. Kerry.

" R. W. 1596," D. W. On the west wall, T. B. 1692. The window jambs of the bell-chamber are literally scored with these mementoes. On the south window we find "R. KEATE, 1784." "I. D. 1696." On the west window, in letters of the seventeenth century, deeply engraven, appears the name of "WILD." On the east window "I. D. 1669." "R. R. 1747." "T. H. 1646."

On the level of the old ringing-loft, before mentioned, these initials are still more numerous; one of them, "I. V. 1599," is very visible from the ground-floor. On the western face of the north pier of the tower arch is the name "Calcroft," lightly but neatly engraven; the characters appear of the early Elizabethan period. On the same level there is another written about the same time, "rokebp." Again, but in an earlier character, we find "Brebis Oratio penetrat celū." Lower down, "THOM: POCOCK," "E. S. 1660." On the east pier of the nave arcade, "W.T. 1626," "E. L. 1690," "F. B. 1654."

Very many of these interesting autographs have been much injured by the destructive "drag" of the church restorer. Such an instrument ought to be entirely prohibited in the restoration of our old churches, teeming, as most of them are, with innumerable traces of bygone generations.

By far the most interesting of all these relics is the device, or cognizance, of the Earls of Warwick, "*The Ragged Staff*." It appears in no less than five places on the tower basement.

The most perfect of these is on the eastern face of the north pier, opposite the font. In the middle of the staff is a small shield bearing a cross.

If the cross be intended for a *cross* "*saltire*," then it must have been carved by one of the retainers of Richard Nevill, Earl of Warwick, the great "kingmaker," who was buried in Bisham Abbey in 1471, and who bore "Gules, a saltire arg^t, with a label gobonné arg^t & azure;" but if not, then it was probably the work of one of the retainers of Robert Dudley, Earl of Leicester, fifth son of John Dudley, Earl of Warwick (created in 1547). The second wife of Robert Dudley, Earl of Leicester, was Lettice, daughter of *Sir Francis Knollys*, Treasurer of the Household to Queen Elizabeth, by whom he had a son named Robert, Earl of Denbigh, who died young and without issue. This Robert died at Cornbury Lodge, Oxfordshire, 1588, and was buried at Warwick.—*Vide* Ralph Brook's Catalogue, 1622.

Warwick. Now, by my father's badge, old Nevil's crest,
The Rampant Bear chain'd to the *Ragged Staff*,
This day I'll wear aloft my burgonet.
SHAKESPEARE, *Second Part of King Henry VI.*

" Arthgal, the first Earl of Warwick in the time of King Arthur, was called by the ancient British 'The Bear,' for having strangled such an animal in his arms ; and Morvidius, another ancestor of this house, slew a giant with a club made out of a young tree ; hence the family bore the Bear and Ragged Staff."—*History of Signboards*, Camden Hotten. 1866.

In a fluting of the south pier of the tower arch the name " **Symson**" occurs ; and, near this, the commencement of another name or word in text-hand, " **ħum**," all in characters of the Tudor period.

Painted Windows.

By one fell stroke, "the storied windows richly dight" were swept way, and plain glass substituted in 1549, at a cost of 15*l.* 10*s.* 6*d.*

We may form some estimate of the beauty of the old glass by its superb surroundings. In many other churches much was allowed to remain, although perhaps a few saintly heads, or a few offending symbols, had to be sacrificed to the spirit of the age ; but in St. Lawrence's not one fragment was left. There is a note at the end of the accounts for 1549 which has been carefully erased, but which is still faintly legible. It shows that, at any rate, the storied panes were not forgotten—" It. to remember what was done w^t all the old glasse of the wyndows in the churche." There is no further clue recorded. Was it sold ? was it broken ? or does it still grace the windows of some continental church ? Whatever may have become of it, there is no lover of art in Reading at the present day who would not gladly hail its restoration, if only to contrast with modern work.

St. Lawrence's unfortunately possesses too many examples of the bad work of the present century. Perhaps the best specimens of colouring characteristic of a particular period may be seen in the lancets over the altar, but this is disfigured by the wretched treatment of the figures in the medallions.

Seats.

Seat rents appear to have been a source of church revenue from very early times.

Anno 1441–2. " Et de iiij^d de dono vx'is Johis Tanner p j setell." A similar sum was paid by the wives of Robert Hover, John Strode, and Thomas Benham, but 6d. was given by the wife of Nicholas Carter—for a *front* sitting no doubt.

The seat rents in 1498 amounted to 6s. 6d. The women only would appear to have been accommodated. The seatholders at this time were the wives of Thomas Smyth, …. Hudson, "bocher," John Carpynter, the mother of Agnes Quedamton, the wife of Will. Hasylwood, John Ffauxbye, Will. Watts, Will. Jonson, Bartylmew Capper, Robard Dyer, John Darling, Will. Dayntre, baker, Mathew and Nicholas Goldsmyth.

> 1515–6. " Also hit is aggreyd that all women that shall take any seate in the seid churche to pay for the same seate vj excepte in the mydle range & the north range be neth the font the which shall pay but iiij^d & that eüy woman to take her place eüy day as they cumyth to church excepte such as have ben mayo^{r}s wyfs."
>
> 1520–1. " Setis." " Itm. of my lord (the abbot) for his moder sete iiij^d."

A touching entry. Hugh Faringdon in his promotion to the abbacy, though a man of humble extraction, did not overlook, or forget to provide for, the comfort of his poor aged mother. .

In 1522 new seats were provided at a cost of 8l. 12s. 2d.

> 1527–8. " Rec. of Mr Barton for a seate for his madens viij^d."
>
> „ " Rec. of Mr Hyde for his mades seat iiij^d."
>
> 1529. " Rec. of Will^{a}m (*barb^r to my lord abbot*), for his wyffes seatt vj^d."
>
> 1532. " The midle rang afore the font."
>
> 1538. " The midle range beneth the crose aley."

From these two entries, and the former of 1515–6, we learn the position of the font at this time. It stood in the *nave* in the *middle range* of seats, and *in the path* from the south door into the north aisle.

The wives of the Brethren of the Mass of Jesus had special privileges.

1545. "Ordinaunce"—"And oũ that it is ordered & enacted that all women of the said pisshe whose husbands nowe be or heretofore have been bretherne of the Mass of Iħc, shall from hensforth sitt & have the highest seats or pewes nexe vnto the mayoᵣs wifs seate towards the pulpitt."

1554. Sep. 29. "At this day it was condescended that thes psons heraft̃ named shall take order for the seats in the churche as well for men as for women—Wiħm Edmūds, John Bell, Thomᵃs Turn̓), and Thomas Sayntmore."

1572. "Itm. The gatheringe at Whytsontyde for all the woomens seates aboue the saide south churche dore as well of the mydle Raynge as the said syde Range in this Whytsontyde was nothinge."

1573 "In consideracion that the colleccions or gatheringes heretofore accostomably vsed for and towardes the mayntenance of the Church as well on the feast of All Saintes, The Feast of the Byrthe of owr Lord god, as on Hocke Monday, Hocke Tewesday, Maye Daye, and at the feast of Penticost com̃only called Whitsontyde togyther wᵗʰ the Chauntery Landes are lefte of, and cleane taken from the Churche to the great Impoverishment thereof, the wᶜʰ heretofore dyd muche healpe the same, It is therefore of necessytye by and wᵗʰ the assent, consent and aggreament of the pisheners then and there beinge p̓)sente for and towardes the mayntenaunce of the contynuall chardges of the Churche by these p̓)sents for eũmore Ordayned, concluded vpon and fully aggreed as hereafter followith, That is, that every woman that heretofore hathe byn sett by any of the Church-wardens, or that of themselves do or have vsed to sytt on the Sondayes or holydayes in any of the seates beneathe the pulpett, and above the southe syde, church doore, or in any of the seates in the mydel Raynge of seats above the saide churche doore Shall yerely paye iiij^d a pece for the church profytt & towardes the contynuall chardgs therof at two Feasts in the yere, That is to say At the feast of the Byrthe of o^r Lord god, and at the feast of pentycost by even porc̃õns. And that all women that be or have byn sett by or wthout the Churchwardens in any of the seates on the south syde Rainge above the pulpett Shall yerely paye vj^d apece at the foresaid feasts by even porc̃õns. The same to be gathered by the Churchwardens or their assignes for the tyme beinge at theire pell &c."

1576. Queen Elizabeth attended divine service at St. Lawrence's.

"Expenses about Ringers the Queene being in Rheding: In bred drinke money and candells to watche the Quenes seate wth the travise and arras hanging in the chaunsell, vij^s iij^d.

"The ratement & payment for Seats in St. Lawrence's Churche & Chancell in Readinge agreed and rated by the p'ishioners to be levied yearly for ever beginning this yere 1607."

In St. John's Chancell.

(4d.) Mr. Romano, Mr. Bird, schoolmaster.

Mr. Dewberye, Mr. Newton, Mr. Morley, Mr. Bun, the groomes.

Mr. Robert Grenefeld, Mr. Bailey, the groomes.

"The North Ile."

SEATS.

1. (At 4d. Parishioners.) Mr. Colthirst, John Walker, Humfrey Ffynmore, Thomas Noye, William Green. (The easternmost seat in the North Aisle proper.)
2. William Thorne, Ffrancis Blake, Roger Walker, John Patison.
3. Edmond Cowper, John Mappleton, John Goodbarnes, Rich. Pynke, Rich. Blakman, John Dewell.

4. Robert Dye, Arther Curtys, Robert Bent, Rich. Springall, Richard Johnson, Will. Sone.
5. Will. Wylande, John Hamblen, Michæll Hamblen, Willm. Willes, John Rumsey, Nicholas Styles.
6. (At 3*d*.) Thom. Richards, John Bagley, Ric. Dell, Tho. Standen, Will. Walker, Robt Griffith.
7. John Charlton, John Bonevant, Will. Porter, Will. Horne, John Burden, John West.
8. John Nashe, Ric. Case, Geo. Millisent, Danyell Pearse, John Ellys, Tho. Thorne.
9. Dan. Clewe, Xpof Thorne, John Jenyns, Peter Burningham, Edward Bagley, Ric. Cooke, John Wylmer.
10. Thomas Locke, Ric. Cottrell, Tho. Hide, John Berrey, Will. Crunage, Mr. Walton.
11. Saboth Ffilpe, Edwd Merifield, Ric. Bunsen, Will. Drusill, Rob. Kenton, John Arther.
12. Nich. Lamphier, Peter Burren, Will. Saunders, Ric. Reddatt, Hen. Randall, Ffrancis Ffrancissar, Wm Bagley, Ed. Bradway.
13. John Malthus, Tho. Humfry, John Watlington, John White, Will. Ledburye, Ric. Bagley, John Coles.
14. Jas. Mason, Tho. Pococke, John Mapleton, jun^r, Edward Symons.
15. John Dawson, John Mylles, Nat. Jemott.
16. Tho. Willys, Symon Maynard, Geo. Woolridge, John Ryder, Will. Milthecoe, Will. Stitche, Hen. Moore, Andrewe Mace.
17. John Howse, Edm^d Bennett, Griffyn Huse, Symon Ffoord.
18. Gabriell Barnes, Tho. Marshall, Abram Paise, Rich. Walker, Edwd Banester.
19. (At 2*d*.) Goodwife Waight, Goodwife Shawe, Goodwife Pommell.
  Mr. Walton, iij.

Middle Aisle.

1. (At xij*d*.) Mr. Thomas Lydell, Mr. Edward Clerke, Mr. Edward Birmingham, Mr. Robt Malthus.
2. (At viij*d*.) Mr. Robt Calton, Mr. Chamberlyn, Walter Watlyngton, Josephe Carter,* John Bagley, sen^r.
3. John Newman, Tho. Burges, Roger Knight, John Johnson.

* Bellfounder.

4. (At vj*d*.) Mr. Burdon, Mr. Wylmere, Mr. Addams, Mr. Westley, Mr. Fforster, Mr. Bowden.
5. (At 4*d*.) Mrs. Bowden, M^ris Mary Calton, Mrs. Griffen, Goodwife Pynke, Mrs. Newport.
6. (At 3*d*.) Goodwife Mapleton, G-w. Cottrell, G-w. Hamblen, G-w. Richards, Mrs. Beake, G-w. Browne, G-w. Bayley.
7. Goodwife Yether, G-w. Locke, G-w. Standen, Jane Bagley, G-w. Stitche, G-w. Collyns.
8. Goodwife Childe, G-w. Pearce, G-w. Merrifield, G-w. Symons, G-w. Clere.
9. Goodwife Randall, G-w. Jenyns, G-w. West, G-w. Burren, G-w. Sedburye, G-w. Bonevant, G-w. Ffilpe, G-w. Horne, jun^r.
10. Goodwife Kenton, G-w. Cane, G-w. Thorne, jun^r.
11. Goodwife Coles, G-w. Lamphies.
12. Goodwife Payne, Ffrannces Jemott, Alice Bagley, Eliz. Hoost, G-w. Reddatt, Priscilla Plant.
13. (At 2*d*.) Robert Robinson, Ric. Harris, Wm Dumper, Thos. Ha3es, jun^r, Wm Joseph, Wm Spencer.
14. Ffrancis Payne, Thomas Illesley, Thomas Watmore, Walter Bailey, John Grippe.
15. Hugh Payte, George Ffeild, Arthur Hooker, Tobye Merritt, Thom. Aley, Wm Mathewe, John Watts.
16. (At 1*d*.) Mrs. Walten, Goodwife Frankley, G-w. Gunnys, G-w. Browne.
17. Goodwife Pococke, G-w. Ffisher, G-w. Banester.
18. Goodwife Willis, G-w. Joanse, G-w. Grenfeld.
19. Griffin Huse, Goodwife Hollys.

"The South Ile."

1. Sr Ffrauncis Knollis.
2. Ladye Knollis.
3. (At 4*d*.) M^ris Clarke, Mrs. Lydall, Mrs. Birmingham, Mrs. Malthus, Mrs. Dennison.
4. Mrs. Calton, Mrs. Malthus, M^ris Honys, M^ris Lane, M^ris Watlington.
5. Widdowe Styles, Goodwife Bagley, G-w. Carter, M^ris Knight, G-w. Johnson.
6. Mrs. Newman, M^ris Westley, Goodwife Ffnymore, Widdowe Thorne, G-w. Samson.

SEATS.

7. Goodwife Wye, G.-w. Thorne, G.-w. Walker, G.-w. Walker, G.-w. Wilmer.
8. M^{rls} Fforster, Goodwife Pattison, Widdow Mansell, Widdowe Curtys, G.-w. Clarke, G.-w. Grene.
9. Goodwife Hamblen, G.-w. Wilmer, G.-w. Bent, G.-w. Mathewe, Mrs. Dewell, G.-w. Goodbarns.
10. Goodwife Sone, G.-w. Rumsey, G.-w. Springall, G.-w. Styles, G.-w. Curtis.
11. Goodwife Greene, G.-w. Porter, G.-w. Newman, G.-w. Curtis, G.-w. Cowper.
12. Goodwife Samson, G.-w. Burden, G.-w. Cooke, G.-w. Walker, G.-w. Buringham, Gooddie Bayley.
13. Goodwife Washe, G.-w. Millisent, G.-w. Myllet.
14. M^{rls} Morley, Mrs. Bailey, Goodwife Walker, G.-w. Burren, & Burmingham.
15. Goodwife Blackman, G.-w. Ffrancissen.
16. (At 2d.) Goodwife Humfrey, G.-w. Bailey, G.-w. Ffielder, G.-w. Price, G.-w. Bramley, G.-w. Buckshieves.
17. Goodwife Moore, G.-w. Watlington, G.-w. Watlington, G.-w. Woolridge, G.-w. Josephe.
18. Wid. Vinege, Goodwife Thornburye, Wid. Hussey, G.-w. Browne.
19.
20. Goodwife Densill.
21.
22. Goodwife Marshall.
23. Goodwife Dell, Alice Hull, Anne Yare, Margery Walker."

1637. "Item pd Wm Meerbancke for rearing the seate higher for the Burgesses wives 9^s 0^d."
In 1860–1, the church was reseated with substantial benches of oak, designed by Jos. Morris, Esq. Arch^t.

The only faculty pew in the church is connected with house now held by Edward Wells, Esq., M.D.

Galleries.

These were removed in 1848 and 1867. The following particulars are given by Mr. Coates:—"In the year 1719 a faculty was granted by the Archdeacon of Berks, for erecting a gallery at the west end of St. Lawrence's Church, and on part of the north and south sides. This gallery was built by a subscription of the inhabitants; and by the faculty a power was vested in the vicar and churchwardens of placing and seating the inhabitants, paying regard to those who contributed most liberally to the erecting of the said gallery. In 1775 it was agreed that, 'As the original contributors to the gallery should drop off, the pews which they occupied should be let, and the profits arising from them should be appropriated, one moiety to the vicar in augmentation of the vicarage, and the other moiety in aid of the churchwardens' levy.'"

"In 1740, Mr. Boudry, then vicar of St. Lawrence's, obtained a faculty to take down a small old gallery at the north-east end of the church, and part of the gallery at the west end of the church, belonging to the Rev. Haviland John Hiley and Mr. Henry Simeon, and to build a new gallery at his own expense on the north part of the said church, and on the west part of the north chancel, with the power of letting the seats, and of receiving the rents and profits thereof to his own use, and that of his successors for ever. A seat was allotted rent free to Mrs. Elizabeth and Mrs. Anne Eades, for themselves and their boarders, as long as either of them should be alive and keep school in the parish. A seat was likewise allotted to Mr. Hiley for his life and one for his boarders, and front seat to Mr. Henry Simeon."

"In 1768 Dr. Nicholson, then vicar, erected a gallery at the east end of the church over the entrance into the chancel, at the expense of 60*l.* advanced by himself, and being assisted by a benefaction of 63*l.* from St. John's College. The rents arising from the pews in this gallery are appropriated to the vicar."

The Bells.

The bells are first mentioned in the roll of 1433, and are severally distinguished by the terms "*little,*" "*middle,*" and "*great;*" from which, it would seem, there were then but *three.*

Something was done to the belfry in 1458, when probably another bell was added: there were certainly *four*

G 2

when Henry Kelsall made his will in 1493, when he made provision for a new tenor in these words :—

> " Item, I will and charge that a Tenour bell to be made according to the iiij bellis that now hange in the stepyll of Saynte Lawrence church of Reding aforseide to the some of —— (there is a blank left in the will). The scripture to be made aboute the same Bell—" *Henry. The Bell of Ihu.*"

As Kelsall was the founder of the " Jesus Mass" in this church (see his will), it is probable that this bell of his was used chiefly for the services connected with the Jesus Altar and the requirements of the Fraternity of Jesus. The bell was not erected before 1498–9, when we find the record of its consecration :—

> " Itm. payed for halowyng of the grete bell namyd Harry, vj^s viij^d.
>
> " And ovir that Sir Wiłłm Symys, Rich Clech and maistres Smyth beyng godfaders and godmoder at the consecracyon of the same bell and beryng al oþ^s] costs to the suffrygan."

William Hasylwood was a bellfounder at Reading from 1494 to 1509, and he may have been the founder of "Harry." He was a parishioner of St. Lawrence's. (His wife was buried in the church in 1502–3.)

> Anno 1508. " It. payed to Wiłłm Hasylwod for a new haly water stok of laton, ij^s viij^d."
>
> (He seems to have married a second time.)
>
> Anno 1510. " It. rec. of Hasylwod is weyff for ringing of the grett bell xij^d."
>
> > " It. rec. of Hasylwod is weyff for hir husbond is grave & for couyng of þ^e same vij^s ij^d."

He was buried in the church.

> Anno 1515–6. "Ordinaċŏ Hit is coven^{a}ntyd & aggreyd by the assent & consent of all the pysshe that what pson wyll have the greate bell of the gyfte of Harry Kelsall to be rong at the knyll or any other tment or obyte, all such psons to pay for the same bell so ryngyng at euy tyme xij^d to the churchwardens for the vse of the same church. And to euy pson that wyll haue hym

tylled to paye iiij^d to the seid wardens. And
that the seid bell be rong or tylled for no pson
but he pay as ys aboue exp^r)ssed.

" P'vyded all wey that the seid bell to be rong or
tylled at all tymes for the obite or myndes of
the seid Harry Kelsall to be kepte. And also
at the obits & mynds to be kepte for M^r
Thomas Justice vicar of the pissh church of
Saynt laurence w^{t}out paying any money ther
for, but to have the seid bell rong & tylled for
the seid ij^o psons at all tymes free."

Henry Kelsall was made a burgess after Michaelmas
Day, 1475.

" Die venlis px post ffm̄ Scī Mich Archī A^o. r.r. E. iiij^{ll}
xv. Eodem die venit Henr' Kelssale & jur' e' com-
burgens^s gild m̄l cat^s & q^o ad fm̄ q̄ tā p^{r}m elect' stat.
maiorat'. Et sol' dī fm̄. Dn̄e Abb' vt V^s v₃ v^a. Et
p jant'lo iij^a iiij^d. pleg. Will. Lynacr, Rob. Prow.
(Corporation Minute Book.)

Elected to represent the town in Parliament, 1482 :—

" Anno E. (iiij), xxii ; Jolies Bakestur Maior ij. Die
Marc crastiō p. ffm̄ Sc̄i E. R. et Confess' A^o s^{a}dict^s
Maior & cōburgens^s Burgi p̄ldict^s eliger' Henr. Kel-
ssale & Willm Erne comburgens' pliamenti px
futur' v₃ vj^{io} die Novēbr' A^o &c." (Corporation
Minute Book.)

Another member of this family occurs in the churchwardens' accounts.

Anno 1503-4. " It. rec. of Randall Kelsall for wast of
torchis at þ^e yer mynd of Harry Kelsall x^d."
(A similar entry occurs the following year.)

Anno 1517. " For the grave of Rand. Kelsalls moder."
vij^s ij^d. (No charge for the bell.)

Anno 19-20 Hen. VIII. (1528).

" It. for the Knell of Randall Kelsall nī" (nihil).

" It. for tollyng at h^s moneth^s mynde nī" (nihil).

The remission of the ringing fee in these cases, in
accordance with the resolution of the vestry—and especially
the responsibility of Randall Kelsall for the mortuary

arrangements of Henry Kelsall, would seem to indicate that Randall was a very near relative, if not the son, of Henry, although he is not once named in the will of the latter.

Some of the bells, including "Harry," appear to have been sold in the beginning of Edward VI.'s reign, but redeemed by the parishioners.

Anno 1550. "Paid & allowed to the churchemen (churchwardens) for the redemyng of bells by them sold, xl^{s}."

Among the "Dett^{s} owyng" in 1554 we have :—

" Item vppon Robt Tylbye & Willm Lyppescombe for redemyng of the greate bell by them sold as apperith vppon ther accompts xxxiij^{s} iiij^{d}." (These persons were the churchwardens in 1550.)

" Harry" survived until 1567, when he was recast for the first time by William Knight, of the Reading Foundry. The whole town and neighbourhood contributed towards the good work. Fifty-five of the parishioners of St. Mary's gave 41s. 8d. (money was then about twelve times its present value) ; seventeen of the inhabitants of St. Giles' subscribed 13s. 8d. ; "The men of the Contrye," including the "Myller of Causham," sent in 27s. 2d. ; a hundred and thirty-four of the parishioners gave 6l. 13s. 4d. ; and the Bachelors of St. Lawrence 16s. 11d. One Martyn Woodnett lowered the old bell, and raised and re-hung the new one for 31s. 8d.

For this recasting William Knight received 7l. 6s. 8d.

The last recorded knell rung on the original bell given by Henry Kelsall was apparently for one of the priests of the old *régime*.

"The Gret bel :—
    In p'mis of Thom^{s} Kenryck for a priests knell, xx^{d}."
"Graves—In p'mis of Thom^{s} Kenryck for ye prestes grave, vij^{s} iiij^{d}."

In 1578 the tenor, with the fourth, or "Lady Bell," as it was called, inscribed, no doubt, with its "Ave Maria gratia plena," was recast by Joseph Carter, one of the parishioners. " Peace and good neighbourhood," an old bell motto, must then have been a reality ; for we again find the parishioners of St. Maries giving "towards ye casting of ye gret bell, xxiv^s vj^d." The following very singular contribution occurs at this time :—

"1580. Rec. of Mr Gryffen for ye penaunce of one Kent allotted to ye gret bell by ye offyciall, vij^s."

At this casting Kelsall was diminished in weight, and consequently in power.

"1581. Rec. of Josephe Carter, belfounder, at seuerall tymes for ye rest of ye mettall y^t was left out in casteyng ye fourth bell and gret bell, vj^{li}."

In 1593, Joseph Carter, the bellfounder, was churchwarden. The following resolution was undoubtedly his suggestion :—

"Toling by the clapp^{r}. Whereas there was through the slothfulness off the Sextine in times past, a kind off toling ye Bell by ye clapper rope, y^t was now fforbidden and taken away : and that the bell should be toled as in times past, & not in anie such Idle sort.—J. Smith, vicar."

1594. "At this accompt also y^t was agreed that our gret Bell should be cast againe and not so much the Tune of the bell was cared for as to have y^t a lowd bell and hard ffar. And the churchwarden, Joseph Carter, consented and agreed to cast y^t before Midsummer ffollowing : And so he was chosen againe Churchwarden the second Time. These being p'sent — Mr. Ffrancys More, Mr. Johnson, Mr. Lydall, goodman Russell, the churchwardens, with others. — John Smithe, vicar."

"The gret Bell waied when he was first taken downe 34 cwt. 38^{li}."

"The same Bell hanged vp againe y^s increased in mettall to 36 cwt. 49^{li}."

"And forasmuch as y^t fell out that he was inforced by misfortune of a ffall in the first casting, to cast him twise againe. Therefore there y^s allowed in curtesie to the said Joseph, being or neighbour, above his bargin of increase, xl^s."

"So the somme of the whole is xv^{li} vij^s ij^d."

Anno 1618. "Itm. p^d to goodman Knight for casting of the 4 bell, 6*l*. 10*s*."

"Itm. p^d moor to him for j hundred & twenty three pound
     of metell put into her, v^{ll} xij^s the hundred, 6l. 15s."
Anno 1647–8. "It. p to Ellys Knight & ffrancis
     Knight for casting the greate bell as by their
     bill appeares, xxvi^{ll} v^s vj^d."
" At a meeting of the parishioners of St. Lawrence, in
Reading, 29th May, 1662.

" *Bells.*
" Agreed that the five Bells in the steeple be made into
     Eight tuneable Bells, and that the Churchwardens
     doe take care to see it done.
" Provided that noe taxe be layd on the parishe towards
     the charge of altering the said Bells & pvided that
     the Churchwardens doe bring & secure the said eight
     Bells in convenient tyme into the said steeple w^{t}hout
     charge to the pishe.

                    Present Mr THOMAS TUER, vicar.
                         D$\breve{c}$or FFRANCIS HUNGERFORD.
                         EDWARD DALBYE, Esq.
                         Mr EDWARD JOHNSON,
                         Mr NICHOLAS POTINGER,
                         GILES POCOCKE,
                         Mr HENRIE FFREWIN,
                         EDWARD KENT, ⎫
                         DAVID WEBB, ⎭ Churchwardens."

1663. " Of the pishioners & others wch was given towards
     the casting ye bells, 62l. 5s. 2d.
     "Item, p^d Henry Knight for casting the 5 Bells
     into eight, 44l. 2s. 4d.
     "Item, p^d Mr Frewin for tinn put into the Bells,
     8l. 13s.
1663–4. " To Thomas Knight for opening the greate bell,
     1s. 6d." (ringing her for the first time).

The great bell was unsatisfactory, so she had to be
recast.

" To Henry Knight, for metall added to the great
     bell, 7l.
1665. " It. paid Henry Knight for 58lb. weight of mettal
     to put in the *two fore* bells, 2l. 18s.
1666–7. " Item p^d to Henry Knight for casting the
     seaventh Bell and other charges, 20l. 15s. 6d.
1703, 6th Sept. " Agreed at this meeting that the great

Bell (being broke) shalbe new cast at the charge of the parish, and the other bells amended.

Mr Abraham Culver, } Churchwardens."
Ffrancis Binfield,

11th February, 1704. "Agreed that the 7th bell be taken downe and new cast, and Samuel Knight to doe it & be paid 18*l*. for the same by the churchwardens. Samuel Knight to be at all manner of charge in taking downe & hanging up the same."

In 1748 the whole ring was recast in the key of E♭, by Robert Catlin, and the two smallest bells added by sub-scription. Before the recent restoration of the bells in 1881-2 they were thus inscribed :—

1. "RICHARD COB . CH.WARDEN . R.C. 1748."
2. "BY ADDING TWO OUR NOTES WE'LL RAISE"
   & SOUND OUR GOOD SUBSCRIBERS' PRAISE"
   1748.
3. "ROBERT CATLIN FECIT. 1748."
4. "PROSPERITY TO ALL OUR BENEFACTORS. R.C. 1748."
5. "IMPRIMIS VENERARE DEUM MANDATA G_B (*sic*) SERVA QUCERES (*sic*) NON ALIOS UNICUS IPSE DEUS. R.C. 1748."
6. "THE REV. THOMAS SHUTE, D.D. VICAR 1748." — R.C. FECIT."
7. "PROSPERITY TO THIS PARISH. R.C. FECIT . 1748."
8. "Mr JOHN KIRK, Mr JOHN HARRIS CHURCHWAR-DENS. THOMAS MEARS OF LONDON FECIT. 1803."
9. "RICHARD WESTBROOK & JAMES WALTER CHURCH-WARDENS THOMAS MEARS OF LONDON FECIT. 1793."
10. "JOHN RICHARDS, JOHN ROSS CHURCHWARDENS . ROBERT CATLIN FECIT - 1748."

On the small bell, which is the representative of the old Saunce or Sanctus Bell,—

"THE REV JOHN GREEN VICAR, JACOB WALTER JOHN NIALE CHURCHWARDENS . THOMAS MEARS OF LONDON FECIT. 1793."

In the month of September, 1881, the author was kindly

permitted by the vicar and churchwardens to undertake
the restoration of the bells, then in a very deplorable condition: they had not been *rung* for several years. The
tenor was cracked through the canons, and the crown had
been strengthened by an iron hoop round the haunch or
shoulder. The best advice having been obtained, it was
deemed prudent to recast her, and a liberal response
having been made by the townsmen and others for this
purpose, it was thought desirable to renew the sixth also—
the worst bell in the ring. With these two was sent the
seventh for tuning purposes ; and this, when the stock was
removed at the foundry, was found to be in precisely the
same condition as the tenor, the fracture having been concealed by its beam. These three were recast, and the
whole of the bearings, stocks, wheels, and other fittings
renewed at a cost of nearly 350*l.*

The weights of the three old bells were—

	cwt.	qrs.	lbs.	
6th	9	0	24	
7th	10	3	14	with their canons.
10th	23	0	0	

The eighth, also sent to Loughborough for the same
purpose as the seventh, weighs 11 cwt. 2 qrs. 7 lbs.

The three new bells weigh—

	cwt.	qrs.	lbs.	
6th	10	0	0	
7th	11	2	0	without canons.
10th	24	0	0	

The bells were recast on Tuesday afternoon, January 10,
1882, at the foundry of John Taylor and Co., Loughborough.
The author hopes to be forgiven for inserting a quotation
from a letter of his to the *Reading Mercury*, &c., descriptive
of the scene :—

"I found the three old bells of St. Lawrence in the
drying chamber or 'oven' broken into fragments, on some
of which I recognized portions of the old inscriptions. In
a short time they were wheeled near the mouth of the
furnace, into which they were eventually thrown. The last
I saw of our old tenor were some dullish-looking fragments
gradually sinking into a seething mass of liquid metal,
glowing with intense brilliancy. The opening was closed
again with bricks and clay, and in about an hour or so
everything was ready. The sight was very interesting.

A narrow channel led from the furnace-mouth to the moulds, and in this duct were placed iron floodgates or stops, by the regulation of which the metal was diverted into the mouths or funnels of the moulds beneath. The precise moment for tapping was one of silent anxiety. At this juncture, with Mr. Taylor's permission, I went near the furnace-mouth, and offered the well-known prayer : 'Prevent us, O Lord, in all our doings with Thy most gracious favour, and further us with Thy continual help,' &c. At its conclusion many of the visitors uttered a fervent 'Amen.' In an instant the boiling liquid gushed forth, and sped hurriedly down the previously heated channel to the first 'swallow hole,' and in a few seconds the new tenor for St. Lawrence's Church came into being in its subterraneous chamber. The first floodgate was then raised, and onward the bright stream rushed into the next mould, and so on successively until the whole were cast ; and thus, within a very few minutes, was born a sisterhood of eight large bells ; three for St. Lawrence's, Reading ; three for Thurleston, Leicestershire ; and two for Baldock, in Herts."

On Shrove Tuesday, Feb. 21, 1882, the new bells were dedicated, and the ring formally opened at 6.30 P.M., a special service having been held on the occasion. The moment the Benediction was concluded, the bells struck up a glorious peal, the flood of music from the grand old tower filling the town and neighbourhood. The tenor was rung by the author for its first time on Monday, Feb. 12, 1882, about three in the afternoon. Who may ring her for the last time God only knows ; but, accidents set aside, she will no doubt hold her deserved position as one of the best bells in the county for centuries to come.

Ringing Annals.

ROYAL VISITS—VICTORIES—CIVIL WAR, TEMP. CHARLES I., ETC.

Anno 1506. "It. payed for bred & ale to þe ryngers in þe rogacion weke ij^d."

Anno 1508. "It. payed for ij^o galons of ale for the Ringers on Dedycaciõ iij^d."

"It. payed to the ryng'ls on Holy Thursday of co"stom to ryng at pcession iij^d."

" It. payed to the same Wiłtm (Poo—sub-sexton)
for rynging on Corp⁹ Xpi day at pcession.

" It. payed for vj^{li} & di Wayght of smale corde
for the Sanct⁹ Bell, & for to toll to Iłiu Masse,
vj^d."

1509–10. " Itm. payed for x Rynggers at the partyng of
the Kyng, & ffor drynke & to the sexton, ij^s
ob^d."

1513–4. " It. payd for a galon of ale for the Ryngers at
the gettyng of Turwyn, ij^d."

(This town was surrendered to the King of England
on the 23rd of August. It was all burnt, save the
palace and cathedral, on the 26th and a few following
days.— *Vid*. Stowe's Chronicle, p. 493).

" It. payd for a galon of ale for the Ryngers at the deth
of the Kyng of Scotts, ij^d." (At Flodden.)

(" On the 9 of September Ring James, the fourth of that name, king of
Scottes, was slain at Bramstone upon Piperd Hill and his armie discom=
fited by the earle of Surrep lieutenant to Henrp the 8 Ring of England."—
Stowe, 495.)

1528. " It. to the quens aumer s$^{'1}$uants, for that the bells
wer not rong at her comyng in to the town,
viij^d."

Anno 24–5 Hen. VIII. (1533–4). " It. for ryngyng at
the birth of the princes *elizabeth* iiij^d." (This
name in another hand, but coeval).

1553–4. " Paid to Ringers at the Kyng & Quenys
cumyng and goyng xx^d."

1560. " Itm. for Ryngynge the great Bell to the
S$^{'1}$mond, vi^d."

1568. " Itm. to the Rynggers at the Queen's comynge in,
xvi^d."

At the foot of the accounts from Michaelmas 1575, to
Michaelmas 1576, we have :—

" Expenses about Ringers, the Quene being in Rheding : In bred, drinke, money, and candells, to watche
the Quenes seate wth the travise and Arras hanging
in the Chaunsell, vj^s iij^d. (p. orig. 361.)

1576-7. " Paid for a verkin of beare at the Ringing for the Quene xxii^d."

1585-6. " Imprimis laid out more than was gathered at the ringing for ye Quenes rainge (reign) viij^s j^d ob."

1587-8. " Paid to the Ringers aboue y^t we gathered on the Quenes daie, xij^d."

1591-2. " Paid for ringing at hir ma^{ties} coming xxij^d."
" Payd for making cleane of the strete at hir ma^{ties} coming & for cariage xx^d."

1602. " It. paid for Ringing when the Queene was in towne v^s ix^d."
" Itm. paid for flowers & Rushes for the churche when the Queene was in towne xx^d."
  ,, " Itm. paid for a cloth to hang before the pulpitt when the Queene was here ij^s vj^d."
  ,, " Itm. paid for ringing at the cominge of the lord keep iiij^d."

1612. Goodman Greene & Ffraunces Blake Ch. wardens.
  ,, " Payd more to the petti Sextone for Ringing a Crownation day and to (two) gallons and a halfe a beare out of my one seller, and had maney vill an slandrows words from this Receaver x^s."

1613. " Payed to them that hope (helped) ring when the quien rode by the towne ij^s."
  ,, " Payed Venter when the quien cam first to the towne 3^s."
  ,, " For bread and beare xvj^d."
  ,, " Moor to Prites two sonnes w^h hop ring ij^s."
  ,, " Payed moor to Venter when shee came to the Abbye for Ring iij^s vj^d."
  ,, " Payed for Ring the 5 of August xiiij^d."

1621-2. " P^d him for ringing the greate Bell at 4 & 8 halfe a yeare 2l. 6^s 8^d."

1633. " M^d that if the sexton of the pish ring aboue an houre and a half any funerall knell, the friends of the deceased shall pay vnto ye church for euery quarter of an houre aboue the time assigned 6^d."

Period of the Civil Wars.

Among the old papers now preserved in the new folio at p. 133, is an original bill of "Venter," the sexton, which may fitly find a place here.   It is dated

"Palme Sundaye,
"Beinge the 26 of March 1643.

"When yᵉ King cam to Twone first, for Rosmery & bays	o	o	8
"When his Maᵗⁱᵉ came from Branfoord for Rosemery & bayes	o	o	8
"It. at Crismas for Rosemery & bayes . .	o	o	8
"It. for carrying of the plate forth out of the vestry & in	o	1	o
"To the clarke for removing the church trunke out of the vestry to the Docʳᵃ house and recarrying it &c.	(sic)		
"It. for carrying of the Church formes to the Abby when the King was there and back againe	o	2	o

In the accounts for the year ending May 30, 1644, we have the following :—(and as all these entries are very important, illustrating the period of the civil wars, I give them as they occur, being evidently written in chronological sequence) :—

"To Pharrowe for making vpp the seats when the parliamᵗ Souldiers were here . .	o	3	4
"To Daniel Browne & goody Venter for makeing cleane the church then . .	o	2	o
"It. for ffrankincense to sweeten the church .	o	1	o
"To him (Edward Venter) for Ringing the last of November when his Maᵗˢ coming hither was expected	o	9	o
"It. pᵈ for Holly & Ivy, Rosmery & Bayes att Christmass	o	1	10
"It. pᵈ to the Ringers on the Kings Coronation day	o	9	o
"It. pᵈ for mending the Seats in the Church wᶜʰ the souldiers had broken downe .	o	1	6
"It. pᵈ for Ewe for the church against *Easter*, and for sticking of itt upp . . .	o	1	8

" It. p^d for ringing when the King came last to
Towne . . . . o 10 o
" It. p$_d$ for Ringing a peale when the Earle of
Essex came to Towne . . . . o 2 6
(Observe the difference in these two last payments.)

In the accounts ending 21st of April, 1645—

" It. p^t to Val. ffallowe for mending seats in
the church wch the souldiers broke
downe . . . . o 3 2
" It. p^d to Daniel Browne for making cleane
the Church twice, & for pitch & frankincense . . . . o 5 o
" It. p$_d$ to ffrancis Thackham for halfe a load
of wood burnd in the Church by the
Souldiers . . . . . . o 6 6
" It. p$_d$ to Val Pharoah for mending Seats in
the Church . . . . . . o 13 9

In the accounts ending 27th of April, 1646—

" It. p^d for 1^{ll} of frankincense and of pitch to
pfume the church . . . . . o o 8
" It. p^d to Daniel Browne for watching in the
church when the soldiers were here, &
making it cleane when they were gone . o 2 6
" It. p^d to the Ringers for Ringing after several
Victories. . . . . . . 1 o 6
" It. p^d for 2^{ll} of pitch & 2^{ll} of frankincense
used in the church . . . . . o 1 4
" It. p^d to Da : Browne for watching & making
cleane the church when the souldiers
were last here . . . . . o 4 o

In the year beginning Whit Tuesday, 1647—

" To the Ringers when the Kinge came throu
the towne . . . . . . o 7 o
" Strewing aubes (herbs) and flowers to strowe
the sitis in the Church win the ginarall
was in the towne . . . . . o o 10
" To the Ringars when the Jinerall war going a
way . . . . o 3 o

1699. " P^d to the Ringers on S. George's Day, 10^s o^d.
1688. The sexton's wages were augmented from 7l. to

20*l.* per annum, "on condition that he ring the
bell at 5 of the clock (morning) and 9 (evening),
in good order, and look after the chimes and
clock as he ought to doe."

During the 15th century the bells were probably rung on
the ground-floor. At the beginning of the 16th century
there was a ringing loft on a level with the sill of the large
west window in the tower.

Anno 1502. "Itm. payed to Wiłłm Cone for settyng on
of a borde vnd'] the loft for þ° ring')s, &c. ix^d."

Numerous initials, with dates from 1599, may still be
seen on the piers and arches above the level of the old
gallery floor.

In the present ringing chamber, which is one of the finest
in the county, is an early record of change ringing painted
on a board. The inscription is as follows :—

July ye 8th, 1734,
The whole Peal of
Grandsire Triples
5,040 Changes was rung in
three hours & ten minutes
by them whose names are
here mentioned.
Henry Samples, Treble.
Gyles Newbury, Second.
Joseph Philip, Third.
Robert Booth, Fourth.
Thomas Shurfield, Fifth.
Henry Peaty (Bob Caller), Sixth.
John Wells, Seventh.
William Ford } Tenor.
Abram Biship }

"This board was restored at the cost of Mr. Alf. Thomas,
Deputy Captain, 1880."

The Clock.

The earliest reference to a clock at St. Lawrence's is in the Roll of 1433 :—

"Et in resol. Johi Tylere p̃ custodia orologii et illuminaciõe lumñ, vij^s."

"Et in stipendio factoris orologii, ij^s."

Tyler occurs as clock keeper until 1441.

The next entry is very interesting, showing the elaborate nature of the mechanism :—

Anno 1498-9. "It. payed for the settyng of Jak (Jack) with the hangyng of his bell & mendyng his hond, iiij^d."

Jack's automatic character must have afforded much amusement to the children of those days, and no doubt equal gratification to their seniors. The mechanism may have exhibited other ingenious attractions besides little Jack with his hammer. The clock was somewhere in the church, and visible, no doubt, to the whole congregation.

Anno 1498-9. "Itm. payed for makyng fast of the cloke howse w^t ij^o pec^s of tymb'r set in to the walls w^t a mason, viij^d.

"Itm. payed to Strawford for settyng of a pece of tymb'r at ye clok ham^s) w^t nayles, iij^d ob.

"Itm. payed for wyer to the same clok, xi^d ob.

"Itm. payd for led to make the payce of the clok, v^s vj^d.

"Itm. payed for castyng the payce iiij^d."

Anno 1510-11. "It. rec^d of Willm Veld for a seate for hymself vnder the clock hows iiij^d."

In 1520 this curious old clock seems to have given way to a successor :

"It. paid to the clockmaker for a new clok in pte of payment of v^{li},—xl^s."

Anno 1521. "In p .mis paid to the clokemakar in pte paymēt of vj^{li} x^s ffor the new cloke & the dyall, iij^{li}."

There is a discrepancy in these two entries : perhaps the
dial was an extra. This clock seems to have been placed
in the tower, as will appear from the following entry :—

Anno 1521-2. " It. payd for glayssyng the stepoll wyndow
oū the dyall wᵗ pᵗ of old glas and pᵗᵉ new
vijˢ vj ."
1522-3. " Payd to Garrett for makg̃ the cloke xxxˢ viijᵈ."

In 1560 a new dial was erected at a cost of 46s. 8d.

Anno 1586-7. " Paid to H. Osmund for mending yᵉ
clocke broken wᵗ the fall of yᵉ gret bell *clapp'*
ijˢ viᵈ."
Anno 1587. The dial was repaired, gilt, &c., at a cost
of 3l. 13s. 8d.
Anno 1596. " Ffor timber and bords for a new clock
howse xˢ jᵈ."

By an Indenture, dated the 15th November, 1673, William
Young of the city of Oxford, Locksmith, engaged with
George Hatton and Samuel Watlington, Churchwardens
of St. Lawrence's, for the sum of 20s. in hand paid at the
ensealing of the deed, and for the further sum of 29l. " to
make, work, sett upp, and finish, &c., a ffirme, good, substantiall and Tuneable sett of Chymes (in Peale) to
two Tunes, viz. : upon the Tune of the cxlviijᵗʰ Psalme, and
the Teune of the cxiijᵗʰ Psalme, or any other Two Tunes
of which the Churchwardens, &c., shall best approve, the
same chymes to strike uppon all the eight bells in the
tower, &c., of equall & good notes." And he the said
William Young also covenanted to make, &c., " a ffirme
good and substantiall Quarterne clock, to strike on the
aforesaid eight bells in an orderly manner as a quarterne
clock ought to doe." The said William Young covenanted
moreover " to putt and sett the clocke now standing in the
Tower in good and sufficient order as the same ought to be.
The said sum of 29l. to be paid as soone as the said chymes
Quarterne clock, and other clock shall be truly and effec-
tually made, sett upp, finished, perfected, and amended as
aforesaid."

William Young's bond was returned to him on the 13th
April, 1680, when the clock was finally completed.

In the year 1881, the old clock which had collapsed
several years before, was removed to afford increased
accommodation in the ringing chamber. It was considered

that from the proximity of the tower to the municipal clock, it was undesirable to provide another, since it would only entail an annual expenditure, which the state of the church funds would hardly justify.

Inventories.

The earliest book of church accounts contains four inventories :—

The first of 1503 is defective ; a part of the inventory of the silver being missing, as well as the altar hangings. The whole has been erased by the compiler of the next inventory of 1517, except the list of "Stained Cloths," which is made to do duty for the latter inventory, where the heading appears, but without the items. The author, however, has appended them.

The second inventory of 1517 is the most minute in detail, and for this reason is here given *in extenso.* It is an invaluable repertory of mediæval ecclesiastical furniture, and will be most interesting to every student of ancient art. The church must have vied with some of our smaller cathedrals in the magnificence of her appointments.

The inventory of 1523 is less interesting : it omits the names of many of the donors specified in the earlier ones.

These three have been most carefully collated. The asterisk (*) prefixed indicates that the article appears in the previous inventory of 1503, and the "o" in the subsequent catalogue of 1523 : the numerals refer to the notes immediately following the inventory, in which every variation is noted.

The fourth is the inventory of the goods assigned to the separate altars, two leaves of which only remain. It was compiled at the same time as the third inventory, as appears from an item in the expenditure of 1523-4 :—

> " It. for makeyng thynventorye of all the church goods, & of all the Implemēts belongyng to all the awlts iij⁵ iiij⁴."

The whole of this has been distributed under the account of the several altars, viz. :—"Oū Ladyes Awlt," "Trynyte Awlt," "Saynte Thom⁵ Awlt," "Saynt Johñ's Awlt," & "the Sepulcre Awlt."

H 2

" Innbentorye of all and sing'lr goodes of the church of Saynt
Laurence in Redyng, renewed & made in the tyme of
John Barfote & John Vansbye p'curators of the seid
churche, the yere of our Lord God a M'CCCCxbij
& the ixth yere of the regne of kyng Henry the biijth."

Plate.

* ° " In p'mis a Crosse of Sylū & gilt w^t mary & John
weying lxxix ounc^s & a q^{a}rt̃ of the gifte of Mast̃
Niclius More late vicar.

* ° " It. a senso^r of Sylū pcell gilt w^{t}out a pan weyng
xxx vnc^s iij q^{a}rt̃ of the gift of—

* ° " It. a nother Senso^r of Silū pcell gilt w^t an Iron pan
in hym weying xxx vnc^s iij q^{a}rt̃ of the gift of—

° " It. a Shipp of Silū weyng ix vnc^s di of the gifte of—

" " It. a nop̃ shipp of Silū weying v vnc^s of the gifte of
Mayst̃ Cletche.

" " It. ij° Canstick^s of Silū weyng xl vnc^s di of the gifte
of Richard Cleche.

" " It. ij° bokes a gospello^r (lxix vnc^s) & a pistello^r
(lxv vnc^s) the one side coued w^t Silū pcell gilt w^t
Imag^s vppon the same & the other side w^t boces of
silū, weyng yn all cxxxiiij vnc^s of the gifte of M^r
Richard Smyth yemā of the robes w^t our souayne
lord the kyng.

" " It. ij° basons of silū weyng xlviij vnc^s & di of the
gifte of Mr Smythe.

* ° " It. a pix of silū & gilt w^t a Silū pyn wayng xvj
vnc^s iij q^{a}rt̃ hangyng yn the Chyrch.

* ° " It. a monstre of silū & gilt weyng xxiiij vnc^s iij
q^{a}rt̃ for the sac^{a}ment of the gift of—

° " It. a Crismatorye of sylū pcell gilt weyng xxij q^{a}rt̃
& di of the gifte—

° " It. a pax of silū pcell gilt weing vj onc^s of the gifte
of—

° " It. ij° Cruetts of silū weing vj vnc^s di of the gifte
of—

° " It. a bell of silū weing viij vnc^s of the gift of— (I.)

° " It. a chalice of silū & gilt w^t a Crucifix on the fote
ennamellid & the trynite ennamellyd on the patent

weyng xxv vnc⁸. (Opposite this, in the margin,
"M͏ʳ Berd hath hym.")

* ° " It. a nother chalice of silũ & gilt wᵗ a Crucifix
graven in the fote & an hand on the patent weyng
xviij vnc⁸.

* ° " It. a nother chalice of silũ & gilt wᵗ a Crucifix ennamellyd on the fote & an hond on the patent weyng
xv onc⁸ iij qᵃrt̃. (" Stolen," in the margin, written
later than 1523.)

* ° " It. a nother chalice of silũ & gilt wᵗ a Crucifix
ennamellid on the fote & pᵉ trynite enamellyd on
the patent weyng xvij vnc⁸ di. (2.)

° " It. a nother chalice of silũ peell gilt wᵗ a Crucifix on
the fote & a v')nacle (3) on the patent weyng xiiij
vnc⁸ qᵃrt̃.

° " It. a nother chalice of silũ peell gilt wᵗ a Crucifix on
the fote & a ũnacle gilt on the patent weyng xij
vnc⁸ di.

° " It. a nother chalice of silũ peell gylt weyng xviij vnc'
di of the gyft of Will₃m Stamford. (4.)"

Reliques.

° " It. a crosse of silũ & gilt wᵗ pᵗᵉ of the Holy Crosse
therin weyng vj vnc⁸ qᵃrt̃.

° " It. a gredyron of silũ & gilt wᵗ a bone of Saynt
Laurence therin weyng iij qᵃrt̃ of an vnc of the
gifte of Thom͏ᵃs Lynde squyer.

° " It. a rownde box of Cop & gilt wᵗ diũce reliques
therin.

° " It. a table closed wᵗ reliques.

° " It. iiij knoppis of Cop & gilt."

Books.

* ° " In p'mis an antipher wᵗ ffull legend of the gifte of
Sʳ John Andrewe sũ tyme vicar ther, the ijᵈᵉ lefe
begynnyng (*Patri et filio*).

* ° " It. a nother Antiphoner wᵗ full legend of the gifte of
Sʳ John Serne sũ tyme vicar ther the ijᵈᵉ lefe begynnyng (*sacerdos ponat*).

° " It. a nother Antiphoner the ijᵈᵉ lefe (*tuũ invocatu
est*).

* ○ " It. a nother Antiphoner the ij^{de} lefe (*tem.z corũ te*).
 ○ " It. a nother Antiphoner the ij^{de} lefe (*eripe te liberante*).
* ○ " It. a portos not Sar' (*Sarum*) the ij^{de} lefe (*sc'pta sunt*).
* ○ " It. a new legend the ij^{de} lefe (*lectuli ligneũ*.) (5.) (6.)
* ○ " It. a queyre the ij^{de} lefe begynnyng (*pastor bone*).
 * " It. a legend Sõõ^r chayned by fore the vicars stall the ij^{de} lefe begynnyng (*vi de Sĉã Kaťĩina*).
* ○ " It. a Martiloge the ij^{de} lefe afť the Kalendre (*dio mari*).
* ○ " It. an ordinall the ij^{de} lefe afť the Kalendre (*pore pasche*).
* ○ " It. a Masse boke the ij^{de} lefe afť the Kalendre (*multitudinẽ asțges*).
* " It. a nother masse boke noted (7.) ij^{de} lefe afť þ^e Kalendre (*hec sacra*).
* ○ " It. a nother masse boke the ij^{de} lefe afť the Kalendre (*asperges*).
* ○ " It. a nother masse boke the ij^{de} lefe afť the Kalendre (*more sanctifices*).
* ○ " It. a litel masse boke notid the ij^{de} lefe afť þ^e Kalendre (*potes expugnans*).
* ○ " It. a nother masse boke notid the ij^{de} lefe afť þ^e Kalendre (*fratres q'cunq3*).
* ○ " It. a nother masse boke not Sar' noted the ij^{de} lefe (*Dñica Prima*).
* ○ " It. a grayle w^t ij claspes of silũ the ij^{de} lefe (*de Sĉa Maria*).
* ○ " It. a nother grayle the ij^{de} lefe (*regimine chori*).
* ○ " It. a nother grayle the ij^{de} lefe (*populus Syon*).
* ○ " It. a nother grayle the ij^{de} lefe (*Dñica prima adventus*).
* ○ " It. a nother grayle the ij^{de} lefe (*non solũ iacuit*).
 ○ " It. a nother grayle the ij^{de} lefe (*humana ðire*). (8.) (9.)
* ○ " It. a manuell the ij ^e lefe (*clericos asțgat*).
* ○ " It. a nother manuell the ij^{de} lefe (*testatem inimici*). (10.)
* ○ " It. a nother manuell the ij^{de} lefe (. . . *culorum Amen*).
 ○ " It. a Sawter & a Colett boke the ij^{de} lefe (*quoniam non est*). (8.)
 ○ " It. a nother Sawter the ij^{de} lefe (*qui confidunt in eo*). (8.)
 ○ " It. ij^e quaires in prent of the visitaĉon of our lady the ij^{de} lefe begynnyng (*decacordo*). (8.)

" " It. a queire of the fest of Cristm⁰s. (8.)

" " It. a pcessionall the ij^de lefe (*Maria ecce*). (8.)

" " It. a nother pcess' writen of the gifte of Richard Turner the ij^de lefe (*ūros es*). (11.)

" " It. a pcess' of the gifte of Ric' Barnys the ij^de lefe. (11.)

" " It. a pcess' the ij^de lefe (*Sp' Sancti*).

" It. a new legend prynted the ij^de leffe (*qui estentib₃*) of the gyft of John Barefote. (11.)

" It. a grale pryntyd of the gyft of Thom⁰s Whyt (*in 2° fo. cōcede quis*). (11.)

" It. a manuell of the gyft of Sr John Rychmond (*in 2° fo. c"cem in frōte*). (11.)

𝔅okes of 𝔓ricksong.

" " In p^imis a grete boce of vellem bourded for masses of the gifte of Wiłłm Stannford.

" " It. a nother boke bourded of paper w^t masses & antempins (? *antiphons*).

" " It. an old boke bourded w^t antempins.

" " It. a noy⁹) of vellame bordyd w^t antems & exul-tavits. (Note 53.)

Copes.

" " In p^imis a Cope of panys of cloth of gold, of crymson velvet & blew velwett of the gifte of Mr Thom⁰s Justice vicar. (12.)

" " It. ij Copes of tissue (13) red and grene of the gifte of the pissh.

" " It. a Cope of Blew velwett w^t floures imbrowdred of the gifte of Thom⁰s Clarke, Hosier. (14). (C. W. in 1443).

" " It. a Cope of crymson velwett w^t orphrays imbrowdred & angels floures imbrowdred of the gifte of Mr Thom⁰s Justice vicar.

" " It. a Cope of White Damaske tissue w^t orfrey of crymy-syn tissue of the gifte of Cristian Wilcox.

" " It. a Cope of White Damask tissue w^t orfrey of Bawdekyn & rosis of gold of the gifte of Raphe White of Okyngh⁰m.

" " It. ij Copis of red velwett w^t orfrey of grene velwett sett w^t floures of the gifte of John Euard, ffuller.

* ° "It. a Cope of cloth of bawdekyn (15) w^t birdis &
floures of gold of the gifte of John Kent.

"It. a Cope of blake velwett w^t qarterys of the gifte of
Mr Smyth (subsequently erased).

° "It. a Cope paned w^t blew velvett & black & orfrey *of
grene saten a brydges of the gift of* the x brethern
embrod^s)yd w^t the name of Ihc. (The words in
italics erased, and the remainder in another
hand.)

° "It. a Cope paned w^t black velwett & plonkett saten
w^t orfrey of grene saten a brydges of the gifte of

° "It. a Cope of blake saten & blonket s^s)senet paned w^t
orfrey of grene saten of brydges.

° "It. ij° Copis of white saten a brydg^s the orfrey Crymson
Saten sett w^t floures of the gifte of Richard Turner
& Richard Barnys.

° "It. ij° Copes of satten russet & crane the orfrey red
damaske & satten of the gifte of Maist^r Smyth.

° "It. ij° Copes of saten a bryges white & grene
paned w^t orfrey of tawney saten of the gifte of M^r
Smyth.

* ° "It. a Cope of Crymson Bawdekyn, the orfray of
yelow saten. (16.)

* ° "It. a Cope red Cloth of Bawdekyn of the gifte of
Joh^{a}nne Barbo^r.

* ° "It. a Cope of Black worsted w^t branchis & birds
of red.

* ° "It. a Cope of white Silke w^t this lre ꟻ Crownyd.

* ° "It. a Cope of Blew cloth of Bawdekyn.

* ° "It. a Cope of red Silk w^t signes of the Son of the
gifte of Dan Rob̃t Redyng Monke.

* ° "It. a Cope of black worsted for obitts.

Vestemēts.

° "In p^{l}mis A sewte of vestements of Crymson Tissue
w^t grene orfrey of tyssew of the gifte of Willm
Wattis.

• "It. a Sewte of blew velwett w^t floures imbrowdred
of the gifte of Thom^{a}s Clark, Hosyer.

° "It. a Sewte of white damaske the orfrey of Bawdekyn w^t roses of gold of the gifte of Water Barton.

* ° " It. a Sewte of red Cloth of bawdekyn w^t birds & floures of gold of the gifte of John Kent.

° " It. a Sewte of Red Cloth of Bawdekyn w^t whyt ross^s of the gifte of Joh^enne Barbo^r.

° " It. a Sewte of Black Velwett w^t garters of the gifte of Mr Smyth (in a later hand in the margin, "deliud to Jhc awt.") (17.)

° " It. a Sewte of Black worsted w^t braunches & birds of red.

* " It. a Chesible suspended w^t ij° tunycles of ray silk (erased).

* ° " It. a Chesible w^t a rest & all thappell of blew silk the orfrey red velwett w^t Imag^s & Crownes of gold. (In margin—" Delyud to Seynt Thomas Awter.")

* ° " It. a Chesible w^t all thappell of blew silk & roses of gold the orfray of the Salutacōn of our lady.

* ° " It. a Chesible of blew silk w^t popyngcays of gold w^t the appells (" sospended" in margin.) (18.)

* ° " It. a Chesible of Crymson Silk w^t grypes w^t narow Crosse of white." (In margin—" Delyud to Seynt Thomas Awter.") (19.)

* ° " It. a Chesible w^t all thappell of grene & black silk myxt w^t gold braunches suspendid the orfrey red velwett w^t ihc in gold of the gifte of Cristian Merch^am. (" Suspendyd.")

* ° " It. a Chesible w^t thappell of red silk suspend w^t lres of gold J & S of the gifte of John Serne. (" Suspendyd" in margin.)

* ° " It. a white Chesible w^t a red Crosse & all appell for lent.

° " It. a Red Chesible w^t narrow Crosse (20) & all appell for good ffriday. (21.)

° " It. a Chesible of grene bourd Alisaunder w^t thappell the orfrey of Crymson silk (22) of the gifte of John Ffrank (" to Seynt Thomas Autre.") (23.)

* ° " It. a Chesible of Cloth of bawdekyn the orfrey of cloth of bawdekyn w^t thappell of the gifte of John Derby Alderman of London. (24.)

* ° " It. a Chesible of grene Damaske the orfray red Silk w^t an Image of Saynt Laurence of the gifte of Margarett Parker (25) of faryngton.

* ° " It. a Chesible of Whit Damaske w^t braunches of gold the orfrey blew velwett w^t thappell of the gifte of John Thorne Abbott of Redyng.

" It. iij° vestments (26) w^t thappell^s of whit saten a brydg^s
w^t orfrey of grene saten of the gifte of Mr Smyth.
(In a later hand " delyv$^)$)yd to iij low autres.")

° " It. a sewte off Russett Tynsyn w^t orffreys off blewe
Tynsyn.

° " It. a sewte of purpyll velwett In brodryde w^t Antony
Crossys & bellys.

° " It. a Cotte (*coat*) ffor Marmawdlyn* of clothe of gold
(*erased*). (*These three last entries in a later hand.*)

° " It. a crosse for a chysybyle of old rede veluet enbrod$^)$)yd
w^t 𝕴𝕙𝕔 & stars of Cowrs golde.

(27.)

" It. an aw^t cloth of crymsyn veluet & whyt damaske
enbrod$^)$)yd w^t flo^{rs} of Venes gold. (The two last
entries in a smaller and neater hand.)"

Awter Clothes.

° " In p^{l}mis an Awter Cloth of panes of cloth of gold &
velwett imbrowdred w^t Arch^{s}ngells & floures of the
gifte of—

" It. ij Aw^t Clothes of tissue red & grene w^t a cou for the
halpase of the same & ij° Curteyns of Sarsenett red &
grene of the gifte of John Pownsar (erased).

" It. ij° Awter Clothes of white Damaske w^t grene floures
w^t ij° Curteyns of white & grene sarsenett of the pissh
gifte (erased).

° " It. ij° Awter Clothes of velvett blew & blak of the gifte
of Mast^r Smyth.

" It. an Awter Cloth of saten blew & yelow paned w^t ij°
Curteyns crymson blew & yelow paned of the gifte of
Mr Smythe (erased).

° " It. an Awter Cloth of black velwett & bawdekyn paned
w^t an Image of Saynt Laurence of the gifte of M^r
Smythe.

° " It. an awter cloth of sarsenet orenge colo^r & blew w^t
curteyns of the same of the gifte of Mr Smyth.

° " It. an aw^t cloth of grene tyssew w^t ij C^{r}teyns of whyt
& gren s'ssenet.

° " It. an awter cloth of Damaske blew & red w^t garters.

° " It. an awter cloth of blew Sarsenet w^t a frontell of saten
a brydg^s blew & red. (*In the margin*, " Seynt John's
au^t.")

* St. Mary Magdalene.

" " It. an awter cloth of black velwett & bawdekyn w^t an Image of Saynt Edua^{r}d (28) and for the nether pte of the same an Awter cloth of Sarsenett orenge colo^r & blew paned w^t curteyns of the same of the gifte of Mr Smyth.

" " It. an Awter Cloth of blew & Rede Saten w^t an Image of Saynt John & Curteyns of blew taffeta to the same.

" " It. ij° Awt^r Clothes of Crane colo^r velwett & whit Damaske panyd w^t floures imbrowdred & ij° Curtens of whit & crane colo^r silk of the gift of   for Saynt John Awt^r.

" " It. ij° Awt^r clothes w^t thappell of the same for o^r Lady awt^r.

" " It. ij° Awt^r clothes of blew saten a brydg^s imbrowdred w^t floures w^t an Image of Saynt Clement for o^r Lady Awt^r & ij° Curteyns of blew taffeta of the gifte of John Turner. (29.)

" " It. an awt^r cloth of Crymson & tawney velwett ymbrowdred w^t ffloures of gold & for the nether pte of the same Crymson saten & cloth of bawdekyn for the Sepuler Awter (*margin*—"at Sepuler aut^r).

" " It. ij awt^r cloths w^t red cross^s for lent w^t C^{r}teyns to the same.

Quysshons.

" " In p^{l}mis a quysshon the one side cloth of gold & the op.^{t}) syde crane colo^r saten of the gifte of Mr Smyth.

Corpas Cases.

" " It. a quysshon the one side blak velwett & the other sy^d ray Silk.

" " It. a quysshon the one side plonkett saten a brydges the other syde of Chalkyd fu∸tian.

" " It. a smale quysshon the one side velwett & the other side red saten.

" " It. a nother the one side velwett & the other side tawney saten.

" " It. ij pillows, the one side of them of cloth of gold & silu & the other side grene Saten a brydg^s.

" " It. ij pillows of blew velwett tissew—(*added in another hand*—"the other syde gren brydg^s saten").

° " It. ij corpas casses of cloth of gold pirlyd w^t tres of
𝕽 & 𝕾 uppon the same imbrowdred w^t iiij^{or} knoppis
of silū & corpas to the same.

° " It. iij pillows of russett ray for weddyngs. (30.)

° " It. iij pillows of blew silk. (31.)

* " It. a corpas case of tissew (*added*—" d'd to sent
Thomas awt̊").

" " It. a nother of red silk w^t lyons of gold. (32.)

* " It. a nother of *blew silk & whit w^t bests of gold*.
(33.) (The words in italics erased, and appended is
—"p^{r}poll the grownd w^t flo^{rs} of Russet.")

* ° " It. a nother w^t the Salitacon of o^r Lady.

* ° " It. a nother of red silk w^t branches of gold w^t red
birds a bout.

* ° " It. a nother of whit silk w^t a red Crosse of Silk.

* ° " It. a nother of cloth of bawdekyn w^t ij° lyons. (34.)

* ° " It. a nother of red silk the one sid, & bourd Alisaunder the other side. (35.)

° " It. a nother of blew cheverns of gold with the bake
syde Russet satten." (Probably the arms of the
donor 'a₃ . . . . chevrons or.') (36.)

Ornaments.

° " It. a sepulcre Cloth of right Crymson Satten im-
browdered w^t Imagerye w^t a frontaill of panys
conteyning in length iiij yards of the gifte of M^r
Richard Smyth w^t ij° clothes of lawnde for the
sepulcre.

' " It. a canape of tissue for the Sacrament & a lawnde
w^t iiij botons wrought w^t gold & tassells of gold for
the pix.

° " It. a Canapye of Crymson velwett imbrowdred w^t
gold floures & the Holy lombe in the mydle of the
pcuryng of Mr Smyth & the wifes.

° " It. a cloth (37) of ray Silk to bere the crismatory
at Est^r. (38.)

Palls.

° " It. a pall of Black velwett w^t garters of the gifte of
Mr Smythe.

° " It. a pall of blew velwett imbrowdred w^t floures of
gold of the gifte of Thomas Clarke hosier.

° " It. a pall of bourd Alisaunder. (39.) (40.)

* " It. a pall of whit Silke lyned w^t lynen cloth for weddings. (41.)

*° " It. a pall of bord Alisaunder lyned w^t red boke-ram. (42).

° " It. a Cloth of gotis to ley in the weddyng cheyre. (43.) (44.) (45.)

Banners.

° " It. a banner for the Crosse of red Sarsenet w^t Imag* of the trynyte & of o^r lady.

° " It. a nother for the crosse of grene silk.

° " It. v baners of silk w^t the Armys of Englond. (46.)

° " It. a baner of whit silk w^t a Crosse of red. (47.)

° " It. a strem') of silk.

" It. a strem') of linen.

" It. a strem') of linen.

" It. a dext cloth of Crymson Bawdekyn (erased).

° " It. ij° dext Clothes of Dornex.

° " It. a knop of gold w^t tassells of blew sylke.

" It. a purse of crymysin cloth of gold pyrled for the osts. (48.) (49.)

" It. ij great stand')s w^t ij small kandylstyks of laten.

" It. ij sensars of latten.

" It. ij cross^s of cop & gylt w^t ij staves longeyng to the same.

" It. a crosse foot of coop and gylt.

" It. ij pax^s of coop.

" It. a fyer pan of yron.

" It. a crysmatory of coop & gylt.

(The last eight items have been appended to the original.)

Awter Clothes of Lynen.

" It. anAwter cloth of Diap in length v yerds & in brede a yerd & di.

° " It. an awter cloth of diap in length iiij yerds iij q^art^s & in brede a yerd & di.

" It. an awter cloth of diap in length iiij yerds & di & in brede a yerd and di.

° " It. an old awter cloth of Diap in length iij yerds & in brede a yerd.

- " It. an old awter cloth of diap in length ij yerd⁵ & di & in brede a yerd.
- " It. an Awll cloth of Canvas in length iij yerds & in brede a yerd.
- " It. an old awll cloth playne in length iij yerds & in brede a yerd.
- " It. an old awll cloth of diap in length iiij yerds & in brede a yerd,
- " It. ij° old awll clothes of diap in length a pece ij yerds & di & in brede a yerd.
- " It. an old awll cloth of diap in length ij yerds & in brede a yerd.
- " It. a diap awll cloth in length iij yerds qᵃrł & in brede a yerd qᵃrł.
- " It. an awll cloth of fyne Holond of iij yerds in length & a yerd in brede.
- " It. a nother of the same cloth of a yerde iij qᵃrł long & a yerd brode.
- " It. an awll cloth of Holond new in length v yerds & in brede a yerd.
- " It. a nother of the same cloth in length iij yerds qᵃrł & in brede a yerd.
- " It. an awllr playne in length ij yerds & a qᵃrł & in brede a yerd.
- " It. a nother of playne in length iiij yerds & in brede a yerd di qᵃrł.
- " It. a nother of playne in length iiij yerds & in brede a yerd.
- " It. a nother of Holond in length iiij yerds & in brede a yerd scante.
- " It. a nother of Holond in length ij yerds & di & in brede a yerd. (50.)

Tewells.

- " It. a Towell of fyne Diap in length xj yerds & in brede iij qᵃrł m̄lkyd wᵗ ffl.
- " It. a nother of diap in length ix yerds & in brede qᵃrł & di qᵃrł m̄lkyd wᵗ R.
- " It. a nother of Diap in length ix yerds iij qᵃrł & in brede di yerd & di qᵃrł wᵗout mark.
- " It. a nother of diap in length ix yerds iij qᵃrł & in brede di yerd m̄lkyd wᵗ ℬ.

ᵛ " It. a nother of Diap in length iij yerds iij qᵃrᵉ mˀˡkyd
wᵗ a gredyron.

ᵛ " It. a nother of Diap old iiij yerds in di length & in
brede di yerd & di qᵃrᵉ mˀˡkyd wᵗ ᵭᵭ. (51.)

ᵛ " It. a nother of playne in length xij yerds & in brede
di yerd mˀˡkyd wᵗ ᴿ. (52.)

Stayned Cloths.

(The items are not supplied by this inventory, but are
taken from that of 1503, the whole of which has been
erased except the following particulars) :—

" Also ij staynyd clothis wᵗ ryddels to þᵉ same & a couˀyng
for the halpace on the hy awltᵉ stayned wᵗ red
damaske warke & an ymage of Seynt Laurence in
the myddᵉ.

" It. a cloth staynd wᵗ þᵉ byrth of oʳ Lorde for þᵉ fonte
and a noyˀ] cloþ for þᵉ same of lynnꝫ wᵗ panys
white & blew.

" It. an aultᵉ cloþᵉ staynyd wᵗ an ymage of oʳ lady of
Pyte & ijᵒ angels and a noþˀ] wᵗ þᵉ sepulcre & ij
angells for þᵉ hy awltᵉ in lent.

" It. an autᵉ cloþᵉ of ray silk for the neþˀ] parte of the
hy awter wᵗ a frontell of styrrs of gold.

" It. a noþˀ] awtᵉ cloþᵉ staynyd wᵗ an ymage of oʳ lady
onely.

" It. a noþˀ] autᵉ cloþᵉ stayned wᵗ oʳ lady Seynt Gregorꝫ
Pyte & Seynt Anne.

" It. a noþˀ] awtᵉ cloth of þᵉ salutacõn & of þᵉ byrþᵉ of oʳ
lorde.

" It. a covˀllyꝫt of blak & grene wᵗ ꝣ & rosys white &
red of the gyft of Alyce Adene.

" It. an awtᵉ cloth stayned of thassūpcion of oʳ lady
seynt Anne & seynt Margaret."

Notes to the Preceding Inventory.

(1.) The original Inventory of 1523 ends here, but the
following is appended in a later hand :—
" It. a stãding cup of silꝰ & gilt wᵗʰ a couˀ of the
gift of Mastres hide " " xvj." (? oz.)

"It. a pomand'] of silu̅ & gilt of the gifte of
   Mastres White." "ix."
"It. a sensure of silu̅ & pcell gilt of the gifte of
   Mastres Barton."
"It. xviij silver aglotts gilt for the sepulcre."

(2.) "Stolen" is written opposite this in the inventory of
     1523 but in a much later hand. (c. 1547.)

(3.) "Vernacle." An engraving of the head of Jesus : so
     called from the "*vera icon*," or true portrait of
     Jesus, on the napkin of *St. Veronica* preserved
     at St. Peter's, Rome.

𝔄𝔫𝔡 𝔈 𝔰𝔞𝔩𝔩𝔢 𝔪𝔞𝔨𝔢 𝔪𝔶𝔫𝔢 𝔞𝔟𝔬𝔴𝔢 𝔡𝔢𝔟𝔬𝔱𝔩𝔭 𝔱𝔬 ℭ𝔯𝔦𝔰𝔱𝔢
𝔄𝔫𝔡 𝔱𝔬 𝔱𝔥𝔢 𝔥𝔞𝔩𝔭 𝔟𝔢𝔯𝔫𝔞𝔠𝔩𝔢 𝔟𝔢𝔯𝔱𝔲𝔲𝔰 𝔞𝔫𝔡 𝔫𝔬𝔟𝔩𝔢.
                    (Morte Arthur, MS. Lincoln, f. 56.)

(4.) In the Inv. 1523 is appended—
     "It. a chalice of the gifte of Mastres Cambie silu̅
     & pcell gilt weyng xij vnc⁸ & j q⁴t̃."

(5.) The Inv. of 1503 has inserted here—
     "It. ij quayers of the Visitaċon of o⁽ lady the
     ij° lefe of þᵗ one begynnyng (*Elizabeth humili
     celi gl'ia*).

(6.) The Inv. of 1523 here inserts—
     "It a new legend prynted in the secundo leff
     (quiestentib₃)."

(7) Inv. of 1503 inserts here—"in which ben red þᵉ
     epystyls."

(8.) This item inserted in the margin of the 1503 Inv.

(9.) Following this entry the Inv. of 1523 has :—
     "It. a new grayle in print in the seconde leff
     (concede qũis)."

(10.) The list of service books in the Inv. of 1503 ends
      here.

(11.) These entries are appended in another hand to the
      Inv. of 1517, so they must have been added
      between this date and 1523.

(12.) The Inv. of 1523, at the head of the list of Copes,
      has in a later hand "It. a cope of cloth of gold
      of the gift of Mʳ Ths Justice." He died in
      1547. See *Mr. Justice's Altar*.

(13.) In Inv. 1523—"iij Copes."

(14.) Inv. 1503 adds—"and Elizabeth his wife."

(15.) Inv. 1503 terms it "a rede cope of cloth of gold,"

which must be regarded as the interpretation of the term " Bawdekyn" used in 1517.

(16.) There were two of these in 1503 for the "rectores chory"—*i.e., chori.*

In a copy of the Salisbury Processional in York Minster Library, in the particulars of the ceremonies at the Font on the morning of Easter Day, the positions of the " Rectores principales" and the " Rectores secundarii" are indicated by crosses 'potent.' The former stand on either side of the priest on the west side of the font : on the east of it stands the bearer of the office book, facing west : again, to the east, are three boys appointed to sing the Alleluias: to the east of these again are the " Rectores secundarii," who are again distinguished by the same crosses 'potent.' At St. Lawrence's these functionaries appear to have been provided with special stools in the choir, their office being to conduct the responds, anthems, graduals, and other musical portions of the service. It would seem they bore a " Tau" cross in processions. Anno 1510–11. " It. payd for coũing & dressyng of the ij° stoles for the Rectors xix^{d}." They are mentioned again in 1530. (See *Will of Richard Bedowe*).

(17.) Invent. 1523 " at Ehe awter" in the margin.

(18.) Inv. of 1503 adds—"the orfrey on the bak a narow crose with warks."

(19.) Inv. of 1503 inserts in a later hand, " delyũd to ou^{r} lady mass," but in 1523 it was attached to St. Thomas' Altar, q.v.

(20.) Inv. 1503, inserts " of warks," and

(21.) adds,—" ffests of m^{a}rtyrs."

(22.) Inv. 1503, " w^{t} warks."

(23.) Inv. 1503 inserts,—" It. a chesyble of grene borde Alysaunder, the orfrey crymsyn sylk w^{t} warks & armys on the back w^{t} all apparell." A pen has been drawn through the whole, but in the margin is written " delyũed to Ehe auter."

(24.) This John Derby built an aisle or chapel on the south side of St. Dionys' Backchurch in London, and was buried there about 1466. (Stowe's Survey).

Anno 1498–9. " It. payed for mending of Darbyes Vestment iiij^{d}." St. Law. accts.

A William Derby was M.P. for Reading anno

I

5 Ric. II. (1382). In the roll of subscribers to the new roofing of the church in 1410 he is termed a "Glover."

(25.) "Margaret *Brode*" in Inv. 1503, and "*Parker*" in 1523, but obviously *copied* from this of 1517.

(26.) " It. iij° Chesabylls" in Inv. 1523.

(27.) The Inv. of 1503 is defective : there is no list of altar cloths.

(28.) " St. Thomas" in Inv. 1523.

(29.) " At oʳ ladys awͭ" in margin of Inv. 1523.

(30.) There were "iiij" in 1503.

(31.) The 1503 Inv. adds "and one of red sylk."

(32.) Inv. 1503, "a lyon." Inv. 1523 "lyones."

(33.) Inv. 1503 (*sic*).

(34.) Inv. 1503 adds "regant."

The next item in this inventory of 1503 (an addition in another hand) is—

"Also a nother corpax cace the one syde of cloth of gold and the other syde of blak velwett wᵗ ⅼres of gold ɼ & ꝭ of the gyft of quene Elizabeth by the pcuryng of Mʳ Richard Smyth yomā of the quenys robys wᵗ iiijᵒʳ knoppis of sylver wᵗ a corpas cloth to the same."

In the "Memorials for a History of Henry VII.," there is frequent mention of this great benefactor to St. Lawrence's :—

Anno 1 Hen. VII.—1485. Easter Term. "To Richard Smyth of the Queen's Wardrobe, for black silk of damask and crimson satin bought for the use of the lady the Queen, 11*l.* 5*s.* 6*d.*"

20 June, 1486. "Grant to Richard Smyth ('in consideracioun of the true and feithfulle service whiche oure welbeloved Richard Smythe Yoman of the Robes withe oure derrist wif the quene hath doone vnto us and during his lif entendeth to doo') of the herbage and pannage of the park of Wiggenok, Warwick, during the minority of Edwᵈ Earl of Warwick to his own proper use without yielding or paying anything therefore to the king. 17 June. P.s. No. 959 Pat. p. 4. m. 16.

Further deliveries from the Great Wardrobe 2 Hen. VII.

" To *Nicholas Pownser*, Ralph Newham and their thirteen
companions yeomen of the King's Crown for
the allowances of their watches; To *Thomas
Slythurst* yeoman of the King's Chamber for
the allowance of his watch; To *John Bigge*,
Richard Noresse, and their twenty companions
pages of the King's Chamber for the allowances of their watches ; To William Smythe,
Richard Bigge, and their six companions pages
of the King's Chamber for the allowances of
their watches ; To William *Betell*, Hamlet
Clegge, *Richard Smyth*, and their twenty-six
companions servants of the Lady Queen—
Cloth of Russet as a gift from the King for an
allowance of their watches.

(If *Betell* stand for *Bedell*, then we have no less than six
surnames (in *italics*) of families residing in St. Lawrence's
parish at this time.)

(35.) Inv. 1503—" ray borde alysād')."
(36.) Inv. 1523. " It. a nother of p^{r}poll the grownd w^t
fflors of Russet," and " It. vij corpesses."
(37.) Inv. 1523. "A sewdary of Ray silk," *i.e.*, a sudarium
or maniple.
(38.) Inv. 1523. " It. a white canopy for lent."
(39.) Inv. 1503 "lyned w^t blew bocram."
(40.) In Inv. 1523 the " borde Alys^{a}under" is erased, and
" red sarcnett w^t a yelow crosse" substituted.
(41.) This is erased in Inv. of 1523, and above it is
written " It. a litle pawll of bawdkynd w^t a
rede crosse for children."
(42.) Inv. 1503 has another entry, "It. ij rydels of whyt
sylk" (rydels=curtains).
(43.) Inv. 1503 adds " Of the gyft of Joh^{n}ne Barbour."
Its significance is obvious ; but this is quite in
accordance with the form of espousals in the
Salisbury use, in which the bride vows to be
"bonour and buxum *in bed*, and at bord."
(44.) Inv. 1523. " It. a cloth w^t gootes to ley in the
weddyng chare."
(45.) To the list of 1523 is appended in a later hand,
" It. a pawl of blak bockram w^t a white crosse."

(46.) " vj banners" in Inv. 1523.
(47.) "ij" banners in 1523.
(48.) "pyrleyd for visytacons"—1523.
(49.) After this is a separate inventory (1523) as follows :—

KANSTYKS OF LATTEN.

" It. ij greate standards of latten.
" It. ij small Kanstyks of latten.
" It. ij sensures of latten.
" It. ij Crosses of copp & gylte wᵗ ij staves to the same.
" It. a Crosse ffoote of Copp & gylte.
" It. ij paxes of Copp.
" It. a Crysmatorye of Copp & gylte.
" It. a fyar pan of yron.
" It. xxvij flatte canstiks & ix peacs of branches."

(50.) In the list of 1503 is one "merkyd wᵗ a bochers ax," and another "of the gyfte of Dan John Cheveley" the total number then was "xix."

(51.) In the margin of Inv. 1503 is an entry which illustrates this mark :—" It. a tewell of dyap of v ȝerds in length of yᵉ gyft of Thomˢ *Phylipps* wyfe."

(52.) The Inv. 1503 has at the end of its list of " Tewells," " It. a noῤ⁾ tewell of pane wark blew & white of ijᵒ yerds & di."

" It. a wasshyng tewell made of cresoms (chrisoms) of ij yerds & iij qᵃrt ⸴s."

(53.) Anno 1531–2. The church books were rebound and repaired.

" The costˢ of the Books.

"Payd for iij buk skynes ijᵒ stag skynes, &
  viij shepe skynes . . . xviij⁸ vjᵈ
"Payd for xxi rede skynes . . . vij⁸
"Payd for glew . . . . . . xijᵈ
"Payd for small threde & pak threde . . ij⁸ ijᵈ
"Payd for a dosyn of parchment skynes . ij⁸ ijᵈ
"Payd for xv vellam skynes . . . x⁸
"Payd to the Joynn'⁾ for bordes to the bokes xxᵈ
"Payd to the boke bynder for byndyng of
  the bokes . . . . . xxiiij⁸
"Payd for byndyng the new grayle &
  lymyng thereof . . . . ix⁸ xᵈ

"Payd for a buk skyn, a shepe skyn, &
    rede skyne . . . . . ij^s viij^d
"Payd for naylls & glew for the Saut^s in
    Saynt Johns Ch^{a}uncell . . . iiij^s j^d
              Sma pagĩs . . v^{ll} x^s iiij^d ob.
" Payd to ffrere Peter for wryttyng & notyng
    the new grayle & for the vellam
    therto . . . . . . xlvj^s viij^d
"Payd for vellam for the great leager . iij^{ll} xxiij^d
"Payd for fflorisshyng the same boke w^t
    stuff therto belongyng . . . iij^{ll} ix^s j^d.

Church Plate.

The church plate before the Reformation must have been very magnificent (see Invent. 1517) : its total weight was 583 oz. ; but by 1523, it amounted to 604 oz. ; besides the additional weight (not stated) of the " standing cup" with its cover presented by Mistress Hide, and eighteen silver shields gilt, for the sepulchre, which must have augmented it to at least 700 oz.

In the accounts for 1538 we have the following :—

" Rec. for plate sold (that is to witt)
    ij Kandlestiks weying xl. unc^s & di.
    a Pax weying six vnc^s.
    ij Cruetts weying vj onc^s & di and a bell weying
    viij vnc^s.
              Sma x^{ll} xviij^s vij^d.
    It. for a gilt cup w^t a cover vj^{ll} xiij^s vij^d.
    It. for a Crismatorie iij^{ll}.
              Sma xx^{ll} xj^s xj^d."

This seems to have been done to discharge some old debts—*e.g.* :

    "Payd to Ric. Dodgeson for detts owyng to hym
        the last yere xl^s viij^d.
    " Payd to IHS Masse for old detts vj^{ll} xiij^s iiij^d.
    " Payd to o^r Lady Masse that was borowed iij^d."

After this we find 32*s*. 8*d*. in hand added to the next year's receipts.

There was another sale of church plate anno 36 H. VIII. (1544), as if the Churchwardens John Bell & John Buckland & the parishioners had some presentiment of the coming spoliation.

" Rec. for c͠tayn plate sold that is to witt :—
A bason weying xxiiij oncˢ.
A senser weying xxx oncˢ.
A pomander weying iij oncˢ di.
A shippe weying ix oncˢ & di.
A Crismatorie weying xxij oncˢ qᵃ.
The sylũ vppon ij bokˢ weying xliiij oncˢ.
An old Crosse wᵗ nayles & other small pecˢ weying
 iij oncˢ qrt̃ at iijˢ xi ob. the once wᶜʰ cuñ̃ythe to
 the sm̃ of xxviˡˡ xiijᵈ iiijᵈ ob."

Note.—In November 1545 the king received from Parliament a grant of Chantries, &c., with a further power of seizure at any time.

Another sale took place 1 Ed. VI. (1547), Edward Butler & John Poyntz being churchwardens.

" Rec. of Nicholas Bull of London, Goldsmyth for c͠tain
 plate to hym sold as followith (that is to witt)—
ij Sensars of silũ waying lxvij oncˢ iij qᵃrt̃.
A Crosse of Silũ waying lxxiij oncˢ iij qᵃrt̃.
A bason of Silũ waying xiij oncˢ di.
A Shipp of Silũ waying v oncˢ iij qrtˢ which
 cuñ̃yth to c. liij qᵃrtˢ at iiijˢ xᵈ the once.
     Sma xxxvjˡˡ viijˢ viijᵈ."
" Rec. more of the same Nicholas Bull for a Monstrat
 of Silũ & gilt waying xxij onc' & for
A Chalice of silũ & gilt waying xx oncˢ which amountith
to xliij oncˢ at vˢ iiijᵈ the once.
     Sma xiˡˡ ixˢ iiijᵈ."

The churchwardens this year have a balance of 31*l.* 13*s.* 4*d.*, which was delivered to John Poyntz, the senior C.W. for the coming year, " in the presence of the parish."

Under the head of " Expenses" the following year, we have—

" Paid & delyũd to Bell by the assent of the pisshe towards the pavyngs of the strets xiijˡˡ vjˢ viijᵈ."

The silver barely escaped the clutches of the Royal Commissioners. The same year we have—

" Paid for makyng of Inventories for the Church goods
to the Comyssion's at ij tymes iij iiij."
" Paid to M Bell, Mayor, of that was made of a Chalice
for pavyng in the strets liij iiij."
" Paid & delyured to M Bell, Mayor, by M Nicholas
vppon the ij Chalises by him sold towards the
pavyng of the Strets by the assent of the
pisshe v."

Nicholas Nicholas died 2–3 Ed. VI. (1549–50). His widow
" Thomosyn" was charged by the C.W. with a debt of
8l. 12s. 6d., which her late husband had received for silver
and not refunded. She begged to be allowed 30s., which,
she said, her late husband had paid to Sir William Webbe
and to Sir Harper (chauntry priests) in part of their wages.
There seems to have been some doubt as to this payment
of 30s. to these chaplains : it is couched in the words
" supposed to be paid" in a memorandum of 1549.

Anno 4–5 Ed. VI. " M^d at this accompte it was aggreid
that if John Radley wold pay to the Churche
at the next accompte xl^s he to haue a gen'all
acquitaunce for all matiers cons'nyng M Turner
& M Beard & all other matiers for the payment
wherof he pmysed to seale an obligačon."

A Bridal Cup bequeathed to the church in 1534 escaped
the Commissioners, and remained intact until 1612.

St. Michael, 25 Hen. VIII. " At this day it is aggreid
that the Gilt Cupp of the gifte of M^res Hide
alweys to remayne in the custodye of the
Mayo, if the Mayo dwell in the pisshe. And
if the Mayo dwell out of the pisshe, then to
remayne & be in the Custodye of hym that was
last Mayo in the same pisshe, to th'use declared
in the will of the seid M^res Hide, whiche ordre
taken by John Reade at Skynn then Mayo,
M Barton M Euard M Turner M Vansby M
White & dyuce others of the pisshe."

In another hand follows :—

" M^ris Hid dissesed in ye yere 1534."*

* The date is wrong. She died in 1532-3, anno 24 Hen. VIII.

To this the following note was appended in the reign of
Elizabeth : the 'hand' corresponds exactly with the entries
made in 1564.

> "The said Cuppe was given for the vse to be carried
> before all brydds that were wedded in St Lau-
> rence Church, And nowe is turned to be occupied
> there at all tymes when nede is to occupie more
> then one comvnyon cuppe at one tyme, to vse
> & occupye it y^r as a comvnyon cuppe, &c."

The custom of drinking wine in the church at marriages
is enjoined in the Hereford Missal.   By the Sarum Missal
it is directed that the sops immersed in this wine, as well
as the liquor itself, and the cup that contained it, should
be blessed by the priest.   The form of benediction ran
thus :

"Benedic Domine panem istum et hunc potum, et hoc
vasculum sicut benedixisti quinque panes in deserto, et sex
hydrias in chanaan Galileæ, ut sint sani et sobrii atque
immaculati omnes gustantes ex iis," &c.

The beverage used on this occasion was to be drunk by
the bride and bridegroom and the rest of the company.
The pieces of cake or wafers immersed in wine on this
occasion, properly called 'sops,' were probably identical
with the "Bride Pastes" mentioned on p. 49.

This wedding cup was in existence in 1607, as appears
by the Inventory of that date :—

> " A fayre cupp with a cover.   Whosoeu is mayre in this
> parishe keepeth him."
> 1612. " The church Cupes was made newe *with covers to
> them boath* in the year of our Lord 1612 by M^r
> Doctor Deneyson and William greene and
> ffrancis Blacke C.W. contayning 34 ovnces or
> neare thearabout."

In the Inventories of 1612 & 1613 these two cups are
poised at "xxxiij ovncis, three quarternes, and a half"—
x^{ll} viij^s ix^d.

With these were associated " Too pewter potes, a great
and a leas. A small dyshe to set on the tabell : too paynted
dishes."*

* At Mardale, Westmoreland, is an old Delft dish with the sacred monogram, surrounded by rays, in the centre, formerly used as a paten.

In the Inventory of 1633 we find—

"It. ij comunion Cuppes of silver wth covers weyinge 33 ounʒes and a haulf.

"Item, one silver flaggon weytinge 46 ounʒes.

"Item, one silver bread plate weyinge 9 ounʒes.
} of the gift of Richard Johnson in 1631.

Anno 1638. "Memorand. The Challis Cupp of Mr Arthur Curtis wch cost 5l. by the addition of more money (3l. 14s.) by Richard Curtis, was counted & made 2 Cupps weighing 34 ounces ij dwts. wch cost 8l. 14s.

"Itm. one flagon silver of ye gift of M^r Jo. Sanders weighing   ounces   prise 26l."

In the accounts for this year is an item of 2s. paid for the carriage of the flagon, so that we may presume that Mr Saunders presented this flagon the same year.

The Inventory of 1648 has—

"Item, two silver Cupps wth covers weighing 33 ounces & a halfe (pcell gilt) (the Cups of 1612).

"Item, *two other* silver cupps wth covers weighing 34 ounces 2 dwts. of the gift of Mr Arthur Curtis & his sonne Richard Curtis.

"Item, one silver flaggon of the gift of John Saunders Esquire weighing 72 ouncs.

"Item, one silver flaggon weighing 46 ouncs.

1 silver bread plate weighing 9 ouncs and a halfe.
} of Mr Johnson's gift."

The Inventory of 1772, with Notes.

Plate.

oz. dwt.

"One large Silver Dish, the gift of Mrs Barbara Foster, weighing   62   0

This dish has a double ogee-shaped

edge with gadroon bordering. On a raised centre is a widow's escutcheon bearing a tower embattled between three buglehorns stringed; impaling, three bars with three lions' heads erased in chief. Underneath is inscribed " *The Gift of Mrs. Barbara Foster to St. Laurence's Church in Reading.*" The Hall mark is the " r" within the cinquefoil shield of 1752–3.

" One large D° Flagon the gift of John Saunders, Esq. . . . . . w^t· 72 7

This beautiful vessel, as we have seen, was presented in 1638–9, and bears the Hall mark for that year. On its front is engraven a shield, bearing—' Per chevron, three elephants' heads (two and one) erased.' The Saunders of Leicestershire, Oxfordshire, & Warwickshire have—' Per chev. sa. and ar. three elephants' heads erased, two and one, counterchanged.' Underneath is engraven " *The guift of John Saunders Esquier once an inhabitant in the pishe of St. Lawrence in Readinge.*"

" One smaller Do. Do. the Gift of Mr Richard Johnson 45 18

This very beautiful flagon is inscribed a little above the centre " Ex Dono Richardi Johnson Martii 25 Anō Dñi 1632." It bears the Hall mark of 1631–2.

" One D° Paten (or Bread Plate) the gift of Mr Richard Johnson . . . . . w^t· 11 0

The following inscription is engraven round the centre, " ⊕ Ex Dono Richardi Johnson Martij 25 Anno Dñi 1632." It bears the Hall mark of that year.

" Two D° Cups and Covers the Gift of Messrs Arthur & Richard Curtis . . . w^t· 34 9

Both these chalices, with their covers, bear the same Hall mark,—the curved oz. dwt.

"**V**" of 1637-8. One is inscribed "Ex Dono m^{rl} Arthuri Curtes," and the other "Ex Dono m^{rl} Richardi Curtes." They are interesting and beautiful examples of church plate.

"One other D° Paten (or Bread Plate) Bought in 1708 . . . . . . w^{t.}   11   7

This is very like the earlier one of 1632. An inscription encircles the centre, "Hæc Patina ex oblationibus collecta erat Anno Dom. 1708." Round the outer lip are the words, "Panis quem frangimus nonne participatio corporis Domini est."

"Two D° Dishes (to collect the offerings) one bought in 1701, the other in 1735 . w^{t.}   24   4

Under the bowl of the older one is engraven

William Grover } *and*
John Knight   } *Church Wardens.*
1701.

The other bowl is of the same size and pattern. Underneath, it has

"St. Lawrance, Reading
Philip Phelp) Churchwardens
John Jacob)   1735."

It bears the Hall mark for that year.

Both have the sacred monogram I.H.S in the centre within, surrounded by the words, "Benificentiam & Liberalitatem oblivisci nolite," obviously added about the beginning of the present century.

"One D° Bason and Stand, the Gift of Mrs Elizabeth Thorn, 1767, for the use of Baptism . . . . . . w^{t.}   21   8

The church was broken open March 2, 1788, when this bason and stand were stolen.

"One silver head on a staff, made use of by the

oz. dwt.

Sexton or Beadle, when attending the minister. Bought in the year 1767." Weight not taken   .   .   .   .   .

Total weight   .   .   .   . 281 13"

The head now in use is something like an inverted pear surmounted by a cross. The upper portion is divided into four sections by two bands of beadwork intersecting each other at the cross, and terminating downwards in a similar band passing round the ball at its greatest circumference. As the Hall mark on the socket is that of 1790-1, the old mace must have been renewed at this time. The present mace weighs 11 oz. 9 dwts.

To this must be added a funnel-shaped silver strainer, bearing the initials 𝔄. 𝔖., and the Hall mark of 1730-1.

𝕸onuments.

𝕯estruction of 𝕸onumental 𝕭rasses.

There are indications in the old accounts of gross neglect, if not of wanton destruction, of the ancient brass memorials, by the authorities before the Reformation.

As soon as the plates became detached from their ledgers, they were not replaced, but sold.

1524. " Rec. for broke mettell of the graves weying ix^{li} xviij^d."

1558. " R. for xvj^{li} waight of grave brasse at j^d ob   ij^s."

This is not so clean a sweep as was made at St. Mary's in this town about 1547—

" Receyvid of John Saunders for iij c^{wt} lacking ix^{li} of metall that was taken upp of the graves, and of olde candlestycks at vj^s the hundred xlvj^s ij^d."

(St. Mary's C.W. accounts.)

Slab broken — once 4 feet by 8 feet.

p. 125

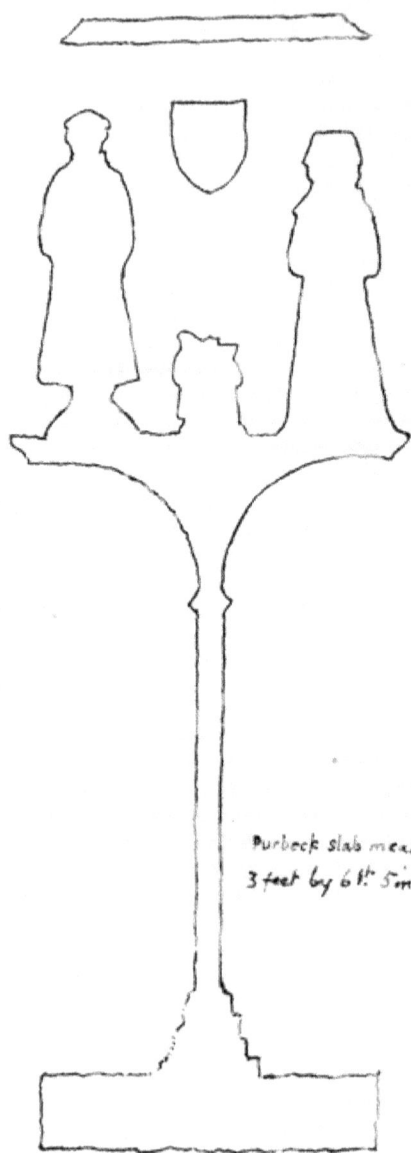

Purbeck slab measures
3 feet by 6 ft. 5 in.

C. K. del.

p. 125 (bottom.)

The earliest survey of the monuments in St. Lawrence's was made by Capt. Symonds, an officer in the Royal Army, 3rd April, 1664. His "Church Notes" are now in the British Museum. (Harl. MS. 965.) They are specially valuable as indicating the original position of the memorials. His observations will be found in the following pages in connection with the monuments to which they relate. He attributes the spoliation of some of the gravestones to the "Roundheads" and "Rebells" who were quartered in the church the year before his visit—apparently deriving this information from the clerk.

A notice of these despoiled memorials will be interesting. The best of them form the pavement of the vestry at the west end of the north aisle.

The largest stone now lying under the north wall was sprinkled with small scrolls, and indications of eight of them remain. There was a shield at each corner of the slab. At the top is the matrix of what may have been a figure of the B. Virgin and Child, though more probably of St. Catharine, for the depression has a circular projecting outline towards the feet, as if indicating a wheel standing by the side of the figure (see under *Altar of St. John Baptist*). Beneath this were the principal effigies of a man and his wife, each about three feet six inches in length. The lower portion of the slab has been cut off, and with it the feet of the principal figures, together with the inscription, a few scrolls, and two shields. It was certainly one of the finest brasses in the county. (*See Illustration.*) These indications assign the memorial to about the year 1475. In Ashmole's time it was in the vicinity of St. Thomas' altar. It may have been the memorial of *Thomas* Clarke, hosier, a great benefactor to the church. He was churchwarden in 1436, 1440–2. Amicia, his mother, died in 1442.

He and his wife Elizabeth presented a cope of blue velvet with a chasuble, two tunacles, and apparels, besides a pall of the same work. The chasuble, or "Vestment," is described as of blue velvet, embroidered with flowers. The pall was also embroidered with flowers of gold.

Another large slab has the matrix of a fine bracket brass very similar to the memorial of John Bloxham and John Whitton, at Merton College, Oxford, but without canopies. The matrix is in excellent preservation, and has a sharp

well-defined margin. A slender stem rising from a graduated base resting on the inscription plate supports a
cross bracket, on which stand the effigies of a man and his
wife, with a son and two daughters between them. Above
the children, and on a level with the upper portion of the
adult figures, is a shield. A narrow horizontal inscription
label, nearly as wide as the bracket, runs across the head
of the memorial. The outlines of the *figures* are very
similar to those of brasses at Bramley, Hants (1452), and
Taplow, Bucks (1455). (*See Illustration.*)

Another stone lying near the west door of the north
aisle in the vestry has a much worn impression of a bracket
brass, almost a fac-simile of the last, but with only two
adult figures.

Another stone adjoining the last, and very much worn,
has indications of a brass consisting of the effigies of a man
and his wife standing on an inscription plate, c. 1512. The
figures are slightly turned towards each other. The man
was habited in the long civilian's cassock, with the large
sleeves of the period. The hair was straight and long,
reaching to the shoulders.

A stone lying under the vestry screen has the much worn
matrices of two shrouded figures about two feet in length.
Their winding-sheets have been gathered and tied at the
head and feet. The figures are slightly turned towards
each other, and their emaciated forms were visible through
an opening in the shroud as usual. It was placed in the
church about the year 1500.

Close by the south wall of the tower is a despoiled
memorial of a very interesting character. The brass plates
have perished long ago; the very matrices are completely
trodden out; the glistening rivets alone remain to tell the
story. The upper portion of the stone has been occupied
by an inscription plate beneath two whole-length figures.
In the centre of the slab are three rivets, one of which
forms the apex of a triangle, the other two being in base.
This location of rivets is distinct from the rest of the plan,
and suggests a subject of special character. If the plate
indicated had been a shield, the rivets would have been
reversed; the single rivet would have been in base near the
point of the shield, and the other two in chief. A plate in

the form of a *bell* would fully comply with the rivet scheme, and identify this slab as the memorial of Henry Kelsall, who gave "The Bell of Jesus" in 1493. Kelsall was buried on the north side of the Altar of Jesus, and the spot was occupied after the Reformation by children. How long they sat there, there is no evidence to show, but probably quite long enough to account for the very worn condition of the stone.

The gift of the bell, too, would seem to have had a special commemoration at the bottom of the slab, by an inscription ribbon of brass fastened by a single line of rivets, and supporting a slender cross beneath the suggested bell. It was very customary in the Middle Ages to represent on the tombs of benefactors the particular object presented by them to the church : thus, the tomb of Amboise, the founder of the great bell of Amiens Cathedral, bears the figure of the bell : a brass at Broxbourne, Herts, 1531, represents John Borrell in armour holding a very ornate candlestick in his right hand, indicating his gift to the sanctuary. Founders of churches in the same way are often represented with a diminutive figure of a church in their hands : at North Creak, Norfolk, it is placed on the right arm of the effigy.

When Symonds made his "Church Notes" in 1642, a tomb was remaining which he was informed was Kelsall's, but tradition has long since ceased to point out his memorial, and the unfortunate removal of the monument from its ancient site has rendered its absolute identification less certain. Still the evidence adduced is almost conclusive. Symonds writes—

"Another flat stone in ye north yle of the church neare the chancel fairely inlayed wth brasse, the picture of a man wth a priest & beades by his side & a woman : the inscription wch was under them was stolne by the Rebells of London about May, 1643.

"A picture of a man and these verses are on ye west side of *this* stone *still* :—

Jhu pat in Bethelem was barne
Sabe bs pat foe be not forlorne
So pat foe map haue frp'cion
We pray pou at his bitt' passion

And dyed for manys redempcion
And bring or sowle to eternal saluac'on
Of thy celestiall deite
ffor us say a pat⁽ᴿ⁾ noster & an Abe.

4 ▽ stolne

For Kimsall
who gave the great
bell   saith the
clerke.

There is another fine marble slab under the north arch
of the tower showing the matrix of a man and his wife with
an inscription at their feet, c. 1510.   In 1741 this stone was
converted into a memorial for Thomas Awberry.

Epitaphs and Monuments.

From Rev. C. Coates' " History of Reading."   With Notes
by the Author.

Within the rails of the altar, on a flat stone, is this
inscription :—

" S. H. S.
Beatam anhelantes resuscitationem in vitam
æternam, obdormiscunt
Franciscus Hungerford M.D. et Elizabetha
uxor ejus, in agro Wilt utrique nati
ex qua suscepit ille septem filios
et quinque filias quorum decem supervixerunt
illi, parsque totius numeri dimidiata
quam proxime hic sepulta jacet.
Connubii inter eos vinculum, obstructum fuit
anno decollationis Caroli Primi
regis optimi et martyris :
dissolutum ; primo, uxoris interitum 1696 :
annoque sequenti, mors, illum, meridie noctis
integra, solute dormientem, in medela artem
quasi pertimescens, inopinanter, arripuit.
Edwardus filius eorum unicè superstes et heres
pietatis et amoris ergo hoc mærens posuit.

Ob. { ille / illa } 1702 anno ætatis suæ { octogesimo currente. / sexigesimo sexto."

(Arms—corrected from Burke—'Sa. two bars arg^t, in chief, three plates, impaling three lions passant guardant. Crest : Out of a ducal coronet or, a pepper garb of the first between two sickles erect, ppr.'

The Wiltshire branch bore the same arms as the Hungerfords of Farleigh Castle, co. Somerset, where numerous ancient monuments of the family remain in the castle chapel.)

On a flat stone :

" Spe resurgendi
Hic prope depositi sunt cineres Edwardi Dalby
Ar. qui obiit 30 Martii anno Dñi 1672,
ætatis 56.

Et Franciscæ uxoris eius, filiæ superstitis et heȓdis
Caroli Holloway, ar. servientis ad legem :
Hæc obiit 17 Augusti anno Dñi 1717,
ætatis 90.

" Et Elizabetha filiæ eorundem, qua obiit
8 Februarii, anno Dñi 1686, ætatis 23."

Arms : Barry wavy of six, Or, and Gules, impaling—a fess between three fleurs de lys : in a canton dexter five ermines.

Crest :—A demi griffin segreant.

(This stone is now in the churchyard and forms a cover to the passage to the heating apparatus. It is a fine stone and in excellent preservation.

The pedigree of Dalby, of Reading, is given by Ashmole in his " Visitation of Berks.")

On a flat stone :

"JOHANNES HUNGERFORD
de Blackland in Comitatu
Wilts, hic jacet sepultus. Obiit
xxviij die Maii, anno
CIƆIƆCLXXVIIJ." [1678.]

(The arms are those of the Hungerfords of

K

Heytesbury—'per pale indented gu. and vert. a
chevron or,' impaling—'party per fesse indented,
a chevron.' This memorial now lies in the S.E.
corner of St. John's Chapel.)

On a flat stone:

"John Nichols, D.D.
vicar of this parish
died June 25, 1788
aged 65 years."

(This stone now forms a portion of the upper
step into St. John's Chapel.)

On a flat stone:

"Mrs Ann Harward dy'd February
the 27th, 17—, aged 69."

(Missing in 1883.)

On a black marble gravestone on the north side of the
altar:

"M.S.
Carolus Morus
publicus auctoritate regia notarius
supremæ curiæ admiralitatis Angliæ
pro-registrarius, honestissimus
vir charitate insignis, et amico fidus
sub hoc marmore, spe resurgendi
sepultus jacet.
Vitam hanc caducam, secundo die mensis
Octobris, anno salutis restauratæ 1673
pro beatiori in cœlis mutavit."

Arms—A chevron between three heathcocks.
Crest—A blackamoor's head.

(Probably buried beneath the new altar pace.)

On a flat stone:

"Here lieth the Body of Richard Curtis Esq.
who departed this life August 30th 1731
aged 56 years.

Also of Elizabeth his wife
who died September the 22, 1769, aged 93 years."
(This monument is missing.)

On a flat stone :

"In memory of Mr William Watlington
who died Oct. 3, 1776, aged 52 years.
Also in memory of
Mrs Catharine Watlington,
who died Sept. 1, 1779,
aged 51 years."
(Now missing.)

On a black stone :

"In memory of Mr Abraham Watlington sen^r
late Alderman of this Borough, who died
Nov. 13, 1766, aged 69 years.
Also Elizabeth his wife died June 8, 1768,
aged 84."
"And Hannah, their grand-daughter, died July 10,
1768, aged eight months and ten days."
"Also of Mr Abraham Watlington jun^r, son of the above,
who died Dec. the 10th, 1773, aged 51 years."
(Now missing.)

On a slab beneath a recess which formerly contained an
urn on the N. side of the Altar :—

"Jeremiah Nicholson D.D.
rector of Kiddington, Oxon,
and vicar of this parish
died July 18, 1771, aged 47 years."

On a white marble tablet :

"Near this place
lie the remains of
the Rev. Mr Philip Whitehead A.M.
vicar of Basildon
in this county
and formerly many years
curate of this parish

K 2

who departed this painful life
June 2, 1767
in humble hopes of a joyful
resurrection at the last day."

(On the north wall within the vestry.)

On a mural monument :

"VNDER THY FEETE READER
SLEEP THE REMAINES OF
RICHARD FYNNMORE HIS
FATHER⁸ BENIAMIN & HIS
BROTHER⁸ IOSEPH WHO COM
ING FROM OXON TO THE BV
RIALL OF A FRIEND FOVND HERE
HIS OWNᵉ GRAVE & SO MINGLED
DVST WITH HIS ANCESTORS
FEBᵗ 6 THE YEARE OF CHRIST
1664 & OF HIS AGE 40.
ONE SON HE LEFT AND I.F. A
MOVRNEFVLL WIDDOW WHO
PLACED THIS TO HIS MEMORY."

(The slab, of blue slate with gilt letters, is broken
into five pieces, and now lies on the step under
the screen at the entrance into St. John's Chapel.
Wylliam Ffynmore was C.W. in 1565-6.   He
gave 5ˢ towards the recasting of Kelsall in 1567.
Humphry Ffynmore, probably his son, was C.W.
in 1604.   In his accounts for 1605 he writes :—

" Rec.of my *brother* Willyam Ffynmore executor
to my mother Anne Ffynmore 12ᵈ"—for tolling
his mother's knell.

William Fynnmore was elected to a scholarship
at St. John's, Cambridge, from Reading Grammar
School, in 1578.   He was B.A. in 1583, and afterwards Bachelor of Law.)

On a veined marble tablet :

" Edward Hungerford, Esq.,
Lyes interred in the grave of his father Dʳ Francis
Hungerford, near this place. Ob. 6 Feb. 1732 at 70.

By whose will (which was proved in the Prerogative Court) two hundred pounds were given to the maior, aldermen, and burgesses of Reading, and since paid to them by his executors, Mr Thomas Blagrave, and Mr Robert Deane, in trust, that the interest thereof should for ever be paid to the vicar of this parish half-yearly, so long as he or his substitute shall daily, between the hours of two and seven in the afternoon, read in the church the Common Prayer and Evening Service according to the Liturgy of the Church of England."

(This slab has been inserted above the arches in the south wall of St. John's Chapel.)

ST. JOHN'S CHANCEL.

On a monument of white and Sienna marble:

" To the memory of

Lieut. Col.	Mrs Mary Case
Cha. Marsh	died Sep. 9. 1773,
Died June 1, 1748	aged 61.
aged 38.	Samuel Case Esq.
Mrs Alice Marsh	died March 10 1778,
died Nov. 9, 1781,	aged 66.
aged 70.	

Arms: Quarterly Arg^t & gu : in the first quarter a horse's head.

Crest—A horse's head issuing out of a mural crown.

(The uppermost monument in the S.E. corner.)

On a white marble tablet:

" Sacred to the memory of
The rev. John Spicer M.A.
rector of Tidmarsh and Sulham,
prebendary of Salisbury,
and for many years master of the
free grammar school
in this his native town.

His genius, learning, friendship,
charity and genuine patriotism
render his death which happened on Nov. 27, 1784,
in the 72nd year of his age,
a public and private loss."

(Now on the north wall in the vestry.)

On a brass plate in a gravestone, on which is the figure
of a man in a gown :

𝔚ere 𝔜nd𝔯 this 𝔐𝔯ble stone lieth 𝔚ater barton gent 𝔚hich
desesid 𝔶𝔢

𝔛𝔛𝔙 day of 𝔄pryll in the yere of our lord God 𝔐𝔩𝔜𝔯xxxbiij on

𝔚hos 𝔖oule 𝔄nd all 𝔠rysten 𝔖oules 𝔍hu 𝔥aue 𝔐ercy
𝔄𝔐𝔈𝔑

𝔠elestĩ qu°dã : bitã quí duxerat ista : bermb𝔷 ecce states : ĩa
reqiescit humo.

This monument is perhaps the most interesting memorial
in the county.   Two years ago it lay on its ledger in front
of the altar, having been removed here from St. John's
chancel in 1848.   From the number of small perforations
in the lines of the engraving, the author supposed it to be
a 'palimpsest' or 'rescript,' and having obtained permission to remove it, his surmisings were verified.   On
the reverse the plates exhibit portions of the effigy of Sir
John Popham, Kt., with the whole of his monumental
inscription.

The plates have been recently enclosed or bordered in
frames of brass, mounted on strong hinges, and attached to
slabs of red freestone, which have been inserted in the north
pier of the chancel arch.

The cost of this work was chiefly borne by the members
of the Popham family of Littlecote, near Hungerford, whose
kind co-operation and assistance in this restoration the
author desires thankfully to acknowledge.

From the will of Walter Barton, printed in this volume,
much may be learnt of his family and status (see Index).
The following notices are from the church accounts :—

1518. "It. of the gifte of M𝔯 Barton toward the making
of the vestr' xl𝔰."

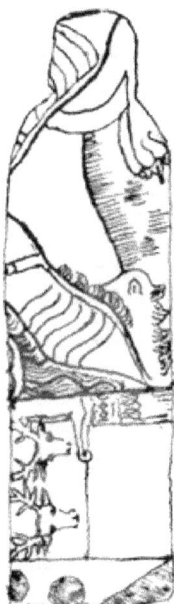

Foot of Effigy – 1st Lion

Part of Tabard.
Fourth Quartering
Zouch. Popham.

Hic iacet Johis Popham miles qudm dns de Torney in Normandia / et dus
de Charderton de Dene et de Alyngton et Albi in Anglia qui obiit · 8 iij·
die mensis · Aprilis · Anno dñi millmo CCCC xxij, cui aie ppiciet de 2

p. 134.

1518: "It. paid for xx q^{rt} of lime viij^{d} a qr to Mr Barton xiij^{s} iiij^{d}."

1519. "It. of Mr Barton toward the repačon of the quere vj^{s} viij^{d}."

1523. Inventory—"It. a sensure of silū and pcell gilt of the gift of Mastres Barton."

(She died in 1545.)

1542-3. "Payd for lynyng for the ij tynacles that Mr Barton dyd give ij^{s}."

In 1578 a Mr. Barton and Mr. Walter Bureton or Buryngton, both "living in the contrye," probably at Streatley, gave xij^{d} each towards the recasting of "Kelsall."

Walter Barton's landed property at Streatley was inherited by the Buriton family. Mr. Haines in his list of monumental brasses (ii. 16—1861) gives the following as remaining in Streatley Church at that time :—

"1. Griffin, son of Thom. & Eliz. Clarke, 1583.
2. Margt. wife of Wm. Buryngton, gent, 1570 effigy covered by a pew in chancel.
3. Thomas Clarke, gent, 1600, and wife Eliz. a dau. & coh. of *Griffith Barton* Esq. (*named in Walter B.'s will*), 1598, with 4 chil., Griffeth, Agnes, Eliz. & Margt., in the chancel.
4. Thomas Buriton Esq. (son & heir of Wm. 3rd son of Thomas Buriton, of Hereford, Esq.) 1603, & wife Joan (Wier) by whom he had 6 sons (then dec.) and 11 daus, partly covered by a pew."

The church has been *restored* since 1861, and some of these are now missing.

Sir John Popham was buried (according to John Stowe's "Survey of London," p. 478^{b} edit. 1633) in the cloisters of the Charterhouse, London, where was a monument to his memory. How comes it, then, at St. Lawrence's? The Charterhouse was dissolved in 1536-7, when the monuments, &c., were sold, Sir John Popham's brass among the rest. It must have been purchased by an engraver, who in the following year received an order for a memorial for Walter Barton.

The artist fortunately took as much of Popham's brass as suited his purpose, selecting the inscription-plate for Walter Barton's epitaph.

Barton's *effigy* is formed of two pieces of Sir John's brass, one containing part of the feet of the knight reposing on a lion, and the other, the arms of Popham impaling Zouch.

> "This impalement of Popham (viz: arg¹, on a chief gules, two stags' heads cabossed or) with Zouch (viz : gules, a chevron arg¹ between 10 bezants, 6 in chief and 4 in base), is described by Bysshe and Ashmole in their Berks Visitation of 1666 as being painted with others in the upper windows of the hall at Aldermaston House, which belonged to the Forster family."

(Edw⁴ Bellasis, Esq., ' Bluemantle,')
College of Arms, London.

The old ledger on which Barton's brass was laid, was undoubtedly the very slab which covered the body of Sir John Popham. In adapting it for a second memorial, the old matrices were chiselled out and the stone rubbed down, but the bottoms of most of the rivet-holes containing the leaded rivets remain, indicating the *bearings* of the original. The principal figure stood beneath a canopy. The knight was habited in a tabard of arms, and the fragment taken from the left-hand side of the figure exhibits the fourth and part of the third quarterings with the hilt of the contiguous sword. The tail of the lion passed under the foot of the knight and terminated in a graceful curve by the side of the sword. The sollerets, exhibiting seven laminæ, are finely pointed.

The slab is of Purbeck marble.

Sir John Popham's epitaph, on the reverse of Walter Barton's, is as follows :—

"𝕳ic iacet 𝕵oḥ𝕖s 𝕻opḥam 𝕸iles q°nd⁴m d̄ns de 𝕿urney in 𝕹ormandia & d̄ns de 𝕮ḥardeford de 𝕯ene ac de 𝕬lbyngton & 𝕬libi in 𝕬nglia qui obiit xiiij°

die 𝕸ens' 𝕬prilis 𝕬nno 𝕯n̄i 𝕸illmo 𝕮𝕮𝕮𝕮 lxiij° 𝕮ui⁹ āie ppiciet̄ d°e⁹"

Besides this accidental association of the name of Popham with St. Lawrence's, there is an entry in the old accounts which points to a closer connection :—

Anno 1498. "Itm. payed for mendyng of Poppams Vestment ij⁴."

The "*vestment*" or chasuble seems to indicate some mass of requiem performed here for some member of the family, and, as it required mending in 1498, it was presumably of considerable age at that time: indeed it may have been given by this very Sir John or his executors for his commemoration.

There is a picture of Sir John Popham on horseback in the vestry, presented by Rev. Sir W. H. Cope, Bart., of Bramshill, a copy of an illumination in a MS. in the British Museum. Here the knight is represented in a tabard of arms, with horse trappings similarly emblazoned. His sollerets appear precisely as on the brass, but the arms have the addition of a bezant between the bucks' heads. Might this have been added while Treasurer to the King's Household?

The Pophams have been seated in the south of England from a very remote period.

GILBERT POPHAM, of Popham, in Hampshire, living in the time of King John, espoused Joan, dau. and heiress of Robert Clarke (a feoffee in trust for the manor of Popham, as appears by charter of the Empress Maud), and had a son and successor,

ROBERT POPHAM of Popham who had two sons— 1. John; 2. Hugh.

JOHN, who succeeded his father at Popham, was great-grandfather of

SIR JOHN POPHAM, who died 16 Ric. II., leaving by Sybil his wife, dau. and heiress of Sir Lawrence St. Martin, two sons, John (Sir) and Henry.

This SIR JOHN POPHAM was constable and governor of Southampton, and of Touraine and Bayonne in France in the time of Henry V., and according to his epitaph, "lord of Turney in Normandy." He was made Treasurer of the Household in the succeeding reign.

John Stowe, in his account of St. Sepulchre's in the Bayly, writes—"One of the Popham's (undoubtedly this Sir John) was a great builder there: viz. of one faire Chappell on the south side of the Quire as appeareth by his Armes and other Monuments in the glasse windowes thereof, and also the faire Porch of the same church towards the south: his Image faire graven in stone was fixed over

the said porch, but defaced and beaten downe : his titles
were these by offices : Chancellour of Normandy, Captaine
of Vernoyle, Perche, Susan, and Bayon, and Treasurer of
the King's Houschold. He dyed rich, leaving great treasure
of strange coynes, and was buried in the Charter house
Church by West Smithfield. The first Nobilitating of
these Pophames was by Matilda the Empresse, daughter to
Henry the first, and by Henry her son : one Popham a
gentleman of very faire lands in Southamptonshire dyed
without issue male, about Henry the sixth, and leaving foure
daughters, they were married to Fostar, Barentine, Wodham, and Hamden. Popham Deane (distant three miles
from Clarendon) was sometime the chief Lordship or
Mannour house of those Popham⁰s."

HENRY POPHAM, brother of this Sir John Popham, died
17 Hen. VI., leaving by Joan, his wife, a son,

SIR STEPHEN POPHAM, who married Margaret, daughter
and heiress of Nicholas Read, of Somersetshire, and had
four daughters, his coheirs (spoken of by Stowe), viz :—

(1.) Margery, married Thomas Hampden, Esq.
(2.) Eleanor, married to John Barentine, Esq.
(3.) Elizabeth, married to John Wadham, Esq.
(4.) Alice, married to Humphrey Forster, Esq., which
accounts for the arms of the Pophams at Alder-
maston House, the seat of the Forsters.

The Pophams of Littlecote are descended from Sir
Hugh, second son of Robert, the son of Gilbert, at the head
of this pedigree.

According to Capt. Symonds, this monument in 1644
was contiguous to that of John, Rector of Erley, and John
Cerne, Vicar of St. Lawrence.

On a brass plate in a gravestone, where was the figure
of a man, is this inscription :

Here lyeth the body of JOHN JOHNSON, late
of Reading, mercer, who having lived 50 years left this
earthly tabernacle.

He was a lover of the Gospell, and a good benefactour to
the church and poore of this parish. Obiit 24 Martii,
anno Dom. 1614.

𝔄nd of 𝔍ohn his son, who, libing fibe yeares, deceased the 2ᵗ day of 𝔍une, 𝔄.𝔇. 1614.

Thus blossoms young by death's means untimely fall from tree,
Thus God each man's nature's course doth evermore decree.

(The whole of this monument has disappeared since 1802. *Vide* "Views of Reading Abbey.")

On a marble gravestone:

" ANTONIUS MASONUS DE MARGARETA
conjuge sua charissima
quæ obiit Martii 6°
1630.

Here, and in Heaven, rest my blessed wife
Who was the crowne and comfort of my lyfe,
In grace by grace to glory let me follow
My spouse, Thy saint O Thou whose name I hallow."

Arms—A lion rampant, impaling—paly of six; over all a bend dexter.
(Missing.)

On various flat stones are the following inscriptions:

" Here lieth the body of Mary Deane, widow of John Deane Esq., late of Mattingley, in com. Southton. Obiit 5 Mar. anno Dom 1706, ætatis suæ 81."

" Here lie the bodies of John and Richard Wilder late of this parish—1727."

" Here lieth the body of Richard Wilder, coach harness maker, Citizen of London, and Freeman, late of the parish of St. James, in the liberty of Westminster, who departed this life the 17th day of December, 1735, aged 47 years. Also John Wilder and Deborah, his father and mother.

" Also to the memory of William Wilder, who died Dec. 11, 1731."

" Here lyeth the body of Robert Blake, gent, twice mayor of this borough, who departed this life March 26, 1727, aged 95.

" Here also lie the bodies of Ann and Mary, daughters

of the said Robert and Mary his wife, who departed this life Sept. 21, 1732, aged 24.

"Here also lieth the body of Mary, the wife of the aforesaid Mr. Robert Blake, who departed this life the 25th day of June A.D. 1734, aged 65 years."

IN THE VESTRY.

On a black gravestone :—

"Anne Watts
aged 9 years
died the 24th day
of October 1723.
Also
Elizabeth Watts
wife of
John Watts, who died
Sept. 25, 1732, in the 60th
year of her age.
Also
Eliz. Collis her daughter
ob. Oct 15, 1738
æt. 41.
Also
the body of the abovesaid
John Watts
late of this
parish esq, who departed
this life May 2, 1750,
aged 78 years."

THE CHANCEL.

"In Ashmole's time there was 'a fair grey marble tomb' raised in the chancel, whereon in brass plates were the figures of a man in a gown, and his wife, in the habit of the time, with the following inscription :—

Here lyeth the bodyes of Edward Butler late of Readyng gent,
and of Alice his

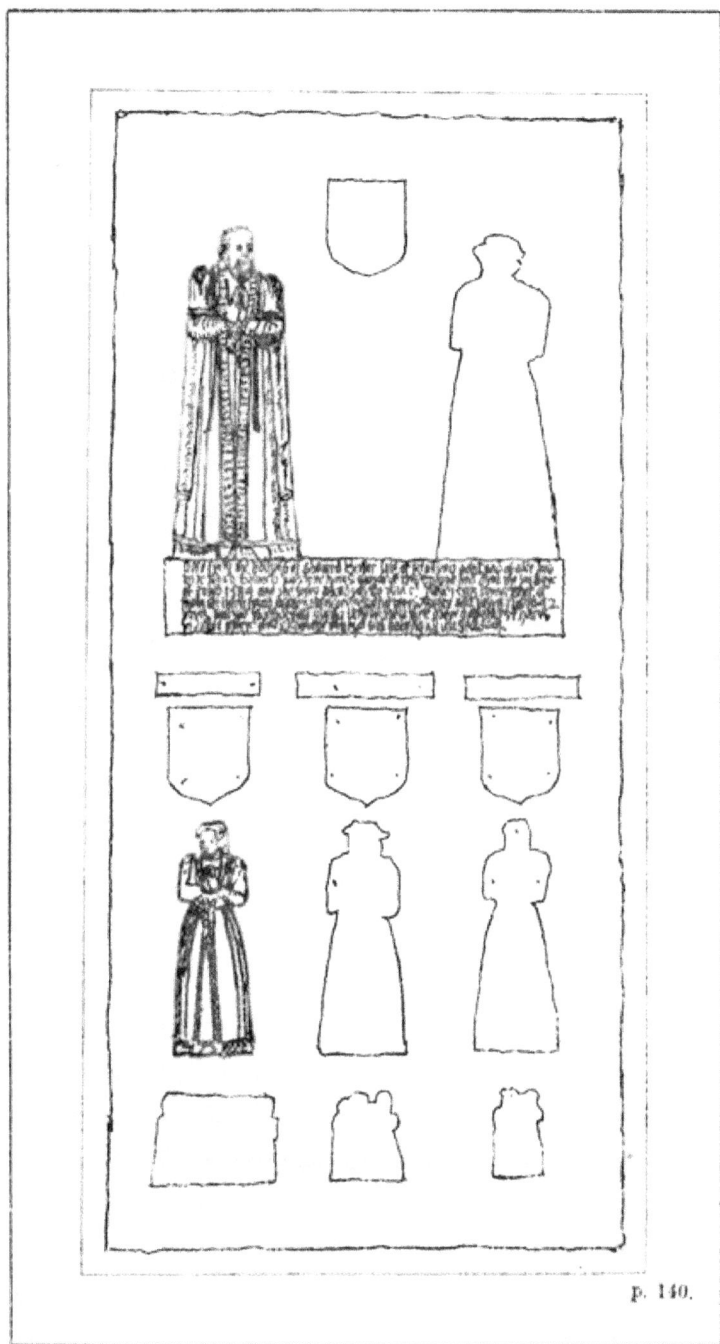

wyfe, which Edward was fyve tymes Maior of this Towne,
and dyed the bij daye
of Julye 1584. and the sayed Alice dyed the xbiij of Julye
1583. beying either of
them att there sayed deathes threscore & twelve yeres Apeere,
and habyng lyved 42
yeres maryed together, and lebyng behynd them three onlye
daughters & heires
vid' Alice, Marye, and Elyzabeth maryed, and habying issue
as followeth :

Alice, married to William Buttell, esq.

Under this name was the figure of a woman standing
holding up her hands in a praying posture, and under
her, three sons and four daughters in the like postures.

Mary Butler, married to Will. Powell Doctour of
Dibinity.

The figure of a woman in the like posture, with two sons
and one daughter.

Elizabeth Butler, married to Richard Staberton
esquire.

The figure of a woman and two daughters in the same
posture of devotion.

On a rim of brass, fixed in the ledge of the stone, were
these verses;—

Chryst to me as lyfe on earth
And death to me is gain ;
Because I trust through him alone
Salbation to obtaine,
So brittle is the state of man
So soon it doth decay
So all the glory of the world
Must pass and fade away.

This monument has been laid flat, and the stone is almost

covered by pews, so that only two lines of the inscription are now legible." (Coate's "Reading.")

Capt. Symonds' account of this monument (1644) supplies a few interesting items :—

> "A faire Altar Tombe betweene the 2 middle pillars of the chancel. This single escocheon (on a bend between 6 covered cups, a mullet for diff.—Butler) is 3 times of each *side*, and at each *end* of the Tombe.
>
> "Upon y^e *surface* of ye Tombe wch is grey marble is the 2 pictures of a man & woman : under them this inscription, and betweene them the afore mençõed coate."

> He then gives the arms of Bottell impaling Butler (1.) Gu. a chev. betw. 3 combs argt. for Bottell ; (2.) a cross botonnée ; (3.) a cinquefoil w^t a lion passant in chief; (4.) blank.

> The next shield is Powell impaling Butler—Per pale, 3 lions rampant counterchanged—for Powell.

> The third shield is Staverton (arg^t a chev. sa. betw. 3 maunches vert.) impaling Butler as before.

The "mensa" of this once "high" tomb, now stripped of its brasses, lies apparently over the grave of Edward Butler. In 1848, the three remaining plates were removed to a stone lying near the south stalls in the choir. In 1882 they were removed for their better preservation to the south wall of the chancel within the sacrarium, the inscription plate having been carefully restored by the author.

> 3 May, 1614. "Att this accompte my Doct^r offred in the behaulf of Mr Samuell Powell to paye x^s a yere to this churche duringe his lief by pmise for the supporting of Mr Butler's toombe. But for some causes it was referred to be considered of vntill another tyme by consent of the pishioners p'nte, and soe the money was refused."

> Low Sunday, 16 April, 1615. "As touching Mr Butler's toombe he shall pay xx^s p añn for eu, or ells the toombe shall not be repayred, but at the next occasion to be pulled downe."

> 1618. "For Edward Butler's Tomb :
> At this accompt it was geven to the parishioners to vnderstand that diuers of them have byn

earnest wth Mr Samuell Powell to geve some yearly portion towardes the support of his grandfather's Toombe w^{che} was erected in the Churche Chauncell to the hurt of the parishe (there beinge noe allowance to maynteyne it). And that the said Samuell Powell for and towards the mayntenaunce of his grandfathers toombe will from thencefourth yerely to the churchwardens of this parishe give xx^s for ever. And that he will take order as by his counsell he shoulde be advised to bynd some of his land in Readinge to and for the true payment thereof for ever.

p Wi⊬m Wylmer."

In 1697 the churchwardens returned that the sum of 7l. 10s. 4d. was due to them for the standing of Mr Butler's Tomb.

In 1719 the arrearage amounted to 13l. 17s. 4d.

The following notices of the Butler family are from the church accounts:

1498. "It. rec. for the Sepulcr of Thomas Butler vj^s viij^d.

  „   "It. rec. for wast of Torchys at the burying of the same Thomas ij^s j^d."

1524. "Xpofer Butteler C.W."

1531. Great Bell. "Rec. for the Knyll of X^{o}fer Butler xij^d—Grave and covering vij^s iiij^d."

1539. "Rec. for the grave of John Butteler & for couïng thereof vij^s iiij^d."

1544. "Rec. for the grave of M^{res} Butler vij^s iiij^d."

1546–7. "Edward Butler C.W." In 1556, he contributed three perches of the wall round the new churchyard at a cost of 21s.; and in 1562 he purchased the "lofte ouer the chancell" (? the sepulchre loft) for 10s.

Joan Butler was buried the same year.

1567. Edward Butler gave 10s. towards the recasting of Kelsall. This was the largest contribution.

1582–3 "In p^{r}imis R. for m^{rs} Butler her knill ij^s vj."

1583–4. "R. for m^{rs} Staverton her knill ij^s vj^d."

  „   Itm. m^r Edward Butler his knill ij^s vj^d."

On different flat stones are the following inscriptions:

"John Eade, born April ye 30, 1715,
died April ye 11, 1716.

Τωυ τ8τωυ εστιυ ἡ βασιλεια τ8 θε8."

" Thomas Addams, M.D.
departed this life 26 April, 1785.
He was a most tender husband
an affectionate father, and a
sincere friend.
Rebecca Addams, wife of Dr. Addams,
departed this life 28 Dec. 1778.
Rebecca Addams sister to Dr Addams
departed this life 8 April 1769.

Arms—Quarterly Argent and Vairy: over all a bend
dexter with a crescent for difference."

On a black marble gravestone:

" Here lieth the body of Thomas
Constable, who departed this
life March the 2nd, 1719, aged64.
Here also lieth the body of Catherine
Constable his wife who departed
this life, the 16th of September 1720,
aged 63."

On a black stone:

" Here lieth interred the body
of Mr Peter Burningham of London
merchant, who departed
this life the first day of June
anno Domini 1689,
aged 41 years."

(The foot of this memorial is covered by the new
altar steps.)

On a black stone :

" Here lieth the body of Mr John Knight
linen-draper, late of Reading, who departed
this life the 25th of July, 1714,
aged 58 years.   And by him his father and
mother and five sisters lie."

From Reading Churches
published in 1802.

Derunt; hir donor et fir oftendet conat z
ut fiyt ponu: ponitur omnis hauor z
sunstuis ens qui translate fin perlege plaza
sum quod erg; hierū tz qd es y ere picn ora
hic uacet dns Johis Roberd qui obyt Secio
die marcij anno dm cnilliho exces xviij

< Kerry del.

Harl MS. 965
Anno 1644.

p. 146.

On a flat stone :

"To the memory of Mrs Anne Moulton
who died June 2, 1750."

"Here lieth the body of Mrs Elizabeth Dudley
the daughter of William Dudley Esq. of
Aldersgate Street London. She died September the 27th anno Domini 1652."

On a gravestone (now near the stalls on the north side
of the chancel—C.K.) is the figure of a priest in his vestments, on a brass plate, and at his feet these lines :—

Vermibz hic donor: et sic ostendere conor
Ut sicut ponor: ponitur omnis honor.
Quisquis eris qui transieris sta perlege plora
Sum quod eris fuerã q'd es y me p'tor ora.
Hic jacet dũs Johẽs Andreb qui obiit Tercio
die Marcii Anno dñi Millm CCCC xxviij.

(In the inventory of 1517 is the following entry :—" In
p^{r}mis an antipher w^t full legend of the gifte of
Sr John Andrewe sũ tyme vicar ther the ij^{de} lefe
begynnyng [patri et filio]." In the previous inventory of 1503, after the words " w^t full legend,"
occurs—"To lye before the vicare."—See *List of
Vicars.*)

Capt. Symonds states that this monument adjoined the
slab of William Goldore and John Sampford in 1644. He
also gives a sketch of the *shield*, which has long been missing—viz., 'a cross saltire,' drawn as though there had
been a *chief* on the shield. Burke, in his "Armory," gives
the arms of Andrewes (of London), " Ar. a saltire az., on
a *chief* gu. three mullets or."

The inscription only remains. There is apparently an
excellent copy of the *effigy* in "Views of Reading Abbey,"
vol. i. p. 44, edit. 1805.

On the side of the chancel, over the priests' door, is a
marble monument, on which, under an arch surmounted

L

by a pediment, which is supported by foui pillars of the
Corinthian order, is a female figure kneeling at a desk with
this inscription :—

IN A VAULT
(FOR WHICH A FACULTY WAS PROCURED)
TEN FEET FROM THE SOUTH WALL AND TWENTY-FIVE
FEET FROM THE EAST WALL OF THIS CHANCEL,
LIES INTERRED
ANNE HAYDON,
WIFE OF GIDEON HAYDON ESQ.
A GENEROUS RELATION,
A SINCERE FRIEND,
AND A GOOD CHRISTIAN.
SHE GAVE IN HER LIFE TIME 120*l.*
TO THE VICAR OF THIS PARISH ;
THREE FIFTHS OF THE INTEREST AS A YEARLY RENT
FOR THE VAULT ;
AND TWO FIFTHS TO BE LAID OUT YEARLY (IF NEED BE)
IN REPAIRING THE VAULT AND THIS MONUMENT
FOR EVER.
OB. 15TH OCT. 1747, ÆT. 61.

Arms—Argt. three bars gemelles azure ; on a chief or,
a fesse dancette gules : impaling, argt. on a bend
azure, three dolphins embowed, or.

(The vault containing the remains of Mrs. Anne Haydon
is marked by a large slab of black marble, bearing the following inscription :

" Under this stone
lie two sisters
MARY WATERMAN
Relict of WILLIAM WATERMAN *Esq.*
Ob. 6 Mar. 1736, Æt. 61.
And also
ANNE HAYDON
Wife of GIDEON HAYDON *Esq.*
Ob. 15 Oct. 1747. Æt. 61."

Above this inscription are two shields of arms—
those of Haydon, above mentioned, and of Waterman,
viz. :—

" Paly of six, arg^t and gules, three crescents counterchanged ; impaling arg^t on a bend azure, three dolphins embowed, or.")

On a white marble tablet :
" Thomas Shute, D.D.
Vicar of this parish, died Aug. 19, 1763,
aged 56 years."

(During his time, in 1748, the old ring was recast, and
the number increased from eight to ten. His name was
inscribed on the sixth, recently recast (see *Bells*). His
monument is now on the north wall within the vestry.)

In the south wall of the chancel is a monument, on
which are the figures of a man and woman kneeling at a
desk ; behind the man are three sons ; and behind the
woman, six daughters. Beneath are these verses :—

QUAM FUERAT VITA CHARUS, QUAM MORTE LYDALLUS
NARRET PASTOR, PLEBS, PAUPER, ET ISTA DOMUS.
ISTA DOMUS TESTIS PIETATIS, PAUPER AMORIS,
PLEBS OPERUM, FIDEI PASTOR, IN HISQUE DEUS.
HANC LECTOR BENE QUI NOVIT FOBOLEMQUE, VIRUMQUE
SÆPE HOS, AUT SIMILES, EDIDIT ORE SONOS
O TER FÆLICEM MATREMQUE PATREMQUE PROPAGO,
CUI TALI EX TALI CONJUGE TALIS ERAT.

At the foot of the monument is this epitaph :

EST HOC CANDIDE INSPECTOR THOMÆ LYDALL
GENEROSI, MAJORATUM APUD REDINGENSES TER
PERFUNCTI (QUI DOMUS HUJUS SACRÆ CONCION-
ATORIS PAUPERUMQUE AUXIT REDITUS) ET MAR-
GERIÆ UXORIS ET LIBERORUM PIE CONSECRATUM
MEMORIÆ MONUMENTUM.

(In 1644 this monument was *over* the chancel door.
The shields on the arches above the two principal
figures would seem to have been misplaced at the
removal of the monument ; for the arms of Lydall,
" Azure, a saltire or : on a fesse of the last three
torteaux," are over the wife, and a shield presumably hers—viz., " Arg^t, three crosses pomee fitchee,
and a chief sable," appears over the head of Lydall.
Jane, daughter of Mr Thomas Lydall, was married to
Mr William Kendrick, whose monument is in the
chancel of St. Mary's in this town.
Thomas Lydall by will, dated Mar. 6, 1606, bequeathed

the sum of 20*s*. yearly to the church, whereof 10*s*.
for the repairs of the church, seats, and bells, and
10*s*. to be paid to the vicar.
He died in 1608.)

In the same wall is another monument where is the
figure of a woman kneeling at a desk : at the top is a hand
holding a wreath of laurel, and under the figure is the
following inscription :—

MARTHA, UXOR CAROLI HAMLEY
CORNUB. HIC JACET SEPULTA. FILIA ERAT THOMÆ
SEAKES DE HENLEY SUPER THAMES IN COMIT.
OXONIÆ, QUI OBIIT DECIMO SEXTO DIE MENSIS
JANUARII AN. DNI 1636. HOC MONUMENTUM
STRUXIT EJUS MARITUS CAROLUS AD CONSER-
VENDAM EIUS MEMORIAM, QUÆ LIBEROS NULLOS
POST SE RELIQUIT PRÆSERTIM VERO IN TESTI-
MONIUM SUMMÆ DILECTIONIS.

On a tablet of white marble :

" In this chancel are deposited
the remains of Joseph Radcliffe
of the Inner Temple, Barrister at Law
who departed this life, the 27th day of
July 1760, aged 64 years.
And of Mary his wife
a descendant of the family of
Sir Thomas Button of Cotterel in
the county of Glamorgan,
eminent for her true piety,
who died the first day of December
1758, aged 65 years."

(On the north wall in the vestry.)

On a white marble monument placed in a recess in the
south wall is this inscription :

" Sacred to the Memory
of William Douglas, batchelor
an honest man, and an eminent conveyancer :
remarkable for his
zeal for his king, love for his country,

duty to parents, generosity to relations,
sincerity to friends, integrity to clients,
benevolence to the distressed, love to all men.

So great his patience,	So generous his soul,
yᵗ he bore the acute pains	that to educate and maintain
of yᵉ gout for forty yⁿ	all his relations
with thankfulness.	was his chief pleasure.
So good his judgment,	So chearful his temper,
that he never made	that his conversation
in all his practice	was coveted by all.
any one material error,	Now, blest of God,
nor lost one sum	enjoy thou the reward
entrusted to his care.	of true Christian charity.

D. Jan. 30, 1732 A. 70.   W. Boudry, Nephew, P.

(This memorial to this most exemplary person is now
in the tower.)

On a white marble tablet :

" In memory of
Mrs. Mary Love
who died
Sept. 27, 1777."

(She bequeathed the sum of 300*l*. in money to the
corporation of Reading, with which was purchased
377*l*. 7*s*. 2*d*. " New Four per Cents." which in 1786
realized 15*l*. 1*s*. 10*d*. per annum ; on condition that
after the repairs of her monument, the annual
surplus should be distributed in bread and money
among such poor who did not receive relief from
the parish.)

Near the pulpit is a monument which has the figure of
a man to the middle under an arch, holding one hand on a
globe, the other on a quadrant. He is habited in a short
cloak and ruff, surrounded with books on each side of him.
On one side is a female figure holding a cube in her hand
as offering it to him ; and under her feet is the word
'CUBUS.' On the other side is another female figure,
offering in the same manner ; and under her 'TETRA-
HEDRON.' On the top of the monument are two reclining
figures inscribed 'OCTAHEDRON,' 'DODICADRON,' and
between them is a figure, now defaced, resembling a
Minerva inscribed ' ISOSEDRON :' these are the names of
the five regular solids in geometry.

Beneath the whole is this inscription in an oval :

"JOHANNES BLAGRAVUS
TOTUS MATHEMATICUS
CUM MATRE SEPULTUS.

HERE LIES THE CORPES, WHICH LIVING HAD A SPIRIT,
WHEREIN MUCH WORTHY KNOWLEDGE DID INHERIT;
BY WHICH WITH ZEALE OVR GOD HE DID ADORE ;
LEFT FOR MAIDSERVANTS, AND TO FEED THE POORE.
HIS VERTUOUS MOTHER CAME OF WORTHIE RACE,
A HVNGERFORD, AND BURIED NEARE THIS PLACE.
WHEN GOD SENT DEATH THEIR LIVES AWAY TO CALL,
THEY LIVED BELOV'D, AND DIED BEWAIL'D OF ALL.

DECEASED THE 9TH OF AUGUST
ANNO D'NI. 1611."

The ancestor of this family was Ralph Blagrave, a lawyer, of Uttoxeter in Staffordshire, whose second son, Robert, settled in London and married Anne Pyke, the daughter of a gentleman in Surrey, by whom he had John Blagrave, of Bulmarsh, who married Anne, daughter of Sir Anthony Hungerford, of Downe Amney, in the county of Gloucester.

This John had four sons : Anthony, who married Jane Borlase ; John, the mathematician, the subject of this memorial ; Edward, and Alexander, the chess-player, a yeoman of the guard.

The mathematician is supposed to have been born in Reading, but in what year is not known. In 1585 he published "The Mathematical Jewel—Margarita Mathematica per Johannem Blagravum Readingensem, conditum, editum et sculptum"—a folio—" Imprinted at London by Walter Venge, dwelling in Fleet Lane, over against the Maiden-head." He likewise published "Baculum Familiare Catholicon sive Generale—A Booke of a Staffe newly invented by the Author, called the Familiar Staffe ; as well for that it may be made familiarlie to walk with, as for that it performeth the geometrical mensurations. Newlie compiled and at this time published for the speciall helpe of shooting in great ordinance, and may as well be employed for measuring of land. By John Blagrave of Reading, gent. 1590, 4to." Dedicated to Sir Francis Knolles. The last work he published was " The Art of Dialling, in two parts." London 1609. 4to.

It is not known whom he married. The lady was probably a widow, as her daughter is called in his will " My wife's daughter Jane." He died at his own house at Southcot, August 9, 1611, and was buried at St. Lawrence's Church, near his mother.

By his will he bequeathed to Joseph Blagrave and his heirs for ever, a messuage or mansion house in Swallow-field, with all his lands in Swallowfield, Eversley, and Reading, *in trust*, to pay on Good Friday in every year to the Mayor and Corporation of Reading the sum of 10*l*., to be bestowed as follows :—"Twenty nobles of the 10*l*. to some one poor maiden servant that hath served, dwelled, and continued in any one service in any of the three parishes in Reading, in good name and fame, the full term of five years at the least, for her help and performance in marriage, but every fifth year the maid to be chosen from Southcot. Also 10*s*. to the parson of St. Lawrence for his sermon on Good Friday, and that after sermon, there be 20*s*. given to the poorest householders in the said parish of St. Lawrence who shall accompany that maid to whose lot the 20 nobles fell to her dwelling house. Also 3*s*. 4*d*. to the ringers : Also 20*s*. parcel of the 10*l*. to 60 poor people of St. Mary's parish, and 6*s*. to 24 poor of St. Giles'. Lastly, the clerk of St. Lawrence's, and the youngest churchwarden, to have 3*s*. 4*d*. apiece to join with the minister, by direction of the mayor in the distribution of the 10*l*."

By a codicil annexed, the testator declares his intention that the mayor and corporation should reserve 200*l*. arising out of several rent-charges before given them, during several leases, to be employed in purchasing and pulling down the middle row of houses between the " Pump" and the "Cage," in order to enlarge the market-place. Then at the end of another seven years the corporation was to receive another hundred pounds of the rents and profits of the lands mentioned in the will, to "buyld a very faire walk under the south side of St. Lawrence's Church in Reading, ten foot broad at the least, and in length from the *church porch* to the west end of the belfry."

In the year 1613 the 200*l*. were applied in removing the tenements in the market-place; and in 1620 the church walk was built, which cost 28*l*. 19*s*. *more* than the 180*l*. which he had left for that purpose. (Coates' " Reading.")

One of the houses removed from the market-place in accordance with Mr. Blagrave's bequest belonged to the church, and at a meeting convened on the 2nd August, 1612, it was decided that the mayor and corporation should erect another house in the parish for the church, " with brick chimney and lofts as habitable, and of the same value to the church as the one to be taken down."

On a white marble monument :

" To the Memory of
Charles Fanshawe, Esq.
Rear Admiral,
who died February 16,
1757,
Aged 57 years."
(Now in the tower.)

On a white marble tablet :

" Near this place
are deposited the remains of
ROBERT WALSHAM, Esq., who died Nov. the 11th, 1791,
Aged 72.
Also of
ANNA WALSHAM, who died Sept. the 16th, 1792,
Aged 74.
To the memory
of their truly honoured and beloved Parents
this grateful Tribute
was placed here by their children,
Anno 1797."

On a white stone near the belfry :

" In memory of
William Spencer
late organist of this parish
who died April 3d 1782,
Aged 58 years."
(In the tower.)

On a white marble tablet against the north wall :

" Hic
ubi excessit e vivis,
requiescere voluit
quod mortale fuit
GULIELMUS KEATE
de Wellia
in agro Somerset, M.D.
Probitate
ut annis venerabilis ;
Ob. Sept. 10. A.S. 1790.
Ætat. 81."

IN THE SOUTH AISLE,

On different flat stones, are the following inscriptions :

" Here lieth the body of Elizabeth, the wife of Captain George Purdon, daughter of the Revd Dr Samuel Bishop and Penelope his wife, who departed this life the 11th day of Sept. 1708, aged 29 years ; as also three of her children ; viz. Penelope, Samuel, and Alicia Purdon : as also the above mentioned Penelope Bishop, widow. Ob. 9th Jan. 1716, ætat. 71."

" Near this stone, in a vault 8ft. by 4, situated 11 feet from the south wall, lyeth the body of Mrs Jane Whiting, who departed this life April 10th, 1745. Here also lies Mrs Mary Love, who had a faculty for this vault ; and died Sept. 27, 1777."
(Now in the tower.)

" Here lie the bodies of two maiden sisters ; Mrs Elizabeth Reeves, aged 58, who died in St Mary's Parish, Oct. 23. 1743 ; Mrs Margaret Reeves aged 55, who died at Caversham the . . . . day of January following."

" Here lieth the body of Mr Benjamin Pocock Surgeon and Apothecary of this parish, who departed this life July 11, 1755, aged 33 years.

This modest stone, what few vain marbles can,
May truly say, ' Here lies an honest man.' "

" Here lies the body of Mrs Elizabeth Milbourne the
daughter of Captain Milbourne and Elizabeth
his wife, who died Jan. 10, aged 12 weeks and 14
days."

On a black marble gravestone :

" To the memory of
Mr John Wilcock Druggist,
who exchanged this life for a better
April 24, 1776
aged 62.

Also of Mrs Mary Wilcock
wife of the abovementioned
who departed this life
March 8, 1777,
in full assurance
of a blessed immortality
aged 61.

Likewise to the memory of
Mary Marshall,
niece of the above Mrs Mary Wilcock
who died May 7, 1787
aged 27."

" Here lieth the body of Richard Piggot, son of
Richard and Hannah, who departed this life May
30, 1703," &c. (defaced).

" To the memory of Mrs Sarah Elkins, relict of M^r
Robert Elkins of London, who after a well spent
life here, exchanged it in hopes of a better on the
22^d of June 1774 in the 85th year of her age."

(Now in the S.W. *angle* of the tower.)

" In memory of Mr French, Chymist of this parish,
who died June 5th, 1770, aged 30.

" Also George Peter French, son of the above, who
died January 8th 1783 aged 13 years."

" Here lieth the body of Joseph Irving who departed
this life Jan. 13th 1773 aged . . . . years."

"John Rowland died Jan. 4th 1784, aged 74 years."

"In memory of Mr Thomas Garrard who died February 7th, 1773, aged 50 years."

"Also of his son George Garrard, who died the 11th of Dec. in the 17th year of his age."
(Now in the tower, almost obliterated.)

"In memory of Mr Peter Hansell, who died March 13th, 1772, aged 65 years."

"Sacred to the memory of Mr Simmoneau Pine, of Bath, whose virtues, and spirit to exert them, gained him the love of all who knew him. He died at Reading 23rd of August 1772, aged 49."

BETWEEN THE AISLES.

"In memory of Thomas Sentence who died April 9th 1781, aged 12 years."

IN THE NORTH AISLE

are several flat stones with the following inscriptions:—

"Here lieth the body of Thomas Awberry. He died May 20th 1741, aged 69 years.

"Near this place lieth Elizabeth his wife and 6 of their children."

(This stone now lies under the north arch of the tower). Coates writes (1802):—"This epitaph now appears on a large flat stone on which were figures of a man and woman: and *near it* is another stone on which were the figures of a man and woman, with several small inscriptions, and in each corner an escutcheon of arms."—This latter the author believes to have been the memorial of **Thomas Clarke**, Hosier, c. 1475.)

"Thomas Flory died April 25, 1736, aged 3 years and 2 months.

"Thomas and William Flory, twins; William died June the 5th, and Thomas died the 7th, 1741.

"Thomas Flory died Nov. 13, 1746.

"In memory of Deborah Flory, daughter of Thomas and Elizabeth Florey, who died March 22, 1763, aged 20 years. Also Elizabeth Flory wife of Thomas Flory, who died March 20, 1780, in the 76th year of her age. Likewise the said Thomas Flory, who died Dec. 7th 1780, in the 78th year of his age."

"In memory of Mr William Halifax, late of this Parish, Surgeon, who died May 9th 1756, aged 35.

"Also of Mr Thomas Halifax who died March 3, 1789, aged 62 years.

"Likewise of Margaret Halifax, daughter of Thomas Halifax, who died October 13, 1789, aged 25 years."

"Here lie the remains of Mary Pitman, wife of Edward Pitman of London who departed this life March 24th 1773, aged 46 years."—Amos iv. 12.

"In memory of John Aris, gent. Died Jan. 19th 1790, aged 81 years."

"Also of Mrs Mary Johnston. Died June 5, 1791, aged 63 years."

"Mrs Anne Jacob died May the 2nd 1797, aged 77 years."

"In memory of Mr James Quarrington, who was Mayor of this Corporation. He died A.D. 1714. Also Anne his wife, died A.D. 1758. Likewise in memory of Mr Thomas Rootes, he died A.D. 1754. Susannah the wife of the above Thomas Rootes died the 5th day of June, 1763, aged 63 years."

" Here lie the remains of Elizabeth the wife of
J. Hooper, Surgeon, of this Parish, who died
Jan. 20, 1761, aged 31."

" Robertus Robinson, ob. 29 Mar. 1776. Æt. 41.
John Cole.   John Godfrey."

" Kitty White died March 9th 1765, aged 10 months.
Harriet White died Jan. 24th 1773, aged 19
months."

" John Hocker died Jan 25, 1737, aged 4 years and a
half. Thomas Hocker died Oct. 3rd 1737, aged
8 weeks."
(In the tower.)

" John Colly died May .... 1743 aged two years
and three months."

" Here lieth the body of Mrs Anne Pedley widow. She
departed this life the 2nd Dec. 1788, aged 53 years."
(In the tower on N. side of doorway.)

" Here lieth the body of Mary Godfrey daughter of
.... Blagrave of Bulmarsh Esq. by Elizabeth
his wife, and relict of Mr John Godfrey, citizen of
London. Also her son and daughter, John and
Elizabeth. She died June 13, 1738, aged 55
years : her son, Jan. 3, 1738, aged 22 years : and
her daughter in March 1736, aged 18 years."

THE FOLLOWING INSCRIPTIONS WERE REMAINING AT
THE TIME OF ASHMOLE'S VISITATION :

On a marble gravestone :

" Orate pro animabus Johannis Rectoris de Erle, et
Johannis Cerne, vicarii Sancti Laurentii de
Rading, et omnium fidelium defunctorum."
(This brass is lost.)

Inventory of 1517—" It. a nother Antiphoner w^t full legend of the gifte of Sr John Serne sū tyme vicar ther, the ij^{de} lefe begynnyng [sacerdos ponat.]"

" It. a chesible w^t thapp'ell of red silk suspend w^t tres (letters) of gold 𝕵 & 𝕾 of the gifte of John Serne."

(See *Vicars*.)

On a marble gravestone in the chancel :

" 𝕳ic jacet 𝕵ohannes 𝕶ent quondam 𝕭urgensis de 𝕽eding: et 𝕵ohanna uxor eius. 𝕼uorum animabus propicietur 𝕯eus. 𝕬men."

" It. a cope of cloth of bawdekyn w^t birdis & floures of gold of the gift of John Kent."

" It. a sewte of red cloth of bawdekyn w^t birds & floures of gold, of the gift of John Kent."

(Inventory, 1517.)

In 1410 he gave 13*s*. towards the re-roofing of the church.   He died about the year 1415.

Mr. F. J. Baigent in his article on " Sheriffs' Seals," in the " Herald and Genealogist," states that " This John Kent occurs as plaintiff in an action in the borough court of the City of Winchester held 20 Jan, 1405-6." " Johannes Kent de Redyng, *Mercer*, quærens."

He supposes him to have been the grandfather of the boy commemorated by a small brass in the chancel of Headborne Worthy Church, near Winchester, thus inscribed—

" 𝕳ic jacet 𝕵ohannes 𝕶ent quondam 𝕾cholaris 𝕹obi 𝕮ollegii de 𝕨ynchestre & filius 𝕾imonis 𝕶ent de 𝕽edynge cujus anime propicietur deus."

He was admitted as a scholar on the 23 Aug. 1432, and died Aug. 31, 1435.

Simon Kent was mayor of Reading in 1430.   In 1451 he sued John Kyrkeby " maryner " of Southampton for a debt of 8*l*.   This can hardly be the John Kyrkby who was mayor of Reading in 1427, 1429, 1432 and 1434, and whose name occurs among the subscribers to the church in 1440.

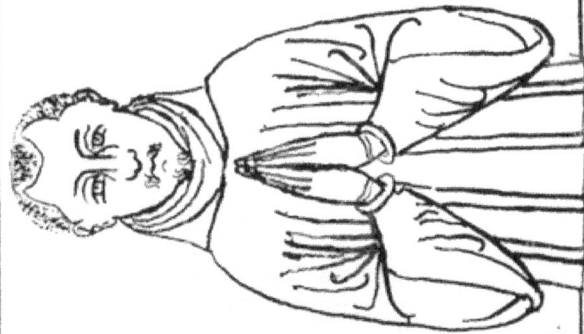

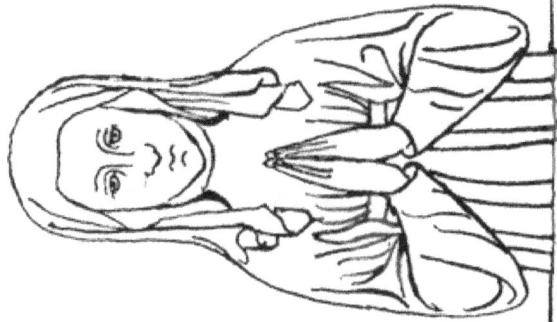

C. Kerry. del.

Hic iacent Johes Raut quondam Burgensis de Redyng Et
Johanna vxor eius. Quoz aïabus ꝓpicietur deus Amen ?

p. 158.

Nicholas Kent was C.W. in 1501; his wife, Joan, died 1503.

John Kent's father (? Nicholas) died 1508, and his wife 1509. He was C.W. in 1515.

Symonds thus describes this monument—

"A flat stone on the north side of the chancel: the two demy pictures of a man & woman: old text."

This brass has been recently taken from the floor and attached to the south wall of the chancel for its better preservation. The almost defaced portions of the engraving have been restored under the author's supervision.

On a brass plate fixed in a gravestone:

"Here lieth buried the body of Richard Cooke, Burgess of Reading; and the bodies of Julian his wife, and Edward his son; the said Richard being buried January 28, 1587."

(Lost.)

On a brass plate fixed in a gravestone:

"Here lieth Master Nicholas More sometyme Master of Arts, and late Vicar of the parish church of St. Laurence; the which deceased the last day of January, in the yeare of our Lord God M.cccc.lxxbij."

(Lost. See *List of Vicars*.)

On a brass plate fixed in a gravestone under the figure of an ecclesiastic in his habit:

"Pray for the soul of Mr Richard Wylcok, Master in Arts, late fellow of New College, in Oxford, who deceased the fourth day of April the year of our Lord 1504."

(William Wylock was one of the subscribers to the restoration of the tower in 1458.

1504-5. "It. rec. of John Wylcox at the burying of M. Richard his son for the grete bell xij^d."

"It. for wast of torchis the same tyme ij^s.

"It. rec. of John Wylcox at the month mynde of M. Ric' his son for the grete bell xij^d."

1507-8. "It. rec. for John Wylcox grave & for leying of the stone on þ^e same grave vij^s vj^d."

This John was a "chaundler and ffishemonger," and a member of the "Mass of Jesus."—See *Will of Kelsall*.

1507-8. "It. payed for the leying of the m͡ble stone on the grave of John Wylcox & for removing of a noþ͡ m͡ble stone & for the leying of þ^e stone on Sir John Styrys xx^d."

1510-11. "It. rec. for the g͡ve of Harry Wylcox &c. vij^s ij^d."

His wife died the same year.

1517. Inventory. "It. a cope of white Damask tissue w^t orfrey of crymysyn tissue of the gifte of Christian Wilcox."

1515-6. "It. rec. for the grave of Christian Wilcox vj^s viij^d."

"It. rec. for the grete bell for the same xij^d."

"It. rec. for the couing of the same grave vj^d."

(This brass is unfortunately lost.)

On another plate, under the figure of an ecclesiastic :

"Hic jacet Dominus Williclmus Goldore quondam bicarius Sancti Laurentii de Redyng: et Dominus Johannes Sampford, quondam bicarius Sancti Egidii: qui quidem Williclmus obiit penultimus die mensis Maij anno Dñi M.CCCC.LXviij."

Capt. Symonds, in 1644, thus describes this memorial :— "A small stone neare the south dore of the chancel wth 2 pictures, *ut supra*."

(This brass is also lost.)

On a plate fixed in a gravestone lying near the south entrance into the chancel was this inscription :—

En Thomas Justice quondam qui rexerat istud
Templum, sub gelido conditur hoc tumulo.
Dum bixit, Christi cultor fuit optimus ille,
Sacri mysterii verus amator erat.
Cujus nunc animo concedas Christe Redemptor
Molliter in gremio posse latere tuo.
Hic die Januarii 12, Ao 1535
diem clausit extremum."

(Lost. See *Altars* and *Wills*.)

" On a large flat stone in yᵉ church *neaxt the chancel, in
the middle yle*, the picture of a man between 2 women."
(Symonds, 1644.)   Of the position of this same monument,
Ashmole writes, " In the upper end of the *body of the
church* near the entrance into the north side of the chancell,
on a brass plate fixed in a gravestone was the following
inscription :—
(It must have lain close to the *north pier* of the chancel
arch.—C. K.)

"Hic iacent Willms Hunt quondam Maior Ville de
Redyng et Alicia et Isabella uxores* eius Qui
quidem Willms obiit bj die mensis Octobris Anno
Domini Millesimo* CCCColxiij° Quorum Animabus propicietur deus. Amen."

(This inscription was remaining in 1860, when the
author took a rubbing of it. It has since been abstracted.
The above inscription has been carefully copied from the
fac-simile then taken: it is contained in three lines: the
asterisks mark their termination. The old ledger of grey
marble, showing the matrices of a man between his two
wives with an inscription beneath their feet, now lies under
the eastern arch of the tower. In the centre of the upper
part of the slab is *a quadrangular* matrix measuring about
six inches by five. There are indications of a corresponding
one near the bottom of the stone.
William Hunt was one of the principal subscribers to the

M

work done to the church in 1440–1. His gift is entered
thus :—

>   "Et de vj⁸ viijᵈ r. de dono Witti Hunt."

He was Mayor of Reading in 1436, 1437, and 1446.

On the south side of Edward Butler's monument on a
brass plate fixed in a marble gravestone :

> "𝔥ere lyeth 𝔖ybbel 𝔖taberton wyfe of 𝔗homas
> 𝔖taberton, 𝔊ent, who lived here on earth in honest
> lyfe, and in good fame, and made a most goodly and
> faithful end, who departed this lyfe the 14ᵗʰ of
> 𝔇ecember 𝔄nno 1583."
>
> (Lost.)

On a brass plate in a gravestone in the body of the
church :

> "𝔥ic jacet 𝔚illielmus 𝔖tonor quondam 𝔅urgen . . . .
> qui obiit 4ᵗᵒ die 𝔐ensis 𝔍anuarii 𝔄nno 𝔇ñi
> 𝔐.𝔠𝔠𝔠𝔠 . . . . ."
>
> (Lost.)

Of this memorial Symonds writes :
" Upon a large flat stone inlayed wᵗʰ brasse the 2 small
pictures worne & taken away, this inscription—though almost
worne away. . . . This is in the middle yle of the church."
"There are divers more flat stones adjoyning, but yᵉ
brasses are stoolne away when yᵉ Roundheads possessed the
Towne 1643."

𝔐odern 𝔐emorials

Erected since the publication of Mr. Coates'
" History of Reading."

On the east wall of St. John's Chapel, within a quasi-
Gothic frame of freestone :

" Sophia, the only child of James Tompson Esq of
Peterborough wife for 52 years of Thomas Ring
Esq M.D., Born Nov. 3 1768. Married Nov. 26,
1787, died May 17 1848 in her 80ᵗʰ year."

Near this, but on the north wall, is a large memorial to
Thomas Ring, M.D., stating that he was born at Basingstoke,
Feb. 3rd, 1761, and that he exercised his profession for 50
years. He was one of the founders and principal supporters
of St. Mary's Chapel, and essentially contributed to the
establishment of the Reading Dispensary and the Royal
Berks Hospital. He died 27th June, 1840.

A little to the west of this, on a white marble slab
within a Gothic frame of freestone :

" To the Memory of
the Revᵈ John Ball, B.D.
Vicar of this parish
presented to the living by
St. John's College, Oxford.
Died Dec. 17, 1865, aged 66.
This tablet is erected by
parishioners and other friends in
grateful recognition of the value
of his faithful testimony as a
minister of Christ, while Vicar of
this parish for more than 30 years."
Heb. ii. 10.

On a brass plate beneath the former :

" To the Glory of God and
in loving memory of
the Reverend Peter French, M.A.
for 47 years Vicar of the Parish of
the Holy Trinity, Burton on Trent,
who died at Reading, Feb. 14, 1878,
aged 78.
In this church of St. Lawrence he was
married, and here received his last Communion
upon the occasion of the Mission.
Feb. 12, 1878."
Psalm lxxiii. 23.

On the respond of the arcade within St. John's Chapel in the S.E. corner :

> " Sacred
> to the memory of
> William Wise, D.D.
> for twenty one years
> the resident Vicar of this Parish,
> and
> fifteen years minister of Hurst,
> where his mortal remains are deposited.
> He died 14 October 1833,
> aged 64 years."

> " Sacred to the memory of Katherine, wife of Henry Deane, Esq., who died 21 Nov. 1836, aged 60 years. Also Henry Deane, Esq., who died 13 Dec. 1855, aged 75 years."
> The vault is 5 ft. on the north side of the communion rails.

On a brass plate on the south wall of the chancel :

> " In memoriam
> ✠
> John Moss
> for 40 years a member of this choir,
> died March 25, 1880,
> aged 73 years.
> ' Lord, I have loved the habitation of Thy house.' "

On a brass plate, formerly fastened to the floor of the south stalls in the choir, and designed to mark the resting-place of some whose monuments lay beneath :

> REV. W. T. M. WEBSTER
> MIRIAM WEBSTER
> MARY HUGHES
> ELIZABETH ELLY

Attached to the staircase of the tower within the nave is a monument of Caen stone, with a fine effigy, life-size, habited in academical costume, and standing beneath a canopy. Beneath is the following inscription :

" M.S.
Ricardi Valpy, S.T.P.
qui
Scholæ Readingensi
annos L amplius prefuit, &c.
In Christo decessit
Londini
V. Kal. Apr. M.DCCC. XXXVI
Ætatis LXXXI.
et in coemeterio suburbano
juxta viam Harroviensem
sepultus est."

MURAL MONUMENTS IN THE NORTH AISLE.

" In a vault on the north side of this church in which
Elizabeth, relict of the late Joshua Loring, Esq.,
is buried, lie also the remains of Eliza Loring,
their only daughter, who died the 24th of
January, 1860, aged 88."

On a brass plate beneath a window-sill :

" In memory of Richard Prichard Smith M.D. Fellow
of the Royal College of Physicians, who for many
years practised in this town, and died Oct. 7, 1867,
aged 72 years. Of his wife Eliza, daughter of Peter
Breton, Esq. who died Nov. 19, 1833, aged 45 years.
And of their children—Arthur who died March 17,
1844, aged 17 years, and Frederick, Emily, and
Eliza, who died in infancy. Also of Katherine,
second wife of the above R. Prichard Smith, and
daughter of Sir Nathaniel Dukinfield, Bart, who
died June 27, 1872, aged 83 years."

In the tower, on the floor at the entrance, and nearly
obliterated :
" Sacred to the memory of
Joseph Palmer
who departed this life
the 15th of May 1802,
aged 75 years.

Mrs Elizabeth Palmer
wife of the above,
who departed this life
October 17, 1809,
aged 60 years."

Arms—A lion rampant with three estoils in chief :
impaling (——?) with a bar in chief. (Not
mentioned in Burke's " Armory.")

On the south wall of the tower :

IN A VAULT NEAR THIS PLACE
ARE DEPOSITED THE REMAINS OF
JOHN BLANDY ESQR.
WHO DIED MAY 28TH, 1821
AGED 61 YEARS.
ALSO OF
MARY HIS WIFE
WHO DIED APRIL 4TH 1802,
AGED 42 YEARS.

SACRED TO THE MEMORY OF
ANNE ELIZABETH
WIFE OF MR WILLIAM BLANDY
WHO DIED JUNE 9, 1830
AGED 33 YEARS.

ALSO OF
MARY
WIFE OF THE REVD. F. J. BLANDY
WHO DIED JULY 25 1837
AGED 41 YEARS.

SACRED TO THE MEMORY OF
RICHARD BINFIELD
ORGANIST OF THIS CHURCH
DURING THIRTY FIVE YEARS
WHO DIED 28TH DECEMBER 1839,
AGED 73 YEARS.
THE ZEAL AND TALENT WITH WHICH HE DISCHARGED THE
DUTIES OF ORGANIST, THE AFFECTIONATE CARE WITH
WHICH HE TRAINED UP A NUMEROUS FAMILY IN THOSE

PATHS OF INDUSTRY AND RELIGION IN WHICH HE HIM-
SELF DELIGHTED TO WALK, HIS PIETY TOWARDS GOD,
HIS BENEVOLENCE TOWARDS HIS FELLOW-CREATURES, AND
THE RECTITUDE WHICH MARKED HIS CONDUCT IN ALL
THE SOCIAL RELATIONS OF LIFE, PROMPTED HIS NUMEROUS
FRIENDS SPONTANEOUSLY TO ERECT THIS TABLET IN TESTI-
MONY OF THEIR GREAT RESPECT AND ESTEEM FOR HIS
MEMORY. HIS REMAINS ARE DEPOSITED ON THE SOUTH
SIDE OF THE ADJOINING CHURCHYARD.

On an oval plate of white marble :

" THOMAS WEST Alderman, died 23rd of April 1803.
aged 55 years."

" MRS. ELIZABETH HAGGARD died 1st May 1822 aged
61 years."

" MRS. ANNE BLANDY, relict of JOHN BLANDY Esq.
and formerly widow of the above named Thomas
West died 4th of January 1835 aged 76 years."

" Mary Francis, wife of Capt. M. Andrews only
daughter of T. S. Salmon M.D. died at Hastings
March 7th 1824. Capt. M. Andrews, of His
Majesty's 44 Reg^{t} died at Llandaur in the East
Indies 21 July 1830."

" Martin Annesley Esq. Senior Magistrate of this
Borough died 29 June 1822 in his 82nd year."

" Thomas Stokes Salmon M.D. died April 30th 1827."

" Lancelot Austwick Esq. died 22 Feb. 1829 in his
78th year."

" Henrietta Venua died Novr 3rd 1824 aged 43 years."
(The stone which covered her grave is now in the
vestry.)

Wills.

The Will of Henry Kelsall. 1493.

(Somerset House.   Reg. " Vox." fo. 5.)

In the Name of God. Amen. The xij daye of
the Moneth of Novembr in the yere of oure lorde Ihu
M.cccc.lxxxxiij, I Henry Kelsall of Redyng of the Dioc. of
Sar' Clothyer, hole and sounde the mynde, not being syke
the body, and in my last days not knowing seke, make my
p'sent testament trypartited in this maner : ffyrst I bequeth
my soule to Almighty God and to our Lady saynt Mary
and to all the saints of heven, and my body to be buryed
in the parisshe chirch of Saint Laurence of Reding aforesaid on the North parte of the Awter of Ihu ther.   Item, I
bequith to the Cathedrale chirch of Sar' xijᵈ.   Item, I
bequeth to the high Awter of Saint Laurence chirch aforsaid
for forgoten Tythis, and evyll tythed xiiijˢ iijᵈ.   Item, I
bequeth to the operacions of the saide chirch xxˢ.   Item, I
bequethe to the operacions of the chirch of sainte Marys
in Redyng aforsaid xxˢ.   Item, I bequeth to the operacions
of saynt Gylys chirch there xxˢ.   Item, I bequeth to the
ffriers Minours there, xxˢ.   Item, I give to Thomas Kelsall
my brother all that same my landis and teñtis Rentis
Reversions and s'juices with all thaier appurtenᵃunces sette
and lying wᵗin the Burgh of Reding forsaid.   And also
all that same my two teñtis with thaier appʳtenᵃnes sette and
lying in the Town of Southampton which teñtis wᵗ thaier
appteñᵃncs late were of Thomas Payne of the saide Town
of Southampton, and after, of Roger Kelsall, Brother of me
the said Henry, and now been myn the saide Henry : and
in oon of the same ij teñtis now dwellyth oon John
Bawdewyn, and in that other teñt now dwellyth in oon
Thomas Crassewell. Also all that same my lands and
teñtis Rents rev'sions and s'jvices medows pastures and
lesures wᵗ thaier app'tenaunces sette and lying in the Ile of
Wyght in the Countie of Southampton in the parisshe of
Whyppyngham there.   And also all that same my grove
or wood lying in the Countie of Southampton wᵗ his
appteñᵃnces in the parisshe of Bramley in the saide countie

called Stertwood there. To be had and to be holde all the
foresaide Lands and teñtis &c. . . . . to the saide Thomas
Kelsall and to the heyres males of his body lawfully begotten," &c. (Then he appoints that if Thomas die without
issue the real estate should go to the next heir male of the
kindred of the said Thomas, but should this utterly fail,
then he wills that the said lands and tenements) "holy
shall remayne to the x personys as underwritten and
named maynteners and susteyners of thaier devocion of
the Masse of Ihu kept and songen in the parrishe chirch of
Saynte Laurence in Reading aforesaide : that is to say
now in the firste Richarde Cleche, draper, John Baxtster,
tanner, John Langham, iremonger, Stephen Dunster,
draper, Rauff Myllington, clothyer, William Tru yoman,
John Wylcokks, chaundler, and ffisshemonger, and William
Scochon, draper, with Richard Smyth gent, and John
Twytt oon of the deuocyoners and maynteners atte first
of the saide Masse of Ihu. And I myself the said Henry
beyng fyrst Mynder Susteyner and Mayntener of my
devocyon of the Masse of Ihu as all these forsaide persons
wele knowen and vnderstonden. To be had and be hold
all the forsaid lands &c. to the x persons forsaid maynteners and susteynors of the Masse of Ihu and to theyre
successors, but if any of these now premises and teñts be
allowed to become ruinous then" (he bequeaths them) "to
the churchwardens of our Lady Chappell of Knottysford
in the Countie of Chesshire and to their successors on condition (under payne of forfeture) that they shall keep a
verely Obite or anniversary in the parisshe chirche of
Sainte Laurence aforsaide for the Sowle of me the said
Henry Kelsale, And for the soules of the which I the said
Henry am bounde to pray for, and for the sowles of all
cristen, to the value of xx^s by the yere as by imperpetuyte.
And also by the oversight of the Curatt of the parisshe
chirch of Sainte Laurence forsaid, whosoever they be, for
the tyme being and that the said curat shall take and have
yerely for Dirige and Masses (this truly to be executed and
done) xx^d for his labour.

Item, I will and charge that myn Executours shall see
that I may have a daylye p^r)ste to sing for me the
said Henry Kelsall in the parish chirche of Saint
Laurence aforsaid by the space of vij yere than next and
immediatly following after my decease, the said p₁ste to
have for the saide vij yere xl^li good and lawful money of

Englond, which xl^{li} shall rest in the hands of the saide
x personnys Maynteners and susteners of the Masse of
Iħu aforseid. Item, I will and charge that myn executours shall ordeyne a stone to be layd upon me the saide
Henry and my wife Agnes in the churche of Saint
Laurence aforseid to the some of vi^{li} xiij^s iiij^d and upon the
saide stone by the ousight of the said x personnys maynteners of the mass of Iħu aforsaide A Reson of them to be made
upon the same stone such as God will induc them
to shewe and sett on. Item, I bequeth to the honoracion and
sustentacõn of the Masse of Iħu of my pper devocõn, two
my best Saltsalers of sylver and gilt, the oon coûed,
and that other not coûed, also two my best standing
cuppes gilt and coûed both. Also my two best
Nutts that I have coûed and gilted: xij sponys
of sylver w^t Wodewoses* vpon the knoppes and
gilted; In this intent that the saide plate afore reherced
shall not be shewed ne lent out of the Rome of the
persons maynteners &c. of the Masse of Iħu, safe
only alwey the saide plate to be had in honoracõn
and worshipping of the saide susteyners &c. of the masse
of Iħu, and to euy of them if nede shall require kepyng
there place. Item, I will and charge that if it be so that
any of the plate forsaide, any parte or all, any lone of the
same to be layd owte of the Rome of the said x persons
maynteners &c., and so proved, that than I will that the
heires male whomsoever they be of the said Thomas
Kelsall holy shall claime again, and recover ageyn to thaier
singuler Avayles by this my last will &c. Item, I bequeth
to the Operacõns of the Chauncell of Saint John of the
parisshe chirch of Sainte Laurence forsaid as to make dexts
there, and to the selyng of the same chauncell xx^{li}. Item,
I bequeth to the chappell of Knottisford aforesaid xl^{li} (to
provide a priest to sing his obit for seven years) which x^{li}
shall reste in the hands of the forsaid x personnys,
maynteners of the Masse of Iħu, and by them to be
deluyered. Item, I bequeth to the mending of the way
betwene Reding and the Thele xl^s, and for mendyng of
the way betwene Reding and Pangbo^{r}ne xl^s, and . . . . .
betwene Reding and Shipping Myll xl^s, and . . . . .
betwene Reding and Burghfield Brigge xl^s, and . . . . .
betwene Reding and Canruende xl^s. Item, I bequethe for

* Wodewoses—*i.e.*, wild men, or monsters.

Stall End. Kelsall's Gift. anno 1493.

p. 170.

the amending of the wey called the Ort lane next to Redinge xl^s. Item, I bequeth to xl maydens euy of them vj^s viij^d. Item, I bequeth to euy godchild of myne beying on lyve ij^s. Item, I bequethe to Thomas Grenewey my suant xl^s. Item, I bequeth to Henry Woodhatch my godson x^{li}. Item, I bequethe to the forsaide Thomas Kelsall my brother a payer of Bryganders covered with velvett, a standerd and a salett. Item, I bequethe to C pore men to euy of them a gown of blak fryse p'ce of euy gown ij^s; they to be deluyered by the discrecõn of myn executours, and the saide x personnes maynteners of the Masse of Ihu. Item, I bequethe to the chirch of Hendley vj^s viij^d. Item, I bequethe to the chirch of Wokyngham vj^s viij^d. Item, I bequethe to the church of Stratfieldsay vj^s viij. Item, I bequeth to the chirch of Stratfeld Mortemer vj^s viij^d .... to the church of Burghfelde vj^s viij^d .... to the church of Tylehurste vj^s viij^d .... of Selhampstede Abbott vj^s viij^d .... of Tydmershe vj^s viij^d .... to the parisshe church of Pangbourne vj^s viij^d .... of Purley vj^s viij^d .... of Whitechurch vj^s viij^d .... of Maplederh^{a}m vj^s viij^d .... of Causham vj^s viij^s .... of Shyplake vj^s viij^d .... of Retherfelde Pypparde vj^s viij^d .... of Lawrence Waltham vj^s viij^d .... of Hurste vj^s viij^d .... of Swallowfelde vj^s viij^d .... of Sonnyng vj^s viij^d .... of Shenyngfelde vj^s viij^d .... of Wargrave vj^s viij^d .... of Sulham vj^s viij^d .... of Knottesford xx^s .... of Rawsthorne vj^s viij^d .... of Moberley vj^s viij^d .... of Overpever vj^s viij^d .... of Netherpever vij viij^d .... of Newe Chapell in the Strete vj^s viij^d .... of Lymme vj^s viij^d.

Item, I bequeth to Margarett Bosden my sister xl^s. Item, I bequeth to Mawde Bosden her daughter xl^s. Item, I bequeth to Margarett Bosden sister of the saide Mawde xl^s. Item, I bequeth to euy soon of my brother Thomas Kelsall xl^s. Item, I bequeth to euy daughter of the said Thomas xl^s—to Jonett Swynton my sister xl^s—to Roger Swynton her son xl^s—to John Saunder my servant xl^s—to Johne Broke my servant xl^s. Item, I bequeth to the mariage of Elizabeth Crantmore xl^s. Item, I will and charge that Charlys Kelsall son of my brother Roger Kelsall shall haue xx^{li} of lawful money of England, which xx^{li} was of the bequest of the said Roger his ffather, which money also shall reste in the handes of the x persons

maynteners &c of the Masse of Iĥu, into the tyme the said
Charles be of the age of xxiiij yere (unless they think he
would well dispose it). Item, I will and charge that Elizabeth Kelsall daughter of my saide brother Roger Kelsall
and sister of the said Charles shall have xx^{li} which was of
the bequest of the said Roger her ffader until she be of age
to be married (the survivor of them to have the other's
share and in case of the death of both, then the wardens of
the Jesus Mass were to apply the 40*l.* for the benefit of their
souls).

"Item, I will and geve to Thomas Kelsall soon of my
saide Brother Roger Kelsall, a place callid the Tower, standing over the Sowth Gate in Hampton aforesaide, w^t a
Skelyng without the wall there, and a long celar by the
Town wall agenst Goddes howse gate—which Tower,
skelyng, and celar, late had the said Roger Kelsall my
brother of the dymyssions and grauntes of the Mayer of
Southampton and his brethren by lese of Indenture. Item,
I bequeth to the Mynchen* of Rumsey, whiche was the
daughter of the saide Roger vj marc. Item, I bequeth to
the Almeshowses in Redyng which wer of the foundačon of
John of the Larder, to euery of the same howses a couerlette,
price of euy of them ij^s viij^d. Item, to euery of the same
howses a pair of Shetis, price of every paier xvj^d. Item, I
bequeth to euery of my Cosynnes sonnys and doughters
lawfully bigotton, betwene Thomas Madok of Knottesford
aforesaide, and Elizabeth my sister nowe being alive, to
euery of them xl^s. I will and charge that a Tenour bell
to be made according to the iiij bellis that now hange in
the stepyll of Saynte Lawrence church of Reding aforseide
to the some of (   ). The scripture to be made aboute the
same bell—' Henry. The bell of Iĥu.' Item, I bequeth to the
sustentation of the forsaide Masse of Iĥu as aforsaid xl^{li}.
Item, I bequeth to the making of the Gyldhall in Reding
when the said hall shall be new bilded xl^s. It. I bequeth
to the daughter of William Swynton xl^s. Item, I bequeth
to Margery Pastlewe vj^s viij^d. Item, I bequeth to Joan
Asshendon vj^s viij^d—to Henry Sadeler vj^s viij^d—to the wif
of John Leche, Hatmaker, vj^s viij^d. The residue of all my
goodes I will that Thomas Kelsall my brother, and Rauff
Whyte of Wokynham whome I make joyntly myn executors,
that they may as God will give them grac to dispose of the

---

* Mynchen—*i.e.*, a *nun.* A. S. Minicen.

said residue to the pleasure of Almighty God, helth unto
my sowle, and my frendis sowles, and discharging of theire
conscience. These witnesses being present, Maister Rauff
Hethcote, Richard Cleche, Rauff Myllyngton, and William
True, with other at Reding the day and yere abousaide."

Proved at Lambeth some time during the months of
January and February 1493–4, which are the dates
of the previous and following probates.

The Will of John Pownsar.

(Probate Registry. Reg. "Ayloofe," fo. 1.)

In the Name of God. Amen. The xxviij Day
of June anno Dñi MCCCCCxvij.

I John Pownsar of Reading in the Dioc. of Sar. Draper,
. . . . do make . . . . this my last wille &c. I bequeth
my soule &c. . . . and my body to be buried in the church
of saint Laurence in Redyng aforsaid before the awter of
Jhus there where convenient place may be had. Item, I
bequeth to the Church of Sarum iiij^d. Item, I bequeath to
the sustentation and mayntening of the Masse of Jhus in
the said church of saint Laurence x^{li}, to be paid in maner
and form folowing yf Isabell my wife lyve sole vnmaried
and contynue Suster paying yerely vnto the said masse
vj^s viij^d, then I will the said x^{li} be paide vnto the Wardeyns
of the said masse to the vse of the said Chauntery and
masse immediatly after the decesse of the said Isabell my
wife, and if it fortune the said Isabell to mary or to leve of
the payment of the said vj^s viij^d yerely, then I wil that the
said x^{li} be paide vnto the said wardeyns unto the vse of the
said Chauntry within ij yeres next and immediatly after,
but if it shall fortune her to mary or to leve of the yerely
payment of vj^s viij^d, Then I will that a prest being honest
and of goode conversacon synge and say masse for my soule
in the said church of Saint Laurence by the space of one
hole yere next and immediatly after my decesse, and he to
have for his salary x marc. Item, I will that an obite be
kept yerely in the said church of Saint Laurence the space
of x yeres next and immediatly after my decesse, for my
soule and my frendes soules, expending thereon yerely
vj^s viij^d. Item, I bequeth to the sustentacon and mayn-
ten^{a}unce of the masse of our Lady in the said church of

Saint Laurence, vj⁸ viijᵈ .... to every godchild alyve
xijᵈ .... to William Hayton and Richard Stamp my ser-
vaunts, to every of them vj⁸ viijᵈ and a hosecloth. Item, I
bequeth to Isabell Barfote, Isabell Rose, and to Alice
Sparowe my servᵃunts, to every of them vj⁸ viijᵈ. I bequeth
to Isabell my wife all that my tenement with thappurte-
nᵃunce sett and lying in the High Strete of Redynge
bitwene the two bridgs there, betwene the tenement of John
Norris Squyer vpon the south parte, and the teñt of the
Abbot and convent of the Monastery of Reding aforsaid
vpon the north parte, to have and to hold the same .... for
ever. I bequeth vnto the said Isabel my wife all that
teñt sett and lyinge in Reding aforsaid in such place there
called Chese Rowe, that is to wit betwene the teñt of John
Norris Squyer upon the Est parte, and the teñt of the Abbot
and Convent of the mon. of Redyng aforsaid vpon the West
parte &c. After the decesse of the said Isabell my wife, I will
that the said teñt remayne vnto John Barfote the elder and
to Richard his sonne and to the heires of the same Richard
lawfully begotten, and for lack of such yssue to John Barfote the elder and of his heires, &c. and for lack of such
issue, I will that the said teñt &c. by the Mayor of the
Borough of Reding and by the x brethren of the Masse of
Jĥus of the church of saint Laurence aforsaid be solde (and
the proceeds disposed of according to their discretion) "for
the welthe of my soule, my wifes soule, and all Xp̄n soules."
(The rest of his goods and debts he leaves to Isabel his
wife, whom he appoints his executrix, and John Barfoot the
elder, the overseer of his will.)

> Witnesses Thomas Justice, Vicar of Saint Laurence
> aforsaid, Thomas Carpenter and William Edmunds.

Proved at Lambeth the 9th December, 1517.

The Will of Thomas Platts.

(Somerset House. Reg. "Blamyr," fo. 11.)

(Orig. in Latin, dated 24 August, 1522.)

In Dei n'oíc. Amen. I Thomas Platts of Reading in the Dioc. of Salisbury of sound mind &c. do make
my last will &c. in this manner. First I give my soul to
Almighty God and to the Blessed V. Mary His mother,

and to all saints, and my body to be buried in the church
of Saint Lawrence in Reading "in edicula Sancti Johañis
Baptiste." I give to the mother church of Salisbury 4ᵈ.
It. I bequeath to the High Altar of the said church of St.
Lawrence for tithes and oblations forgotten, and to pray for
my soul 3ˢ 4ᵈ.   It. I bequᵉath to the light of the Holy Cross
"in alto" 20ᵈ.   I bequeath to the light of the Blessed
Mary the Virgin in the said church 20ᵈ.   I bequeath to
Agnes my daughter 5ℓ.   I bequeath to Joan my daughter
5ℓ.   The rest of my goods not disposed of, I give to pay
my debts and to Margaret my wife that she dispose for
the health of my soul as she shall think most pleasing to
God and most beneficial to my soul; and I constitute
Margaret my wife my executrix.

   "Et pro magna consideracióe quam habui in Waltero
Barton de Reading predict. constituo in supvisorem mei
hujus testamenti ea intencione qᵈ iͥpe intendat et effectualit'
laboret circa reputacióem debitorum meoruni &c.   Hiis
testibꝫ dñs Edwarduo Bowes curato de Braynford, Roberto
Sadler, Wiͭͭo Wryght, Raynold de Reding pred. et aliis."

   Proved at Lambeth 10 Nov. 1522.

The Will of Richard Bedowe,
Vicar.

(Somerset House.   Reg. " Hogen," fo. 22.)

In Dei nomine. Amen. The xv day of November,
in the xxvj yere of King Henry the eight the yere of our
lorde god a thowsande vᶜ and xxxiij, I maister Richard
Bedowe vicar of Saincte Lauraunce in Reading of the
diocesse of Sar. in hole mynde and good Remembraunce,
lawde be to God, make my testament conteyning in hym
my last wille in maner and fourme as folowith. Ffirst, I
commende my soule to Almighty God, and to the holy
company of hevin, and my body to be buried in the chauncell
of sainct Laurence church in Reading beforesaid before the
ymage of Sainte Laurence at the aulter's end.   Item, I
bequeth to the cathedrall churche in Sar. iijˢ iiijᵈ—to the
cathedral churche of Lincolne iijˢ iiijᵈ—to the cathedrall
churche of sainct David iijˢ iiijᵈ—to the reparaco͆s of sainct

Laurence church aforesaid xl⁸. Item, I bequeth to the
maynctenance of Jesu Masse in Sainte Lauraunce church
aforesaid vj⁸ viij^d. Item, I bequethe to the mainctenaunce of
our lady masse in the same church vj⁸ viij^d . . . . to the
parrishe church of Lukenor xl⁸. Item, I bequethe to the
parrishe church of New Radnor a chalice price iij^li . . . .
to Glawster churche a chalice price iiij mͬc . . . . to Lan-
dewy abarargh a vestment of grene satten of burges . . . .
to the parish church of Borroth a vestment of grene satteyn
of burges. Item, I will that my executour finde and provide to my mother during her life all thinges necessary for
hir. Item, I will that my mother shal have during hir life
all the revenues profits and use of all my father's landes
&c. (He mentions his uncle Sir John ap Rice). Item, I
bequeth to the freers mynours in Reading aforsaid xl⁸.
Item, I bequethe to Richard Andro xl⁸ and my gowne that
I were euy day w^toute the furre, and to his wife my shorte
gowne. Item, I bequethe to an honest preest iiij marks
sterling to singe two yeres at Sainte Martyns in Oxford for
the soules of John Powes and his wife and their benefac-
tours. Item, I bequethe to my brother at Godstow to be
praied for iij^li to the poor people of Lewknor shortly after
his burial xl⁸. To the churches of Adwell, Weston, Asten,
Croway iij⁸ iiij^d each . . . . to my cowsen Lewes ap Rice
xx⁸ . . . . to my cowsen David ap lͭen xx⁸. Item, I bequethe all my bokes to All Sowlen College in Oxforde, &c.
Item, I bequethe to Sir John Maynforte for his labour and
for my monthes Dirige, x⁸. Item, I bequethe to an honest
preest to singe and pray for my soule one yere in Sainte
Laurence vj^li xiij⁸ iiij^d. And I will the same preest to say
Placebo and Dirige and cõmendaͨon thrise every weke
during the said yere, w^t Masse of Requiem on the morrowe,
and that to be doon suche dayes in the weke as myn executour shall appointe, and the saide preest to synge longer
for me, if my goodes after my bequestes paid will further
extende. Item, I make and ordeyne maister Thomas ap
Howell my sool executour &c. Item, I make my lorde
Hugh Abbott of Reading and Dr. Gwent, Deane of the
Arches, my supvisors &c. and I geve to eche of them for
their labour a Riall of gold. Item, I bequethe to my aunte
that is blinde x⁸. Item, I bequethe to Saint Laurance
church in Reading aforsaid two of my new joyned stools
for their Rectours. In witness whereof I have sette myn
seale in the presence of these witnesses vnderwriten the

day and yere above writton, Petir Shefforde, Davy
Williams, and John Mainforthe curat.

Proved at Lambeth 21 Jan. 1534.

The Will of William Watts.

(Probate Registry, "Hogen," fo. 28.)

In the Name of God. Amen. The first day of
July in the yere of our Lord God M. fyve hundred and xxxv.
I William Watts of the parishe of Sainte Laurence of
Readyng . . . . hole in mynd and of good remembrance,
laude be to God, make my testament in maner and fourme
folowing : ffirst, I comende my soule to almighty God my
maker and Redemer, to our Blissid Lady saint Mary, and to
all the holy company of hevyn, and my body to be buried in
the parishe church of Saint Lawrance aforsaid before the
quere dore. Item, I will that there shall be bestowed at my
buriall amongst preests clerks and pour people, fyve pounds,
and in lyke maner at my monethes mynde fyve pounds.
Item, I will so shortly as can be after my deceas all my
debts to be paid . . . . and that to be doon w^tout delaye,
which debts be written in my counting boke. Item, I bequeth to the high awlter of Saint Lawrance in Reading
aforsaid for tythis & offerings forgotten vj^s viij^d. Item, I
will that an honest preest shall singe and say masse and
other divine services for my soule and all Xpn̄ soules the
space of oon yere in Saint Lawrence aforesaid, and the
preest to have for his labour vj^{li} xiij^s iiij^d. Item, I will that
Margaret my wife shall have all my three tenements w^t
the appurtenaunces that lyeth between the Vawte and the
George gate, and a parcell of arable grounde lying in
Whitle called the Clayepittes for terme of her lyf and after
her decesse to Henry Watts my cousin keeping an obite in
Saint Laurences churche for xx yeres next and immediately following the decease of Margaret my wyf, to the
value of vj^s viij^d yerely. (To his wife Margaret he bequeaths 20*l.* with all his goods in his house in New Street,
except a gilt piece given to Thomas Knight as well 20
marks to bring up David his brother. To Richard Knight
5 marks. To William Knight 5 marks.) "Item, I bequeth
to the Reparacōs of thornaments that belongith to the
brotherhode of Jesus Masse founded in Saint Laurence

N

churche aforseid five m̄rcs." (He bequeathed 40ˢ to the Lady
Mass for the same purpose, to the reparations of the church
20ˢ, to St Mary's in Reading 6ˢ 8ᵈ, to St Gyles 6ˢ 8ᵈ,
to the church of the ffriars Minours 6ˢ 8ᵈ, to Wokyngham
church 20ˢ.) " To Rafe my sonne every yere 20ˢ." (He
appointed a yearly obit to be kept for his soul in St. Lawrence's so long as Margaret his wife should live, enjoining
her to bestow thereat yearly the sum of 40ˢ among priests,
clerks, and poor people. He constituted Richard Turner
and Henry Watts his executors.

> Witnesses—Water Barton, gent, John Vansbye, Robert
> Watlyngton "and other moo."

Proved at Lambeth 13 Nov. 1535.

The Will of Thomas Justice.

(Probate Registry, "Hogen," fo. 31.)

In Dei Nomine. Amen. The xiiij day of Decem-
ber the yere of our Lorde God a thousand five hundred xxxv.
I Thomas Justice, Clerke of Readinge &c—do make &c.—
Ffurst, I commende my soule to Almightie god and to the
holly company of hevyn, and my body to be buried in the
pishe church of sainte Laurence in Readinge aforesaid
. . . . I bequethe to the pishe church of sainte Maries in
Readinge aforesaid xxˢ . . . . to the pishe church of sainte
Gylys in Readinge aforesaid xxˢ Item, I bequethe to
Alice the wife of Thomas Sayntmonde a salte of siluer wᵗ
the couer pcell gilte and vj spones of siluer and a paier of
shetes . . . . I bequethe to every of hir children beinge
now alive and unmaried a siluer spone and fourtie shillings
in moneye and a pair of shets, and if any of them dye, than
their parte to be divided to the survivours brethren and
susters. Item, I will my two tenements lyinge in London
Strete to Richard my brother, kepinge therfor yerely in the
parish Church of saint Laurence an yerely obite for the
soules of his frendes and myne. The residue of all my
goodes aboue not bequethede after my detts paide, I give
and bequethe to Richard Justice my brother, and to Thomas
Sayntmounde, whom I ordeyne and constitute myne executours to dispose the said residew to my poure kynnes
ffolks, and other poure people of sainte Laurence parryshe
aforesaide, and I give to eiche of them xxˢ for their laboure.

In witness wherof I have subscribed this with myne owne hande the day and yere above written.

Proved the 27 of January,
1535.

The Will of Walter Barton.

(Somerset House. Reg. "Dyngely," fo. 17.)

In the Name of God. Amen. I Water Barton of Radyng in the Dioc' of Sar' being in helth of bodye and in good and parfite memorye ; thanks be to our Lord God, The xxvij day of Octobre the yere of our Lord God a thousand fyve hundreth thirty and sevyn, And in the xxixth yere of the reigne of King Henry the eight, make my testament and last will in maner and fourme as folowith—ffirst I bequeth my soule to Almighty God, and to the suffrage of his blissed mother our lady saint Mary, and to the suffrages of all the holy company of hevyn, And my Body to be buryed there where it shall please god to dispose for me after the discrecion of myn executours. Item, I bequethe to the Cathedrall churche of Sar' vj^s viij^d. Item, I bequethe to Sir John Maynfforthe vicar of Saint Laurence, my Curat, in recompense of my tithes negligently forgotten yf any be, and to pray for me xx^s. Item, I bequeth to Sir Thomas Lathum parson of Englefield to pray for me x^s. Item, I bequeth to maister William Symondes vicar of Busselden to pray for me x^s. Item I bequeth to Sir William Atkynson parson of Uffeton to pray for me x^s. Item, I bequeth to the Vicar of Shepelake to pray for me x^s. Item I will that there be deliuered w'in six days after my deceas to fourscore pore householders being charged with Childeren w'in the towne of Radyng after the discrecion of myn executours to every of them iij^s iiij^d. Item I will that there be said and doon for my soule at my burying, and as soon as may be doon conveniently, so it be doon at my burying and at my monethes mynde and before, a thousande masses. Item, I will ther be delte for me at my burying and before my monethes mynde to poure people dwellyng in the towne of Radyng to pray for me twenty pounds after the discrecions of my executours. Item, I bequeth towarde the mayntenaunce of the Masse of Jhu in the parisshe of Saint Laurence of Radyng vj^{li} xiij^s iiij^d.

N 2

Item, I bequeth toward the mayntenance of the Masse of
our lady w⁺in the said church, thre pounds vjˢ viijᵈ. Item,
I will that all such detts and sumes of money as be expressed hereafter in this quayre be truely contented and
paid as spedely as may be conveniently. Item, I will that
if there shall be hereafter any other detts or restitucons
claymed by any parsone, as I remembre me noon to be,
yet if it may appere to myn executours by any likelyhod
or coniectur that it shuld be, I will it shall be paide . . . .
Item, I give and bequeth to Alys my wife all my stuffe of
householde and all my plate except suche as I shall hereafter declare by this my will. Item, I bequeth to Griffith
Barton my nevewe oon salt of siluer, parcell gilt wᵗ a couer
that is daily occupied on my borde, twelve spones of oon
sorte having knapps gilt wᵗ this Ἧ X in euery ende, and thre
litle cupps of siluer wᵗ a couer that John Hart made to me
when he dwelled at Redyng. Item, I bequeth to William
Buryton my nevewe all my weryng gere. Item, I bequeth
to Alice my wife all the wares in my shop with the dettes
of the whole stock belonging to the same. Item where
William Buryton my nevewe for suche money as he hath
in the said stock and for his labour hath had before this
diverse yeres the fourth parte of the geyn of the said stock
and wares towarde his lyving, I will that after my decesse
yf he wyll and do contynue his occupying wᵗ my said wife
and behave himself toward hir kyndely, that as long as
they can so agree together, that he shall have the third
parte of the geyn and profitte that shall yerely rise vpon
the occupying of the said stock that is to sey, all the profits
that shall growe and ryse vpon the said occupying to be
yerely rekened, and the thirde parte of the said encrase
and geyne to be deliuered to the said William And if they
cannot so agree, then I will there shall be deliuered to him
in Wares detts and redy money the thirde parte of all the
said stock and so to depte the other two partes to be at the
discrecion and will of my said wife to dispoase at hir
libertie, and if they doe contynue togither in so occupying
till my wife decesse, then I will the said William shal haue
the halfe parte of the said stock as well in wares, money
and detts : in euery thing the other halfe therof to be at
the libertie of my said wife to be disposed at hir pleasure.
Item, I bequeth to my said wife all such interest and leeses
as I have in the psonage of Shiplake in the ferme of Burwey
and in the porcon of the tithes of Synshᵃm, soo always

that as long as my nevewe William Buryton and she doo
contynue togither their occupying, I will he shall haue the
half of the profits of the same w^t my said wife and the
hoole after hir deceas. And if they do not so contynue
agree and occupye togither, then I will the said William
Buriton shall have noo parte of the profits thereof but my
wife to have the hool profits during her lyfe And after
hir deceas, my nevewe Henry Barton to have the said
Leeses during the termes of the same.

Item, I bequeth to Thomas Buryton my nevewe
vj^{li} xiij^s iiij^d. Item, I bequeth to euery of his Childern
being in lyfe vj^s viij^d. Item, I bequeth to John Buryton my
nevewe iij^{li} vj^s viij^d, and to euery of his Childern being in
lyfe vj^s viij^d. Item, I bequeth to my nevewe John Blount
fourty shillings, and to euy of his childeren being in lyfe
vj^s viij^d. Item, I bequeth to Thomas Blount my nevewe
xl^s, and to euery of his childern being in lyfe vj^s viij^d. Item,
I bequeth to Richard Blount my nevewe xl^s, and to euery
of his childern being in lyfe vj^s viij^d. Item, I bequeth to
William Buryton my nevewe my leese that I have in the
psonage of Ash^{a}mpsted to help to find his childern and to
bring them up. Item, I bequeth to my nevewe Griffith
Barton all my interest and Leese that I have in the Lordship of Southstoke and the psonage of the same with the
indenture therof to his own propr use. Item, I bequeth to
the same Griffith Barton, to Thomas, Water, and Xpofer,
the sons of William Buryton, all such interest and Leese as
I have in the Lordship of Mykelton, and the parsonage of
the same, to take the profits therof when it shall com,
equally to be divided bitwene them foure, And he that doth
longest lyve to haue and enioy the hoole leese w^t all the
profits of the same, and the indenture therof, and that Leese
not to be solde nor any part therof but to remayne as aboue
expressed w^{t}out any alienaçõn of any parte therof till the
hole shall come to oon of the hands of the said foure
persons. And for suretie therof, I will the said indenture
shall remayn in the sauff custodye of the Maior and Burgenses of Redyng by indenture to be kept, and for the
custody therof assone as the terme of the said indenture
shall begin to take effect, I will the said Maior and Burgenses shall have yerely out of the same vj^s viij^d till the
said indenture shalbe deliuered as is afore written. Item, I
bequeth to William Buryton and to Thomas, Water, and
Xpofer, his three sonnes, all such interest as I have in the

psonage of Cholsey, the profit therof to be equally devided
among them (the maior and burgesses to keep the indenture
as before) Ffor the custodie wherof, I will shall be yerely
deliuered to the maior and burgesses to thuse of their hall,
two quarters of good and sote (*sweet*) whete to be paid
yerely out of the said parsonage and deliuered at Radynge
w'in their said hall as long as the maior and burgenses
shall have the custodye of the said indenture. Item, where
I haue caused my recoverers of my manor of Ildesley to
make a leese w^t me to William Buryton my nevewe of the
fferme of Hodcote for terme of certeyn yeres as appereth
by the said indenture, upon the whiche fferme I have nowe
a stocke of shepe to the nombre of thre hundreth thre score
and aboue, The which Leessees made of trust to myn owne
vse, I will and bequeth the same leese and the hole stock
thervppon to be disposed as herafter doth folowe : Ffirst I
will that my said nevewe shal haue the said fferme and the
hole stock vpon the same, and he to take the profits of the
same to thentent that w^t the same profits he shall con-
tynually maynten the same stock as good as it is nowe,
and the rest of the profits to take to his owne vse toward
the keping of his childern till Alice his doughter shall come
to the age of mariage.   And yf she be ruled in hir mariage
by hir said father then I wille she shal haue the said Leese
and the hole stock to hir said mariage.   And if it fortune
the said Alice to dye before she shalbe maried, or yf she
marye contrarie to hir fathers mynde, then I bequethe the
said leese and the hole stock to Thomas, Water, and
Xpofer, sonnes of the said William, the profits therof over
and beside the maynten^{a}unce of the said stock as is afore
written to be equally divided amonge them, (but if these die
without issue) then I give and bequeth the same leese and
stock to my Cosyn Gruffith Barton." (He then constitutes
his wife Alice his executrix and William Buryton and
Robert Watlyngton his executors.) "And I bequeth to
the same Robert to helpe my wife in hir cawsis iij^{li} vj^s viij^d." ·
He gives the residue to his wife to be disposed for the
benefit of their souls according to her discretion. Witnessed
by Gruffith Barton, John Trumflet, and John Maynforth
vicar there.

Memorand. I bought my landes in Streteley in Jan :
20 Hen : viij, and sens my entre I dyd paye noo quyte rent
to my lord of Derbye, the whiche claymeth yerely out of it
xxxj^s vj^d.   Item, I doo thinke in conscience I do owe to

paye yerely for such londes as I doo holde of hym in all
xvj⁸ vj^d. Item, certeyn londes there callid 'Goldhurds' is
holden of him by the yerely rent of viij⁸ and a pound pep,
and of that londes William Ffrewen of Streteley hath all
the chief londes that he bought of William Watts of
Readyng, and yet I doo knowe I have parte of that londe,
but a great dele the lesse and worste parte, yet I can be
content to bere parte of the Rent; And yf I bere yerely
iiij⁸ I thinke it be w^t the largest. And yf I pay therfor
iiij⁹, then my hole rent to my lord of Derbye for all my
londes shalbe yerely xx⁸ vj^d. So I do owe them for oon yere
at Mich. anno xxi Hen. viij xx⁸ vj^d. and so to Mich. anno
xxvij. The hole sm^a soo owyng vij^li iij⁸ vj^d.

Memorand. I ought to have comon in all my lords
Demaynes as apperith by my evidens of the graunte of
John Mohon one of my lords Auncestours and I am kept
from it. Item, my lord cawsid certen of my ten^aunts and
seruants to be indyted of Ryott and of forcible entre for
pecible entre into two acres of myn owne grownde in the
Suth felde, and therupon ther was an accon taken agayn
them at the comen lawe and an Issue joyned, and my lord
will sue noo further, the fynes of the said judyments and
the costes in the suyte in the lawe in defence of my lords
wrong doon to me in that and in other accons tryed agayns
my lords ten^ants in repleyves and other, cost me aboue tenne
pounds: som recompence I wold I had, and yet, notwith-
standing the trouble and wrong that I haue had, if I may
haue and enjoy my comen and to haue my londes owt of
Waryans according to my right, I wolde my lord were
payde of his Rents being behynde, and so after con-
tynually. Item, John Clerk of Hagburn claymeth owt of
my londes in Sheprege xx^d by the yere, yf he can shewe
me out of what londe it is dewe to be paid or any other
thinge to charge me by, I will he be paid. I am behynde
at Mich. anno xxvj I think vj yeres.

Detts to be paid by myn executours: ffirst I did receyve
of Leonard Rede Esquier more than my dutie by tenne
pounds towards that I lent him vpon a bill of his hande
obligatory tenne mrks and yet I owe him fyve mrks: I dyd
delyuer that fyve marks to my maister Englefelde to paye
him, and the other bill to be cancelled and he must discharge me therof. I will it be paid of myn own conscience,
for I am in dowte whether he be paide. Item, ther is
owyng yet to Pangburn church to buy a Cope, of the

legacy of maister Leynham, xiij⁸ iiij^d. I haue ben in hande
w^t the parishens to bye a cope and they do not. I will it
be doon and paid according to maister Leynhams will. I
will that money to be paid.

> Probatum fuit &c. 16 die mensis
> Maii AD. 1538. apud London &c.

Robert Watlington, Clothmaker, made his will
6th Jan. 1541.

"Item, I bequeth to the high aulter in Saint Laurence
Church for tithes &c. forgotten, xx^d. Item, to the Masse of
Jesus in the Church of Saint Laurence, xiij⁸ iiij^d. Item, to
the Masse of our Lady, x⁸. He bequeathed to his three
'childer' Nicholas, Alice, and Joan, 26l. 13s. 4d. apiece. To
every servant in his house at his departing, 6s. 8d. each. To
poor people at Warfield, 20s. He gave his real property to
Nicholas and his heirs. "It. I bequeath to Nicholas my
sonne my great goblet and my great Andyrons." The
residue of his goods he left to Elizabeth his wife.

> Proved Jan. 30th, 1542.
> Reg. "Spert," fo. 15.

John Trumflet, Mercer, gave to his sister Alice
Trumflet 5l.: to his sister Catharine Sowthy 5l.: to the
four daughters of his wife Alice, viz., Bridget, Elizabeth,
and Margaret, 10l. each. To his son Richard 200l. to be
taken by 40l. a year out of the debt of Richard Watlington.
To the same Richard he devised all his lands, &c. in Binfield, Reading, Arborfeld, &c., his wife Alice to enjoy the
rents during his son's minority.

He gave his best gown to his uncle William, his long
gown lined with chamlet to Thomas Southy, and his gown
of Kentish Russet to his cousin Robert Sheford, his
doublet of Damask to Will Watlyngton, his satin doublet
to John Gateley, and his chamlet jacket to Richard Mathew.
To Robert Style 6l. He appointed Mr. Thomas Vachell
the elder the overseer of his will.

> Proved 25 Sept. 1549.
> Reg. "Hogen," fo. 38.

The Obituary.

A list of the names of those persons whose bequests, inter-
ments, and obsequies are recorded in the Church accounts
from the year 1410, down to the commencement of the
burial registers in 1605.

The persons whose names are marked with an *asterisk*
were buried within the church.

Anno 1410.   Robert Beche bequeathed vj^s viij^d to the
Church.

1433-4.   Ric. Glover bequeathed x^s.
John Barton (butcher) bequeathed vj^s viij^d
to the Church.
Ric. Benton bequeathed iiij^d to the Church.
Tho. Glover bequeathed j^s viij^d to the
Church.
Will. Lousse bequeathed j^s viij^d to the
Church.
John Markham jun^r bequeathed vj^s viij^d
to the Church.
John Chapman bequeathed j^s.
Thomas Cowper bequeathed vj^d to the
Church.

1440-1.   Thomas Hawe bequeathed iij^s iiij^d.
John Kayns bequeathed vj^s viij^d.
Ric. Hawkeley bequeathed iij^s iiij^d.

*1441-2.   Thomas Swayn bequeathed vj^s viij^d.
Amicia, mother of Tho. Clerke bequeathed
v^s.

1498-9.   Thomas Butler*. Webby's wyfe. Henbury's
wife of Caversham. Alysaunder Prentyse*
wyfe. Thomas Payne. Boldys moder.
Richard Ades. Thomas Carpenter's wifes
moder*. Plecyes wife. Alysaunder Prentice*.
Hudson's wife. John Fuller's wife. Robard
Cavyes wife*.

1501-2.   Sir John Hyde, vicar of Sonning*. William
Tru (or Trew)'s wife*. Isabel wife of
Rob. Sadler.

1502-3. Harry son of Robard Prow. Lawrence Morton
gentyllman*. Roger Johnson's wife*. John
Crewse*. Thomas Platts* (see below). Sir
John Pymber (priest)*. John Long Master
of the Grammar school*. My lord Wod's
bequest 6ˢ 8ᵈ. Thomas Rede*. Elizabeth,
wife of Harry Prow. William Hill.
(Elizab. his widow married Mʳ Mayho).
Sir Will Symmys* (interred wᵗ much
ceremony.) Will. Dodson*. William Watts.
Will. Harebotell. Will Hasylwood's wife*.
"It recᵈ of Margaret Platts for a stone to cou͡
her husbonds grave xix ."
1503-4. William Dodson (Isabel his relict). Joan wife of
Nicholas Kent. Thomas Myryman's wife.
Tho. Turner's wife. Florence Rede* (Alice
Sharp paid the burial fees). Nicholas Kents
wife Joan*. William Hill (leaving Joan his
widow.)
"It rec. of Randall Kelsall for wast of Torchis
at þᵉ yer mynd of Harry Kelsall xᵈ."—(H.
Kelsall died in 1493.) John Higson's wife
left 8ᵈ towards a Pax.
1504-5. Richard Wylcox* (son of John. See monᵗˢ.)
Agnes wife of Lawrence Hill. Margaret
Nash's husband. Alice a Dene*. Agnes
wife of John Sharpe*. Thomas Bunting—
fees pᵈ by Symond Lamb. John Darling*
(father of John Darling C.W.). Anne Darling* "my moder" (i.e. of Jno. Darling
C.W.). Agnes, wife of William Watts.
Robert Prows wife*. John Love gave 6ˢ 8ᵈ
to the church by will. White his executor.
1505-6. Helen Langham*—fees paid by John Gryffyn.
William Hall*—fees paid by his widow
Margery.
1506-7. The husband* of Sybell Darling. Dancaster*—
fees by his widow. John Arnold.
1507-8. Master Symeon. A kinsman of Sir Thom:
Walssh. John Wylcox*. Will: Hether—
fees by Mʳ Cleche. The father of John
Kent. Thomas Hart*. Sir John Styry*—
fees paid by John Pouncer. Robert Prow*—
fees by Wⁱⁿ Lendall.

1508-9. John Gryke. John Vyncentt*. Will: Nettar*. William Myllis*. John Kent's wife*. Robert Burlei's wife. Mr Rokys*. Colyar. Cave*. Robert Dodson's wife*. Agnes Darling*. Roger Graney*. Thomas Hart.

1509-10. Mestres Bereman. Nettar's wife. Edwards of the Kinge's Stabull. 'Haselwood's weyff'. Mr May*. Robert Dodson's kynnes woman*. Harry Wylcock's wife*. Haselwood* (the bellfounder).

1510-11. Nycholas Ward s$\dot{}$lv^ant w^t the Kyng*. Raufe Mylyngton*—"It. rec. for the great bell at his berying, and duryng the monethe, and at the moneth mynde, v^s iiij^d. William Cobbe*. John Semper's wife. Rec^d of the greate Bell at Hasylwod's mynd xij^d. Rawlyn's wife*. The wife* of John Turner, baker. Harry Wylcox*. Ireland's wife*. Sharpe's wife*.

1511-12. John Pastler*. John Semper. John Turner*— (his son Richard Turner paid the fees.)

1512-13. Andrew's wife*.

1513-14. Alysaunder Wyld.

1514-15. Cony's wife. John Roke*. Roger Bryce*. Will: Faryngton*. Will Leycet*.

1515-16. Richard Turner's wife*. Will. Lendall*—(Will. Knight paid for his year's mind in 1525-6.) Philip Rysby's wife*. Isabell Hart*. Mr Watt's wife*. Mr White*. Christian Wilcox*. John Roke*—(buried under the seats). Richard Aman's wife*. Roger Brice (bur^d under the seate). Richd Wryght, baker, bequeaths 3^s 4^d to the church.

1516-17. Nicholas Kent. William Stamford* (a benefactor.)

1517-18. Ralph White of Okyngham. Richard Turner's wife. Xpofer Spakeman's wife*. John Pownsar*—(see *Wills*). Will. Layward*. Whit (the bellfounder's) wife*.

1518-19. John Partriche*. John Molyners* (fletcher). Robert Dodson's wife*—(a dyer). Will. Kenes wife*. John Lambs wife*. John Lamb*. John Eton*. Will. Trewe* jun^r. Richard Goodyere's child*—buried w^t Dod-

188 THE OBITUARY.

son's wife. Randall Kelsall's moder*—(no
fees charged for use of the bell—see *Bells*
under 1515.)

1519–20. Rob. Blake's wife*.

The great bell was usually *rung* for a knell,
and *tolled* for the month's mind, and
'terment,' or year's mind. The following
is the only exception :—

1520–1. It. for *Ryngyng* at the t'ment of my lord
Abbott xij^d (Thomas Worcester). Thomas
Barber*. Wrights wife. Sir John Riche-
mond*—buried in St. John's chancel.
John Kent's wife. Mr Carpenter*. Joan
Darling*.

1521–2. Roger Johnson's wife*. William Trewe*.
William Kene. John Gylman. William
Traunder the King's S^r}vant.

1522–3. John Buckworth's wife*. M^res Smyth*. Henry
Horthorn*—(see an account of his family
under *Sepulchre Altar*). William Lasse-
ham*. Nicholas Kene*. Thomas Watts*.

1522–3. The vycar of Hakfeld. M^res Dabscowrt Davyc
Joons*. Thomas Tallyer*. John Whyt-
tygh*m. M^res Vincent*. John Wynyet.
John Voyer's wyff*. Harry Carpent*.

1523–4. Mr. Richard Cleche's wife.* "A straung' that
dyed at the george"*. John Johnson's wife.
Rich. Yeves wife. Mr. Everard's wife (died
some time before). John a Merkbye's
wife.

1524–5. John Paynter*. Isabell Lessham.* Will
Sadler*. Rec. for the grave of Mays^t
Cletch* by his bequest x^s, and for Knell
and Month's mind ij^s iiij^d. Mestres Dawson.

1525–6. John Goodgame*. Will. Fayrchild*. Rob. Dodson* (dyer). Robt. Dwight*. Margaret
Goodyere*.

"Gyven to the church by the same M'gàrett
a pott p'ce ij^s v^d."
Symson's wife.

1526–7. Margaret Weston*. Henry Currers wife*.
Rob. Lykley.* Will. Whytt.

1527–8. John Andrew's wife*. Thomas Everard*. Nicholas Hyde*. Sir Will. Wryght*. Randall

Kelsall*. (no charge for his knell &c.)
Henry Horethorn's wife*. Will Coon*—
(He appears to have executed all the more
delicate wood carving in the church—*c.*
1520.). Ric. Wyers wife. John Andrew's
wife. John Cottelar.

1528-9. Thomas Symson*. Symon Lamb's wife*. Sir
Thomas*, (a priest.)

1529-30. Robert Medwyn's wife*. Ric. Chester*. John
Andrew's wife*. Nich Eves wife*.

1530-1. John Russel*. Lawrence Malt*. Ric. Foxley*.
Thomas Overthrow's bequest 4^d.

1531-2. Mr Ffoster*. Xpofer Butler*.

1532-3. Agnes Vansby*. Agnes Coone*—(see 1527).
Mrs Margaret Hide*. Philip Riseby*.
Robert Philip.

1533-4. Ric. Eve*. Alice Paynter* widow. Sir Robert
Heth*. Als Watlyngton*.

1534-5 Simon Lambb*. Richard Barnes* bequeathed
vj^s viij^d. Mr Richard Bedow, vicar*, bequeathed 40^s. Nicholas Eve*. John Andrewes wife. M^{r}Will Watts*, bequeathed
xx^s. (See *Wills.*)

1535-6. William Knight, bequeathed 6^s 8^d. Anne
Hodson*.

1536-7. Thomas Panter*. Roger Johnson's wife*. An-
teny Brygham. Als Smith*. Will. Smyth*.
John Masthalls wife. Mr Whitton. Will
Smyth's wife*. Robert Watlyngton's wife*.
Sir Thomas Englefold, knight. Barnard
Gorffyn*. Margarett, servant to Ric. Dodge-
son*.

1537-8. Walter Barton* Knyll xij^d.
(" Rec. for the grave of Wat Barton & Couyng
the same w^t a stone vij^s viij^d.")
William Coke & his wife. Welsshe's wife.
Justynyan's wife. Will. Paslow's wife. Rec.
for tollyng at the t'lment for the Brethern
of Ebs masse. (First entry of the kind.)

1538-9. John Barfotts wife*. Karyn Carpent*. William Buryton's wife.* Andrew Wright's
wife*. John Buk. John Vansby's wife.
Will Lyppescombe's wife.

1539-40. Christian White*. Robert Ellys*. John

Butteler*. Hugh Frankleyn's wife. William Turner*.

1541-2. Mistress Margarett Watts*. John Byrds wife*. John Andrew*. John Rede als Skynner*. Dodgesons mayd,*—(see 1536). Thomas Myrthe*. Mr Marble*. Chas. Miller*. John Appowell*. M^{res} Everard*. Elizab. Kempsall*. Nic. Nicholas children*. Ric. Bexe. Margaret Watts. John Bede.

1542-3. Sir Willi3^{a}m,* chapleyn to Sir Willi3^{a}m Penyson, Knyght. Mrs. White*. Mrs. Thornell. Stephen Cawodd. David Willi3^{a}m's wife.

1543-4. Robert Watlyngton*. Roger Johnson*. Thomas Knyght*. Mr Edward the King's servant*. Will. Edmund's wife. "Rec. for tyllyng at the _tment of Mr. Justice_ iiij^d." Will Barbor's wife. John Shawe. M^{res} Cambye. John Kent*. John Vansbye*. James Hoberd's wife. Gilbert Johnson's wife*. Nicholas Niclas' child*.

1544-5. James Wild*. Mrs. Butler*. John Cutley's wife. Mr Potter. Gatlei's wife.

1545-6. Joan Knight*. ("Rec. for the grave of M^{res} Barton and for couyng of the same vij^s iiij^d.") Robt. Roys.

1546-7. John Barfote*. Xpofer Fuller's wife*. Ric. Dodson's wife*. Thomas Mason's wife*. Mr Turner.

1547-8. Gilbert Johnson*. Peter Laurence. Robt. Ellys' wife. M^{res} Watlynton*. M^{res} Nicholas. Richard Novys. ("Rec. for the knyll of Mr Justice xij^d*." "Of the grave of Mr Justice vij^s iiij^d."

1548-9. Hugh Goodwyn*. "One that dyed at Perkyns." John Trumflet*. Rob. Hodson. Margaret Slythurst*. Rob. Stanshawe. Nicholas Niclas*. Robt Bell.

1549-50. Mother Barker. Mother Chamberlayn. Rec. for the knyll of the Vicar. Alice Trumflett*. Edward Phillippes' wife*.

1550-1. Mr Bearde. Thom^{a}s Malthows. Hugh Beke. Robt Blake. Mr Buckland*. Sawnder's wife*. John Wheler*.

1551-2. Thomas Perkyns*. M^res Myrth*. Joh^nne (Joan) Aldeworthe*. Raphe Gladwyn*.

1552-3. William Bureton*. Anthony Chapman*. Will. Davy & his wife*. Will. Avis wife*.

1553-4. Radley's wife*.

1554-5. Richard Mathewe*. Edmund Raynefford*. Peersie the corior*. Yerpes wife*. John Fforman*.

1555-6. John Poynt3*. Will. Parslowe*. Richard Court-ney*. Peter Reade. Edward Butler's childe. Walter Beryngton's childe—(Buryton). Thomas Hunt's wife. William Watlington.

1556-7. John Reade*. Richard Dodson*. Thomas Sent-man*. James Edmonde*. Will. Edmonde*. A boy Thomas Edmonde. Mrs Turner*. Mrs Bell*. Goodwyfe Wyar*. Goodw. Johnson*. Isabell Moore*. Will. Avyys*. Harry Wat-lyngton*. John Myllar. Agnes Myllar.

1557-8. Goodw. Huggens*. Will. Baynton. Ric. Smythe*. Goodwife Watlyngton*. Goodman Chaun-trell*. Robart Myllwarde*. Goodw. Benwell. Goodman Harpyn*. Syr Willyam Webbe. The Curryar*. Mrs Bourne. Mayster Bourne. Goodw. Ffawsby*. Goodm. Constable*. Peter Barber's wife. Mother franklyn. Tayler the smith's mother & father. Goodm. Nightingale's mayde. Mr Perkyns.

1558-9. Mrs Beake. Goodm. Allesaunder. Goodm. Saun-ders*. Geo. Wray. Goodw. Sentman*. John Bowlde. Leonard Brewar. Ric. Whitbourne. Goodm. Tayler's wife. Goodm. Alexander's wife. Harry Touse. John Pyckton. John Cater.

1559-60. John Coopar. G-w. Constable. Mystres Clyfford. G-w. Mathewe. John Andrew's wife. Will. Martyn. Maister Bygg. John Gateley's wife. Edmond Locke. Goodm. fynmore's child. G-w. Cater. G-w. Burgeys. Allesaunder. Will. Haslett's child. John Braysey. Francis Beake. Eliz. Rewby. Annys Church. Ric. Fostbury. John Radley's maid.

1560-1. John Huggens. Jone Coopar. Goodm. Wellsh. Goodm. Hookar. Jeffery Coopar's wife & child.*

1561–2. John Alloway. Richard Knyght. Will. Wilde. Jone Myles. Jone Butler. Agnys Hydar. Thom. Ffawkesby. Widow Cooper*. Goodw. Shaw.*

1562–3. Father Moore. Nicholas Watlyngton. John Webb's wife*. The olde Tanner. Jone ffyne. Mr Will. Watlyngton*. Agnes Gybbens.

1564–5. Mrs Tylby*. Anys Burges. Alice Shawe. John Phillypp. Ric. Wellshe. Annys Clement. Mother Ryther.

1565–6. "Mr Blacgrove's wyffes knyll xx^d." Maister Vachell's daughter. Maister Pollington's wife*. Ric. Lock's wife*. Thomas Benwell. John Downar*. Maister Butler's son*. Thomas Crome. G-w. Dennys. Edwd Phillypp. Tho. Ffraye. G-m. Tanner. G-w. Phillypp.

1566–7. "Of Thomas Kenryck for a priest*—knell xx^d: grave 7^s 4^d." Roger Greete. Gregory's wife. Ellis Burgey's daughter. John Cooper's son. John Gryffyn's wife.

1567–8. G-m. Bush. Rich. Constable*. Tho. Lightfoote. Mother Kenryck. G-w. Levered. Salter's wife.

1568–9. Henry Biggs wife*. "Mystres Okham (of the Abbye)". Martha Hubbard. Mrs Rudge*. Ales Rudge. Mr John Rudge*. Rich. Turner's servant. Jone Jenkyns. James Hubbard.

1569–70. Mr Turnar*. Rob. Grantam. G-m. Wells*. G-w. Battye. Gryffen's wife. Well's dau. Thomas Segar.

1570–1. Mary Buckland*. Goodman Robynson the "fullar"*. Davye Playne. G-w. Ffaythfull. G-w. Arlatt*. Ales Wake. Widow Harryson's child. Joynar's wife. Stonyford's son.

1571–2. Avery Berry's wife's sister. "The Cardmaker." Will. Duddlesoll's chylde. William Budde*. Thomas Philpe.

1572–3. Edwd Vynge. Thom^s Humfery. Gryffen Morgayne. Christopher Porter. Hen. Bryges. Hen. Lendall. Tho. Thorne. Olde Mother Staples. Johanne Harrys. Hen. Cove. Alice Browne. Ric. Burges. Marg. Ryder. Johanne Banester. Steph. Goldinge. Peter Horne.

Hen. Brygges. Old Father Horne. Joan
Browne. Agnes Browne. Adam Denys.
Nich. Turner.

1573–4. Goodman Jefferie*. Goodwife Budde. Mr. Blake.
Goodwife Locke. G-w. Welche. G-w. Prior.
John Roberts. G-w. Johnson. Agnes Grea.
Goodman Woodward. G-m. Jimmatt. Wood-
ward's wiffe. Wtłm Slater. Burgesses
man. Will. Sawyer. G-m. Welles. Robin-
son's childe. Mʳˢ Webbes child. G-m.
Web.

1574–5. Will. Walker. Alice Wells. Roger Clyfforde.
Anthony Beake. Jonas Ffringe. Rychard
Rolte. Margᵗ Wyer. Mary Downer. Ric.
Bourneham. Walter Morris. John Jenens.
Johanne Gamon. Ralfe Deaton. Alex-
aunder Kinge. Agnes Downer. Ric.
Drewe. Avicia Byrcham.

1575–6. Mʳ Bowyer. Mʳ Ockham. Mother Horsley.
Esdras Cooper's childe. Mother Redwood.
G-w. Rutter. Wᵐ Nightingall's man. Ro-
binson. Goodman Thornes child. Goodwife
Bonyvant.

1576–7. Roger Nightingall*. Mʳˢ Hoskins. G-w.
Deddlesall*. Mʳ Doleman's man*. John
Shrive's wife*. John Robinson*. John
Gateley*. the Joyner that died at
Dennetts. Pyther's wife. Mʳ Aldworth.
Edwᵈ Locke.

1577–8. John Ryder. Goodwife Child's mother. Gardener's
wife. Ric. Turner's daughter. Wodenson's
wife. John Williams wife's dau. Will.
Knight's dau. Wtłm Simonds the Turcke
his knell viijᵈ. Will. Rogers. Trapman's
maid. An apprentice of London. One
Hosier's wife of London. Averie Derrie's
dau. Will. Dedollsall. John Dedullsall.

From Mich. 1578 to Mich. 1579. Hen Bigge's wife*.
Christoph. Staper's brother. " Itm. for the
knill of Wm. Lawds mother ijˢ vᵈ." Hunte.
Widow Wolfe's husband.

1579–80. Mʳ Edmonds*. Ric. Welling. John Shrieve.
John Arlette. Geo. Lams*. Will. Walwin's
child. John Griffen.

1580-1. Mrs Lendall*.   Mrs. Turner*.   Blackall the
clothier. Will. Genynge. John Dumper's
child. Jones. Doddese's wyfe.

1581-2. Goodwife Dell. Tho. Walker's wife. Goodman
Dawson. Elizab. Knyght. John Browne.
Hen. Taylor. Jone Wilcox. Will. Walwyn.
G-w. Berde. John Walles. Anne Browne.
Jane Patie. John Lendall. Mr. Hopkin's
child. Marg^t Wilkenson. Alice Evans.
G-w. Horslye.

1582-3. John Huggins*.   Mrs Butler*.   Leonarde Andrew. Ylkenson. Mother Mooraway. G-w.
Nycholson. Joseph Carter's child. Blake's
wife. Olde Woddell. Higg's wife.

1583-4. Ant. Grauntham*. Mrs Staverton*. G-w. Stryke.
Olde ffather Hayes. Rychard Aldworthe.
" Mr Edward Butler his knill ij^s vj^d."
Old Agnes Reed. Hen. Bigg's child. Ales
Rydge. "*My* mother in law Bateman"—
(Ffrancys Sykes and John Moore, C.W.).
Tho. Clawbutt's child. Rob. Monday's
child. Mr Harries' child. Coomes the card-
maker's son. " One of the gromes of o^r
queene's stable." Blackall his child. Hen.
Biggs his child. Bawlterstone's child.

1584-5. John Webb. Thomas Knight's wife. Thomas
Beale. Mr Lydall's child. Nich. Higgs.
Mr Hopkin's child. John Browne.
Thomas Grea. Strik's child. Walter Wat-
lington's child.

1585-6. William Lendall*. Knight*. Green's wife*.
Soffe's wife*. G-w. Stokes. G-w. Morrys.
Greene's wife. Strowde's wife. G-w. Bar-
nard. G-w. Goffe. Goswell. G-m. Thorne.
Gaston's wife. Edwd M^undaie. Mr Ffi-
ppenie.

1586-7. Mother Come's Grave*.   Elizabeth Remish*.
Gilbert Aldworth. Thomas Bagley.
Richard Arlott. Andrew Strike. Nicholas
Saunders. John Stratton. Richard Lock.
Goslen. Wimper's wife. Edward Brambley.
Robert Jonson. Richard Burges. ffather
Randole. Ald. Redwood. Curtise wife.
Oliver Hanley's son. Beenam's wife.

Ffoster's wife. Cater's wife. ffather
Pyther. Ellys Tomson. Widow Whyte.
Old Bennett. Dumper's wife. Mason's
child. Cotterell's child.

1587-8. John Moon's wife*. Avery Berry*. Rowland
Combe. Goodwife More. Mr Kenrick.
Mapleton's wife. Margaret fford. Beatrice
Gilkins. Bigg's child. James Winch's
man. John Child's child. Hugh Prior's
wife. Haile's child.

1588-9. John Maine*. Mrs Child*. Mrs Daver's man*.
Willm Crisselton*. Matthew Reynolds. M^r
Townsend*. Collen's wife. Walter Hawke's
wife. Mr Callys. Mother Pastler. Weaver's
wife. Mother Cooper. Mrs Turner's child.
Richard Weaver. Denshire. Agnes Sturton.
Mathew Renolds. Simon Dee's child.
Michael Hamblen's child. John Brambley's
child. John Russell's child. Mother Patie's
child. John Combe's child. Edwd Nichol-
son's child. Thick's dau. Lane's child.
Mr Whitton's dau. Mr Whitton's child.
Glover's wife.

1589-90. Widow Heynse. Goodwife Ryder. Mrs Radley.
James Baker's wife. Mr Burson. Widow
Crisselton. John Dumper. Agnes Seaman.
Richard Jonson. More's child. Robert
Childe. Miles' dau. John Newman's child.
William Nightingall's child. Leonard Leve-
rett. Edward Lambole's child. Morgan's
son. Nicholas' grand-daughter. Braker's
daughter. Walter Watlington's maid. John
Walsh's maid.

1590-1. Ffather Robinson*. Mrs Powell* (dau. of Ed.
Butler). Eliz. Johnson. William Inglish.
James Sexe's wife. Goodw. Russel. Mother
Browne. Mr Whitehead of the Q. stable.
Jane Nightingall. Jone Goodwin. Mother
Swan. Robert Browne. William Young.
Yeoman's wife. Walter Watlington's child.
John Eelye. Richard Brodde. John Walker's
child. John Butcher in the ffriers. Mother
ffoxe. John Sone's child. Jefferee Jenyns.

1591-2. Edmund Cooper's wife*. Lawrence Barn's wife.

John Gallant's wife.   Christopher Barnard.
Robert Bowyer.   Mr Robert Knoles his
daughter. Goodw. Henden. William Grene's
child.   Matthewe's child.   Alice Knight.

1592-3.   Rouland Come's wife*. Thomas Turner*. Good-
man Moore. Mrs Dorothie Hopkins. Good-
man Pythers. Goodman Cloiton. John Sone.
Fforest's wife.   Mr Witton.   Mr Brighton.
Thomas Turner.   Willm (Mr Daver's man).
Goodwife Venter.   Mother Venter.   John
Servgood.   Thomas Tutler.   Eadde.   John
Russell's child.   John Newson's child. Hen.
Ffreeman's child.   Thorne's child.

1593-4. "Received for Wittm Lawd's grave vij^s iiij^d."*
This William Lawd was the father of the
illustrious Archbishop.   He was a native
of Wokingham.   Mr. Bruce, in his history
of the Archbishop's Benefactions to Reading, states that the father resided in a
house on the north side of Broad Street in
Reading.   Its site is now called 'Lawd
Place.'   He carried on the trade of a
clothier, and filled all the offices in the
town save the mayoralty. His wife " Lucy"
was the daughter of John Webbe of
Wokingham, and sister of Sir William
Webbe, Lord Mayor of London in 1591.
She was first married to John Robinson, a
clothier in Reading, by whom she had a
son William, afterwards a Doctor in Divi-
nity, Prebend of Westminster and Archdeacon of Nottingham, and five daughters,
one of whom was the mother of Dr. Cots-
ford, and the other of Dr. Layfield, both
eminent clergymen.   The Abp. was the
only issue of his mother by the second
marriage. He was born in Reading 7 Oct.
1593.
See under 1570-1 of this Obituary for " Goodman Robynson the fullar" (Mrs. Laud's first
husband), 1578-9 for the Archbishop's grand-
mother (probably buried at Wokingham),
and 1601, for the burial of the Archbishop's
mother. The monuments belonging to this

family in St. Lawrence's would most cer-
tainly be destroyed by the " Roundheads
& Rebells" when quartered in the church in
1643. There is no memorial in this town to
the Archbishop or his family, although this
prelate was one of its greatest benefactors.
Widow King*. Goodwife Ffreuen. Good-w.
Staples. Davye Vaghan. Mrs Hopkins.
Mr Ffilmer. Willm Simmes. Good-w.
Welles. Mr Richard Aldworth, maior. Jone
Knight. Elizab. Millsopp. John Curteis'
sonne. Willm Wigmore. Ellen Walker.
John Cater. Thomas Ayres. Margarite
Martin. Bradley's childe. Fforest's childe.
Anne Wintersall.

1594-5. Richard Rider*. William Thorne's wife. John
Ffoote. William Walwin. Agnes Walton.
Thomasin Carden. William Linger. George
Bradford. Camelle's child. Thomas Willis'
childe. Thomas Cutler.

1595-6. Nicholas Mansfielde*. Henry Bigg*. Thomas
Page*. Old Mr Child*. Anne Warner.
Richard Morrall. Thomas Lewes. Andrew
Taylor. Anne Newton. Anne Watlyngton.
John Watlyngton. John Andrew. Henry
More. Elizabeth Aylerd. Thomas Page.
Marie Jones. Alice Rivers. Thomasin
Sinwell. Robt. Malton's son. Gabr. Barne's
child. Jone Cavie. Collys Browne. George
Androw. Mr Charlton's child. Collin's wife.
Jone Yeomans. Margerie Benson. Alex-
ander Read. Bartlemew Walker. John
Pound. Richard Watlington. Mary Stevens.
Richard Watlington. Robert Hicks. Ed-
ward Skinner. "*In ye Abbey*—Thomas
More's child." Widow Lightfoot.

1596-7. Beniamin Turner*. William Jhonson*. Johane
Gatelie*. Edmund Percke*. Richard Cook's
wife*. Mrs Jhonson*. Mr Beeke*. William
Clemment. Roger Watlington. Elizabeth
Smithe. Nicholas Child's wife. Robert
Mondie the butcher. Robert Johnson's
wife. Christian Neele. Alice Maie. Beniamin
Turner. Christopher Porter. Roger Webb's

child.   Redigunt Clarke.   John Weston.
Johañn Carr. Anne Weston. Alice Wick-
moore. Agnes Willis. Marie Barrett. Chris-
tian Tayler.   Elizabeth Clifford.   Roger
Ffraunces. Richard Fforster. A servant of
Edw. Birmingham's. Roger Bayley. John
Staples' wife.   Johanne Aylard.   Alice
Walker. Patteson's child. William Walker.
John Staples glover. Old Simmes. John
Carre.

1599. Mr Stamp*. Bryde's wife*. Paule Sadon. Katherine
Carter. Miller. Thomas Shepherd. Kathe-
rine Smithe. Eliz. Byde. Rich. Byde's wife.
Anne West. William Walwin. Katherine
Seyman. William Ffindye. Alice Sutton,
widow. Mary *Beallucke* (? Bralluck). Garrett
Smyth. Robt Moore. Thomas Moore. Wil-
liam Thorpe. Thomas Prentall. Katherine
Stone. Eliz. Ebson. George Millesant. Ellis
Marten. Sibill Hass. Nicholas Stone.

1600. Barnard Harrison*. Mr Ellis Burges. Mr William
Lendall. Mr Symson. Mr Barnard's wife.
Roger Walker's sonne.   Andrew Applebee.
Thomas Nightingall. John Walker's child.
John Benge's child.   William Marshall.
Maryan Blinson. Agnes Watts. Robert
Dee's child. Joan Welsh. John Braker.

1601. George Burgess*. Willm Dell*. Mother Andrews.
Mr Richard Johnson.*
"R^d for the graue of Wyddowe Lawd & for
breking the ground vij^s viij^d."* (See under
1593-4.)
Roger Dawson. Robert Maulthus child. John
Pinnsye's child. Agnes Barnes. Margaret
Barfoote. William Walker's child. Ffrancis
Blake's child. John Bent. Robert Smyth.
John Walker's child.

1602. Henry Mayne*. Mr Alexander*. Mrs Moore*.
John Brock's wife*.   Richd Watlyngton.
Thomas Hussey. Mr Alexander. Arthur
Curtice wife. Mr Richard Watlington. M^{rs}
Moore (see 1595-6). Robert Maulthus wife.
Widow Bailey. Richard Wells. John Brock's
wife. Robert Bailey. William Marshall.

Ellyn Barrett. Bailey's wyddowe. Richard Ffowler. William Staples' childe. Dannes wife. Ellen Hawle. John Gylle. Elizab. Hill. John Graye. William Greene's child.

1603. Mrs Carter's sister. Ric. Dell's child. John Symons' child. Edwd Thorbe's child. John Haryson. Danyell Clear's child. Mrs Fillmer. Goodman Collis. Elizabeth . . . . Joane Glasse. John Maynerd. Joan Watlington. Denes Vnderwood.

18 Feb. Mr Myller's chyld.*

Father Thomas Wye. John Hutchens. Anthony Bryant. John Gunter. George Rowdes. Lawrence Wayght. John Gibens. John Bishop. Ayles Noble.

"Rec^d of Sir Francis Knowles x^s." (for a burial).

M^rs An Kendrick. Thomas Levence. John West. John Dawson. Leonard Myller. Ambros Wheyatt. Nathanyell Jemvit.

1604. Goodwyff Kyng's husband, & her man John Swayne. Robert Harmes. Margaret Rumsey. Alse Justice. Nycholas Stoane. Annis Burden*. Joane West. Harry Moore's boy. John Martyn. Wydow Burgis*. Alse Hulbard. Joane Aley. John Rumsey. Ffrancis Wilmat. Gregory Hissby. Mrs Adams. Robert Haryson.*

"Rec^d of my brother Willyam Ffynmore, executor to my mother Anne Ffynmore 12^d."

Goodman Baker. Goodman Bramley. John Irysh. Anne Springall. Georg Porchmouth's child. M^res Harrys. Richard Traphels. Annys Elezander. William Conoway's child. John Bramley. Eleyzander Withers. Ekary (equerry) Collett.

Churchyard.

"M. that in the monthe of August in the yere of our Lord M.D.lvj and in the iij^d & iiijth yere of the regnes of our souaigne Lord & Lady Philipp & Marie by the g^{a}ce of god kyng & Quene of Englond Spayne ffraunce of bothe Ciciles, Jer̃m & Irelond, Defendors of the faithe, Archduke of Austrie, Duke of Burgundie, Millayne & Brabant, Counties of Haspurge fflanders & Tiroll: John Bell then beyng Mayo^r of the Borough of Redyng, Hit was then gr^{a}unted by the Quenys ma^{te} vnto thenh̃itants of the pisshe of Seynt Laurence w^{t}in the seid Borough of Redyng a Certayne grounde Lying next vnto the pisshe Churche ther, ffor to erecte & make therof a Churche yarde for the seid Churche & pisshe, as by the walls & enclosur^s thereof then & ther made it doth & may appere, whiche seid grounde for the seid Churche yarde so gr^{a}unted was & is in recompence to the seid inh̃itants & pisshe of & for another Church yarde of late belongyng vnto the seid pisshe, lying next vnto the late Churche of the late Mon^n ther, and from the seid inh̃itants taken. The charg^s of makyng of the seid newe Churche yarde was borne & paied by thenh̃itants of the seid pisshe in man^r) & fo^{r}me as heraft̃ followith, that is to witt for eu̇y perche of the seid wall contenying xviij fotes, vij^s.

John Bell, mayo^r iij pches, xxj^s.
Wiĺłm Edmunds j pce & di x^s vj^d.
Edward Butler, iij pches, xxj^s.
Thom^s Turner, iij pches, xxj^s.
Thom^s Byggs, ij pches, xiiij^s.
Water Beryngton, j pche & di, x^s vj^d.
Richard Watlyngton, j pche & di, x^s. vj^d.
Thom^s Sayntmore, j pche, vij^s.
Robt Tylbye, j pche, vij^s.
Richard Dodson, j pche, vij^s.
John Radley, j pche, vij^s.
Xpofer Beryngton, j pche, vij^s.
Richard Johnson the yong ., ij pches, xiiij^s.
Henry Osbo^{r}ne, j pche, vij^s.
John Sawnders, j pche, vij^s.
John Coup, j pche, vij^s.
Wiĺłm Lyppescombe, j pche, vij^s."

The new churchyard was hallowed on the second day of May, "beying Sonday in the yere of our Lord, 1557," by "William Ffynche Suffrigan vnto the Bisshopp of Bathe & Welles."

The following entries relate to the old churchyard on the north side of the Abbey Church :

1501–2.   " It. payed for mendyng of the churchyerd wall x^d."

1504–5.   " It. payed to Macrell for pavyng of the aleys of the churchyerd & for beryng away of

1507-8   the same pavyng ij^s."

    " It. payed to Willm. Poo subsexton for sellyng of the nettyls in the church yerd wher the vycar hath gevyn the pfy3t therof for kepyng of the same iiij^d."

    (Observe the vicar's rights in his parochial freehold at this time).

1547–8.   " Paid for repacõns done vppon the wall of the church yard, v^s."

The following record of an encroachment is preserved in the 3rd Register :—

" In April 1699.

    Memorandum that Mr Burgis, draper, then rail'd in a little part of the Churchyard by connivence of the then vicar, for to adde a decency to his Dwelling House, the Landlord of which is Sr Walter Clargis. He is to suffer any parishioner (that desires it) to be buryed there, And any Vicar that hereafter is instituted and inducted into the Church, may chuse whether he wil suffer those Rails to be kept up or not.

        As witnesseth

            Phannel Bacon, Vicar."

Another encroachment was made in the same locality by the builders of the new Town Hall in 1881, when several bodies were disturbed. The churchyard was considerably enlarged on its eastern side in 1791 by the enclosure of a portion of the Forbury. The last interment therein occurred on the 5th of June, 1879.

List of the Church Registers.

1. Baptisms and Births, from 13 April, 1605, to May 5, 1654.
   Weddings, from Apr. 10, 1605, to May 3, 1654.
   Burials, from 12 Apr. 1605, to May 17, 1654.

   > (There are no records of burials from 1644 to 1654.)
   > Of vellum, measuring 15½ in. by 6 in., in good condition.

2. Births, from May 21, 1654, to Oct. 2, 1683.
   Baptisms, from May 23, 1654, to Sep. 22, 1688.
   Publications of Intended Marriages, from June 4, 1654, to Feb. 14, 1668.
   Marriages, from June 20, 1654, to 16 May, 1686.
   Burials, from May 24, 1654, to June 2, 1687.

   > Of vellum 15½ in. by 6 in.—good condition.

3. Baptisms, from April 4, 1686, to 26 Sep. 1724.
   Marriages, from Mar. 27, 1686, to 10 Oct. 1724.
   Burials, from 25 Mar. 1686, to Sep. 27, 1724.

   > In this vol. is a list of "Briefs" from 1686 to 1735. Of paper, and in good preservation, 18½ in. long and 8 in. wide.

4. Baptisms, from 4 Oct. 1724, to Mar. 25, 1772.
   Marriages, from 4 Oct. 1724, to Mar. 25, 1754.
   Burials, from 5 Oct. 1724, to Mar. 25, 1772.

   > 20½ in. by 8 in.—well written—vellum sides, leather back—wants a little repairing.

5. Marriages, from Apr. 25, 1754, to June 18, 1762.

   > Includes the Regist. of Banns to 1771.
   > 15 in. by 9 in.—paper—good preservation—rough calf binding.

6. Marriages, from June 23, 1652, to Mar. 22, 1772.

   > 15 in. by 9 in.—paper—rough calf binding.

7. Baptisms, from Mar. 25, 1772, to Dec. 31, 1812.

Burials, from Mar. 25, 1772, to Dec. 29, 1812.

    15 in. by 10 in.—good preservation, but wants rebinding.

8. Marriages, from 29 Mar. 1772, to 16 Feb. 1779.

    14½ in. by 9 in.—fair preservation—rough calf binding.

9. Marriages, from 22 Apr. 1779, to 29 Dec. 1812.

    15 in. by 10 in.—rough calf—wants rebacking.

10. Baptisms, from 4 Jan. 1813, to Sep. 21, 1834.

    15 in. by 10 in.—forel cover.

11. Marriages, from 11 Jan. 1813, to 9 Feb. 1834.

    15 in. by 10 in.—good paper—forel binding.

12. Burials, from 1 Jan. 1813, to Dec. 20, 1840.

    15 in. by 10 in.—very good paper—forel binding loose.

13. Baptisms, from 22 Sep. 1834, to 24 Feb. 1859.

    Good paper—forel binding loose.

14. Marriages, from 11 Jan. 1813, to 9 Feb. 1834.

    Sound paper—good condition—forel binding.

15. Burials, from 1 Jan. 1813, to Dec. 20, 1840.

    Good paper—fair condition—forel.

16. Baptisms, from Feb. 26, 1859 to present time.

    Good condition.

17. Marriages, from Feb. 9, 1834, to June, 1837.

    Good condition.

18. Burials, from Dec. 22, 1840, to June 5, 1879. (The last interment,)

    14 in. by 10 in. Good.

19. Marriages, from July 24, 1837, to Apr. 21, 1847.
20. Marriages, from Apr. 25, 1847, to Aug. 16, 1856.
21. Marriages, from Aug. 19, 1856, to May 11, 1869.
22. Marriages, from May 17, 1869, to present time.

Collections on "Briefs" in the Parish Church of St. Lawrence—out of the 3rd Register.

1686. Oct. For distressed inhabitants of Whitechapel and Stepney, £3 os. 5½d.

1695. Dec. 22. For inhabitants of Grantchester, Cambridge. Loss by fire 1250£. Coll. 9s. od.

1695. Mar. 15. Fire at Gillingham, Dorset. Loss 3900£. Collected 12s. 6d.

1695. Mar. 20. Inhabitants of York. Loss 18000£. Coll. £3 2s. od.

1695. Mar. 20. Netherhaven and Fiddleton, Wilts. Loss 4590£. Coll.

1696. Mar. 29. For John Avery, of Twyford, Hants. Loss by fire 400£.

1696. July 19. Some inhabitants of Streatham.

1699. May 15. For French Refugees, first to leave the Duke of Savoy's country, £23 9s. 9d.

1703. Apr. 4. For Robt. Bales, Maltster, a loser by fire at Dunnington, Yorks., W.R., 1135£. Coll. 8s. 3d. ("Dinington").

1703. July 4. For church of St. Germains, in Salop, York, 9s. 4½d. Estimated repairs, 4000£.

1703. July 25. For repairs of Lutterworth Church, Leicester, 1528£. wanted. Coll. 9s. od.

1703. Sept. 9. For loss by fire in Fordingbridge, Hants, to amount of 5059£ 19s. od. Coll. £1 7s. 6d.

1703. Oct. 24. Fire in Spitalfields, London. Loss 1200£. Coll. 9s. od.

1703. Nov. 17. Fire at Tuxford, Notts. Loss 2666£ 3s. 4d. Coll. £1 6s. 7d.

1703. Jan. 27. Repairs of Shrewsbury church, Salop. Damage estimated, 4462£ 18s. 6d. Coll. 20 shill.

1703-4. Feb. 6. Fire in Wapping. Loss, 13,040£. Coll. 13s. 1d.

1703-4. Mar. 12. Fire in St. Giles-in-the-Fields, London. Loss, 1543£. Coll. 8s. od.

1704. Apr. 27. Relief of Refugees of the Principality of Orange. Coll. £12 17s. 8d.

1704. Sep. 6. " Collected there in the parish from House

to House for the Relief of Seamen's widdows and orphans upon the account of the dreadful storm vpon November the 26th, 1703, £5 5s. 2d."

1704. Oct. 22. For Will. Brampton, of Stockton, in Stanton Lacy, Salop. Loss by fire, 1536£. Coll. 14s. 8d.

1704. Nov. 30. For Repair of Monks Kerby Church, Warwick, damaged by the wind, to 1497£. Coll. £1 11s. 4d.

1704. Dec. Fire in Great Massingham, Norfolk. Damage 1486£. Coll. 11s. 0d.
South Molton fire, Devon. Loss 2234£. Coll. 10s. 0d.
Stoney Stratford fire, Bucks. Loss, 1669£. Coll. 14s.

1705. Sep. 24. Rebuilding of All Saints' Church, Oxford. Coll. £3 0s.

1705. Nov. 4. Fire at Rolleston, Stafford. Loss 1134£. Coll. 9s. 0d.

1705. Dec. 16. Fire at Kirton, Lincolns. Coll. 10s. 0d.

1705. Feb. 17. Fire, Bankside, St. Saviour's, Southwark. Loss 1131£. Coll. 7s.

1705. Mar. 10. Fire in Bradmore, Notts. Loss 2400£. Coll. 10s. 7d.

1706. Mar. 31. Fire at Chatteris, Isle of Ely. Coll. 7s. 0d.

1706. June. Fire at Inniskillen, Ireland. Loss 8166£. Coll. £2 16s. 11d.

„ July 29. Repair of Beverley Church, Yorks. Coll. £1 0s. 1d. Damage 3500£.

„ Sept. 15. For Mr Will Smith of Anchorwicke, Wyradisbury, Bucks—for a loss by fire. Coll. 16s. 1d.

„ Oct. 20. Fire in Morgan's Lane, Southwark. Damage 2706£. Coll. 10s. 4½d.

„ Nov. 24. Fire at Great Torrington, Devon. Damage 1600£. Coll. 9s. 3½d.

„ Dec. 15. Repairs of Basford Church, Notts. Coll. 9s. 6d.

1706-7. Mar. 9. Repairs of Darlington Church, Durham. Damage 1704£. Coll. 13s. 0d.

„ June 8. Fire in North Marston, Bucks. Loss 3460£. Coll. 7s. 10d.

1706–7. June 22. Repairs of Broseley Church, Salop. Damage 1390£. Coll. 8s. 0d.

1707. July 13. Fire in Towcester, Northampton. Loss 1057£. Coll. 10s. 0d.

    „ July 27. Fire in Shireland, Middx. Loss 3505£. Coll. 10s. 6d.

    „ August 31. Fire at Spilsby, Lincolns. Loss 5984£. Coll. 11s. 6d.

    „ Sep. 21. Fire in Little Port, Isle of Ely. Loss 3931£. Coll. 12s. 6d.

    „ Nov. 23. Fire at Heavytree, Devon. Loss 991£. Coll. 6s. 1d.

    „ Dec. 7. Repairs of Dursley Church, Gloucester. Loss 1995£. Coll. 9s. 1d.

    „ Dec. 21. Repairs of Orford Church, Suffolk. Loss 1450£. Coll. 10s. 6d.

1707–8. Jan. 11. Fire in Woodhurst, Huntingdon. Loss 583£. Coll. 9s. 2d.

    „ Mar. 14. For building a Protestant church at Oberbarmen, Duchy of Berg. Coll. £1 6s. 6d.

    „ Mar. 18. Fire at Soulham, Warwick. Loss 4454£. Coll. 14s. 0d.

1708. Apr. 25. Fire in Charles Street, Westminster. Loss £3891. Coll. 14s. 0d.

    „ May 16. Fire in Bewdley, Worcesters. Loss 1384£ 4s. 0d. Coll. 10s. 9d.

    „ May 30. Fire at Alcumbury-cum-Weston, Huntingdon. Loss 3318£ 10s. Coll. 13s. 6d.

    „ June 30. Fire at Lisburne, Ireland. Loss 31770£. Coll. £3 9s. 0d.

    „ July 11. Fire at Shadwell, Middx. Loss £6137 17s. Coll. 16s. 6d.

    „ August. Fire at Wincanton, Somerset. Loss 2930£. Coll. 11s. 0d.

    „ August 22. Fire at Great Yarmouth. Loss 1228£. Coll. 14s. 4d.

1708. Nov. 3. Fire in Strand, London. Loss 17880£. Coll. £2 16s. 8d.

    „ Nov. 15. Fire in Edinburgh, Scotland. Loss 7962£. Coll. £1 15s. 3d.

1708–9. Jan. 16. Repairs of Brenchley Church, Kent. Damage 1000£. Coll. 11s. 6d.

    „ June 23. Fire in Holt Market, Norfolk. Loss 11258£. Coll. £2 7s. 3d.

1708–9. July 3. Repairs of Llanviling Church, Montgomery. Loss 1325£. Coll. 10s.

,, July 24. Rebuilding Hurlow Church, Essex, burnt down. Loss 2035£. Coll. 17s. 8d.

,, Aug. 14. Repairs of St. Mary Redcliff, Bristow. Loss 4410£. Coll. 12s. 2d.

,, Aug. 21. Several fires in Market Rayson, Lincoln and county adjacent. Loss 1228£. Coll. 11s. 9d.

,, Nov. 4. For the relief of the poor Palatins. Coll. £12 12s. 2d.

,, Dec. 3. Fire in "Stoak," Suffolk. Loss 2463£. Coll. 10s.

1709–10. Jan. 8. For building a Protestant church at Mitlau, in Courland, 15s.

1710. Apr. 30. Fire at Rotherhithe Wall, Surrey. Loss 640£. Coll. 10s.

,, May 7. Fires at Northfleet and Durant, Kent. Loss 1613£. Coll. 15s. 1d.

,, July 2. Repair of church at Ashton-super-Merly, co. Chester. Damage 2710£. Coll. 12s.

,, July 23. Rebuilding of Chalfont St. Peters Church, Bucks. Damage 1521£. Coll. 16s. 9d.

,, Aug. 13. Rebuilding of Stockton Church, Durham. Damage 2580£. Coll. 16s. 4d.

,, Nov. 26. 11s. for a fire in Twyford, Berks and Wilts. Damage 1261£.

,, Dec. 10. 7s. for a fire at Ensham, Oxon. Damage 1474£ 11s. 6d.

,, Dec. 24. 9s. 1d. for a fire in Pavingham, Beds. Damage 700£.

1711. Jan. 7. 10s. for rebuilding of Cockermouth Church. Charge 1331£.

,, Mar. 18. 12s. 7d. for Repairs of Rotherhithe Church, Surrey. Charge 4361£.

,, Apr. 15. 10s. for Repairs of Cardigan Church. Charge 2240£.

,, 21 May. 11s. 8½d. for St. Mary's, Colchester. Charge 6153£.

,, 27 May. 8s. 3½d. for Wishar Church, Warwicks. Charge 1210£.

,, 10 June. 10s. 6½d. for St. Helen's Church, alias Edington, Isle of Wight. Charge 1203£.

,, 24 June. 6s. for a fire in Edinburgh. Loss 3527£.

1711. 24 Nov. 7s. 8d. for fire at Tadmore and Market Rayson, Yorks. Loss 1169£.

„ 9 Dec. 9s. 8d. for Rebuilding of Long Melford Church, Suffolk.

1711–12. 24 Jan. £2 14s. 2d. for Rebuilding Woolwich Church, Kent. Charge 5069£.

1712. May 11. 9s. 4½d. for Charles Empson of Booth, in Howden, Yorks. Loss by fire 2000£.

„ 1 June. 6s. 7d. for a fire in Thames Street, London. Loss 1111£.

„ 15 June. 1712£ 8s. 10d. for a fire at Little Brick-hill, Bucks. Loss 1270£.

„ 6 July. £1 18s. 2d. for Rebuilding the Church of Whitechurch, Salop. Damaged to 5497£.

1712. Aug. 10. For Ric. Salter, Coleman Street, London. Loss by fire 1720£—12s. 0d.

„ Aug. 24. For rebuilding West Tilbury Church, Essex. Damage 1117£—8s. 5d.

1712–3. Jan. 11. For Adderley Church, Salop. Damage 800£—13s. 0d.

„ Feb. 15. For St Clement's, Hastings. Damage 1550£—6s. 6d.

„ Mar. 11. For Battle Bridge, Southwark. Loss by fire 12254£—2£ 8s. 6d.

„ Mar. 15. For Pensford Church, Somerset. Damage 2742£—9s. 6d.

1713. Mar. 29. For Coleorton Church and parsonage. Leicesters. Damage 2412£—11s. 0d.

„ June 10. For Burton-upon-Trent Church (repairing). Damage 3100£—£1 10s. 6d.

„ July 19. For fire at Witheridge, Devon, and at Chilton, Berks. Loss 116£—10s. 0d.

„ Aug. 9. Rebuilding of Woodham Ferrys Church, Essex. Cost 1425£—£1 0s.

„ Aug. 3. A double loss by fire by Will. Adams of Heathill in Sherif Hales, Stafford £2 0s. 3d. Loss 108£.

„ Sep. 13. For rebuilding the Steeple of Warmingham, Cheshire. Cost 885£—10s. 6d.

„ Dec. 13. Repairing Southwell Collegiate Church, Notts. Cost 3800£—£1 10s. 6d.

1713–4. Feb. 21. Fire in St. Mary Church, parish Devon. Loss 1392£—9s. 0d.

1713-4. Mar. 7. Fire at Rudgley, Stafford and at Wrexham, Denbigh. Losses 1691£. Coll. 10s. 3d.

1714. Mar. 21. Rebuilding Quatford Church, Salop. Cost 1366£—10s. 2d.

„ April 4. Repairs of St. Margaret at Cliffe Church, Kent. Cost 1384£—13s. 1d.

1714. Apr. 18. Repairing St. John Baptist Church, Southover, near Lewes. Cost 1510£—12s. 8d.

„ May 2. Repairs of Shipwash Church and Relief of Silvanus Carter, a sufferer by fire. Loss &c. 1155£. Coll. 9s. 6d.

„ June 20. For Leighton Church, Salop. Cost 1516£—7s. 0d.

„ July 4. Rebuilding of Burslem Church, Staffords. Cost 1618£—11s. 6d.

„ Aug. 2. For fire in Blandford Forum. Loss 7880£—£1 11s. 4d.

„ Aug. 15. For two fires in Dorchester, Dorset. Loss 2537£—14s. 2d.

„ Oct. 20. Fire at Bottisham, Cambridges. Loss 3659£—£1 6s. 4d.

„ Nov. 21. Rebuilding Torksey Church, Lincoln. Cost 1182£—13s. 0d.

„ Dec. 5. Rebuilding Ruthin Church, Denbigh. Cost 3128£—13s. 0d.

„ Dec. 19. Repairing New Shoreham Church, Sussex. Cost 2203£—11s. 6d.

1714-5. Feb. 5. Loss by fire of Will. Bowyer, of Whitefriars (5146£)—£2 1s. 6d.

„ Feb. 20. Fires at Preston Bagot and St. Nicholas Warwicks. (1162£)—12s. 0d.

„ Mar. 13. Rebuilding of All Saints, Derby. Cost 5252£—10s. 0d.

1715. May 22. Rebuilding St. Peter's Church, Chester. Cost 1590£—8s. 0d.

„ June 22. Towards the great loss of cows in Middlesex, Surrey, and Essex. Loss 24.539£—£2 16s. 0d.

1715. July 17. For Kentford Church, Suffolk, & of 2 sufferers by fire there (1057£)—12s. 3d.

„ Aug. 14. Sufferers by fire at Dryneton, Staffords. & Shinbridge, Gloucesters. Losses 1378£—13s. 0d.

P

1715. Aug. 28. Rebuilding St. Giles', Newcastle-under-
Line, 12s. 0d.

„ Sep. 11. Rebuilding St. Marie's, Lichfield (4966£)
—14s. 0d.

„ Nov. 20. Fire at Liverpool (3005£)—12s. 6d.

„ Dec. 4. Rebuilding of Blymhill Church, Stafford.
(1485£)—11s. 0d.

1715-6. Jan. 8. Fires at Walker Hith, Lincolns. and
Wrexham (1425£)—10s. 2d.

„ Mar. 4. For two sufferers by fire, one at Mitcham,
Surrey—other at Lythwood in Condover,
Salop (1442£)—11s. 0d.

„ Mar. 18. Rebuilding a church at Sunderland,
£2 0s. 0d.

1716. Apr. 29. Loss of John Aron by fire at Little Drayton, in Idsall als Shiffnall, Salop (1070£)—
10s. 0d.

„ June 3. Fire at Upton in Westham, Essex. In the
same Brief for a fire at Tempsford, Bedfords.
(1940£)—15s. 0d.

„ Aug. 10. Fire in Thames Street, London (7639£)
—£2 7s. 0d.

„ Oct. 3. Fire at Spalding (20,560£)—£2 0s. 1d.

„ Nov. 18. Double fire at Ottery St. Mary, Devon
(4466£)—8s. 1d.

„ Dec. 16. Rebuilding churches of Chelmarsh &
Ryton, Salop (2126£)—12s. 1d.

1716-7. Jan. 28. Reformed Episcopal Churches in Great
Poland and Polish Prussia—£5 6s. 6d.

„ Mar. 3. Fire at Ridgmont, Bedfords.—8s. 3d.

1717. Apr. 29. Fire at Houndsditch, London (5383£)
—£2 0s. 0d.

„ June 16. Benenden Church & steeple, Kent. Loss
by fire (1552£)—14s. 0d.

„ July 7. Oldbury Church, Gloucesters. Charge
1163£—12s. 6d.

„ Aug. 4. Fires at Healthwaite Hill, Yorks. & in
Whittington, Staffords. (1287£)—16s. 2d.

„ Sep. 1. Fire at Harsto . . . . Derbys. (1426£)—
13s. 6d.

„ Nov. 30. Fire at Frampton, Dorset (1560£)—
12s. 0d.

„ Nov. 17. Fire at Ellingham, Norfolk, & at Wisbeach,
Isle of Ely (1611£)—10s. 0d.

1717. Dec. 8. Fire at Putley in Morton Valence, Gloucester, and another at Townjay, Salop, 13s. 0d.

1717-8. Jan. 5. Repairing Arnold Church, Notts. Charge
290£—10s. 0d.

„ Feb. 9. Fires at Newland in Hurst, Berks. & Chip-
ping Wycombe, Bucks. (1020£)—3s. 1d.

1718. May 25. Rebuilding St. Mary's, Newington, Surrey.
Charge 1296£—12s. 6d.

„ June 15. Repairing churches of Ashbourne &
Mapleton, Derbys. Charge 3016£—13s. 0d.

„ July 6. For Grindon Church, Staffords. Charge
1350£—10s. 6d.

„ July 20. Fire at Cherrington, Warwicks. Loss
1476£—11s. 6d.

„ Aug. 24. Enlarging Penrith Church, Cumberland—
14s. 1d.

„ Sep. 28. Fire at Wilcott & Eusden, Salop. Loss
1717£—11s. 6d.

„ Oct. 26. Arely Church and Steeple—10s. 0d.

„ Dec. 7. Rebuilding Sheriff Hales Church, Staffords.
—10s. 0d.

1718-9. Jan. 4. Fire in Little St. Andrew's, Cambridge
—10s. 6d.

„ Jan. 25. Rebuilding Dolgelly Church, Merioneth.
Charge 1449£—12s. 0d.

1719. May 10. Fire at Headington, Oxon, 10s. Loss
1983£.

„ July 12. Fire in Old Radnor. Fire at Habberley,
in Kidderminster (1289£)—14s. 0d.

„ Aug. 9. Fire at Old Weston, Huntingdons.—
12s. 6d.

„ Aug. 30. Fires at Cheltenham & Lechlade, Gloucesters., & at Thornton, Hough, Bickley &
Barnston, Cheshire (1307£)—12s. 6d.

„ Oct. 11. Repairs of church & steeple of Biggles-
wade, Bedfords. Charge 1437£—12s. 0d.

„ Oct. 25. For church and steeple of Deeping, St.
James, Lincoln. Charge 1102£—11s.

„ Nov. 29. Fire at Thrapston, Northampton. Loss
3748£—12s. 0d.

1719-20. Jan. 3. Fire in Bedford Row, St. Andrew's,
Holborn. Loss 4178£—10s. 0d.

„ Jan. 17. Repairs of Hartlepool Church, Durham—
12s. 0d.

1719-20. Feb. 7. Rebuilding Hinstock Church, Salop—
11s. 0d.

  „ Mar. 13. Repairing St. John Baptist's Church,
Chester. Charge 3269£—15s. 0d.

1720. July 10. Repairs of Great Grimsby Church—14s. 0d.

  „ July 31. Rebuilding Oxstead Church & Steeple,
Surrey—12s. 6d.

  „ Aug. 25. Relief of Sufferers by Thunder & Hail in
Staffords.—£3 8s. 3d.

  „ Sept. 11. Sufferers by fire in Paris St. Exon. Loss
1067£—14s. 1d.

  „ Sept. 25. Rebuilding Kingswood Church, Wilts.
Charge 1000£—14s. 7d.

1720. Nov. 13. Rebuilding Burton Church, Cheshire,
(1548£)—13s. 6d.

  „ Nov. 27. Rebuilding St. Olave's Church, York
(1039£)—10s. 0d.

  „ Dec. 18. Fire in Igmanthorpe, Yorks., and at
Norton under Cannock, Staffords. (1133£)—
11s. 6d.

1720-1. Jan. 24. Fire at Meon Stoke, Hants (5173£)—
£3 0s. 8d.

  „ Feb. 19. Shrawardine Church & Parsonage, Salop
(1609£)—10s. 0d.

  „ Mar. 19. Fire at Swaresey, Cambridges.—10s. 6d.

1721. June 11. Rebuilding Fitt's Church, Salop (1509£)
—13s. 10¼d.

  „ July 30. Repairing Tewkesbury Church, Gloucester (3929£)—£1 13s. 3d.

  „ Aug. 13. Fire at Burcott & Wheatley, Oxon
(1847£)—9s. 6½d.

  „ Sep. 10. Fires at Lowth, Lincoln, and Newport,
Salop (1347£)—10s. 2½d.

  „ Sep. 24. Fires at Kemberton, Salop, & Dissenth,
Radnor—12s. 6¾d.

  „ Nov. 6. Kingston-upon-Hull, Yorks. (5840£)—
£2 7s. 2d.

  „ Nov. 26. Repairing Usk Church, Monmouths.—8s. 0d.

  „ Dec. 17. Fire at Amberley, Sussex—10s. 3d.

1721-2. Jan. 8. For Jenkin Vingoe, a sufferer by fire at
St. Ives—11s. 0d.

  „ Feb. 18. A fire at Welshpool—10s. 6½d.

  „ Mar. 11. Fire at Damerham, South Wilts (1365£)
—14s. 9d.

1722. May 6. Fires in Addington, Randwick & Alderton,
     in Surrey & Gloucester (1497£)—9s. 3d.

1722. May 27. Fires in Gratwood, Bilston & Newent in
     Stafford & Gloucester (1184£)—10s. 6d.

„ July 8. Rebuilding of Upper Darwen Chapel, Lan-
     cashire (1032£)—11s. 1d.

„ July 22. A fire at St. John Wapping & Wapping,
     Stepney, Middx.—8s. 0d.

„ Sep. 2. Repairing and rebuilding Bakewell Church
     & Steeple, Derby—13s.

„ Sep. 18. For Sufferers by an Inundation in County
     Palatin of Lancaster (10,227£)—£4 0s. 0d.

„ Oct. 21. Fire at All Hallows, London Wall (1000£)
     —11s. 0d.

„ Nov. 18. Fire at Abbots Bromley, Staffords.
     (2437£)—10s. 4d.

„ Dec. 16. Fire at Caldecott, Herts. (1062£)—11s. 1d.

1722-3. Feb. 11. For "a great Loss of the Inhabi-
     tants in Brithelmston (Brighton) in the
     County of Sussex by the Breaking in of y^e
     Sea."—£2 13s. 11d.

1723. May 6. For repairing the Church of St. Mary in
     Nottingham—£2 0s. 2d.

„ June 13. Rebuilding Ruddington Church, Notts.—
     13s. 4d.

„ July 21. For Repairs of Bangor Church—15s. 1½d.

„ Aug. 15. Repairing Hexham Church, Northum-
     berland—£1 10s. 0d.

„ Sept. 15. Fire at Hearsease, Radnor—12s. 8½d.

„ Nov. 4. For "large repairs" of St. Albans, Herts—
     £2 1s. 0d.

„ Dec. 22. Rebuilding of Lyons als Holt Church,
     Denbigh (1939£)—11s. 0d.

„ Dec. 29. Fire at Shennington, Gloucester—11s. 2d.

1723-4. Jan. 8. Fire at Weatherby, Yorks. (7533£)—
     £1 18s. 8d.

„ Mar. 1. Repairs of Epperston Church, Notts.
     (1311£)—10s. 6d.

„ Mar. 22. The Rebuilding of Ilkeston Church,
     Derbys. (1352£)—11s. 0d.

1724. April 19. Fire at Falmouth, Cornwall—12s. 0d.

„ May 3. Repairing Newport Church, Salop—11s. 6d.

„ May 31. Repairing Holt Market Church, Norfolk
     (1229£)—11s. 0d.

1724. June 21. Fire at Cherry Hinton, Cambridge
        (1045£)—9s. 0d.
  „ July 26. Repairs of Frodsham Church, Cheshire
        (1108£)—7s. 0d.
  „ Aug. 30. Inundation at Halifax (3395£)—14s. 8d.
  „ Sep. 13. Fire at Staverton, Northamptons.
        (2009£)—10s. 4½d.
  „ Oct. 4. Fires at Alrewas, Staffords. & Southburgh,
        Norfolk—9s. 6d.
  „ Oct 25. Fires at Michael Church, Radnor, and
        Grimston, Leicesters. (1047£)—8s. 8d.
  „ Nov. 29. Fires at Camps Hall, Cambridge, and
        Downton, Wilts (1067£)—7s. 0d.
1724-5. Jan. 3. Fire at Cricklade, Wilts (1624£)—
        8s. 0d.
  „ Feb. 7. Rebuilding Neath Church, Glamorgan—
        8s. 1d.
  „ Mar. 21. Fire at Knighton, Hereford & Laint-
        werdine, Radnor (1093£)—8s. 10¾d.
1725. Apr. 4. Repairing and Rebuilding Wirksworth
        Church, Derbys.—12s. 2d.
  „ May 23. Fire at East Morden, Dorset—11s. 0d.
  „ June 6. Rebuilding Bowley Church, Salop—9s. 0d.
  „ July 4. Rebuilding of Langton Church, Lincoln—
        12s. 2d.
  „ Aug. 11. Fire at Market Lavington, Wilts—
        £2 7s. 2d.
  „ Sep. 5. Fire at Crediton, Devon, & Kirk Deighton,
        Yorks.—9s. 6d.
  „ Nov. 7. Rebuilding Bampton Church, Westmoreland
        (1355£)—14s. 6d.
  „ Nov. 28. Rebuilding Darlastone Church, Staffords.
        —11s. 0d.
1725-6. Jan. 16. Rebuilding Waresley Church, Hun-
        tingdon (2003£)—13s. 6d.
  „ Feb. 6. Rebuilding Ormskirk Church, Lancashire
        —10s. 6d.
  „ Mar. 23. Fire at Great Torrington, Devon—
        £2 17s.
1726. June 12. For Folkestone Fishery—15s. 6d.
  „ July 8. Fire in Buckingham (19,141£)—£4 8s.
  „ Sep. 4. Rebuilding Albrighton Church, Salop—14s.
  „ Sep. 25. Fires at Alderford, Norfolk, & Great Or-
        wood, Bucks. (1070£)—14s. 6d.

1726. Nov. 8. Rebuilding St. Nicholas, Worcester—
£1 12s. 2d.

„ Nov. 27. Rebuilding Tibshelf Church, Derby—
11s. 7d.

„ Dec. 18. Rebuilding West Houghton Chapel,
Lancashire (1455£)—8s. 6d.

1726-7. Jan. 29. Rebuilding Backford church, Cheshire
(1532£)—11s. 3d.

1729. Aug 24. Fire at Rickingal & Bolshal, Suffolk—
13s.

„ Sep. 28. Repairs of Tamworth Church, Stafford—
14s. 5d.

„ Nov. 6. Fire at Stilton, Huntingdons.—£1 13s. 0d.

„ Dec. 21. Repairs of Pershore Church, Worcester—
12s. 3d.

1729-30. Jan. 13. Repairs of St. John Baptist, Gloucester—11s.

„ Feb. 22. Fire at Milbourne, Cambridge—13s. 6d.

„ Mar. 15. Fires in Middlesex and Cheshire, viz.,
Hornsey and Wheelock—11s. 2d.

1730. Apr. 5. Rebuilding Worthenbury Church, Flints.
—12s. 0d.

„ May 6. Sufferers by Fire at Copenhagen—
£1 8s. 1d.

„ May 24. Rebuilding Belston Chapel, Staffords.—
12s. 2d.

„ July 26. Fire at Hinckley, Leicesters.—14s. 8d.

„ Aug. 23. Sufferers by fire in Bearley, Warwicks.—
13s. 10d.

„ Sep. 24. Repairs of St. Michael's Church, Southampton—£2 2s. 2d.

1730. June 21. Inundation by sea at Wroot, Lincolns.
(2686£)—14s. 3d.

„ Oct. 25. Rebuilding Colnbrook Chapel, Bucks—
11s. 11d.

„ Dec. 6. Fire in Yarburgh, Lincoln—13s. 0d.

1730-1. Jan. 10. Fire in Kidderminster—7s. 8d.

„ Feb.14. For Denbigh Chapel,Denbighs.—10s. 11½d.

„ May 9. Repairs of Llandulas Church, Denbigh—
15s.

„ May 30. For the Church at Chapel-in-le-Frith,
Derbys.—14s. 0d.

„ Aug. 4. For Cathedral of Llandaff—£2 3s. 0d.

„ Sep. 5. For Teabury Church, Gloucesters.—13s. 8d.

1730–1. Oct. 3. For Misley or Mistley Church, Essex—
10s. 11½d.

   „   For Wyesdale Chapel, Lancashire—13s. 10d.

1731–2. Feb. 6. Sufferers by fire in Shirminster, Newton
Castle, Dorset—10s. 9d.

  „ Mar. 5. Sufferers by fire at Wootton-under-Edge,
Gloucesters.—11s. 0¾d.

1732. Apr. 16. Fire at Calcott, Gloucesters.—8s. 9¾d.

  „ Apr. 23. Repairs, &c. of All Saints Church,
Hastings—11s. 5½d.

  „ Sep. 3. Repairs of Draycott Church, Stafford—
11s. 3d.

  „ Oct. 15. Bishop's Norton Church, Lincolns.—12s. 3d.

  „ Oct. 29. Abbey Langr Cost (? Lanercost) church
—9s. 3d.

  „ Nov. 28. Sufferers by fire at Ramsay, Huntingdon
—£3 9s. 11d.

  „ Jan. 7. Fire at Manton, Rutland—9s. 1d.

  „ Jan. 21. Fire at North Stoneham, Hants—9s. 4d.

  „ Feb. 18. Repairs of Well Church, Lincolns.—
10s. 11d.

1732. Oct. 22. For sufferers by fire at Blandford—
£2 10s. 9d.

  „ Mar. 5. Repairs of Aberbrothock Harbour—
£1 7s. 4d.

  „ Mar. 8. Fire at Austerfield, York—8s. 5½d.

  „ Apr. 8. Repairs of Dudley Church, Worcester—
11s. 3½d.

1733. Loss by fire at (one Brief) Wood Plumpton, Lancaster—7s. 5d.

  „ Whitefield, Somerset—8s. 9½d.

  „ Waddington, Wilts—9s. 11d.

  „ Barton-upon-Humber, Lincolns.—8s. 11d.

  „ Erchfont, Wilts—16s. 2d.

  „ Aylesbury, Bucks—15s. 5¾d.

1733. Upon the Brief for Rufford Chapel, Lancaster—
£1 15s. 7d.

  „ Conington Church, Cambridge—9s. 1d.

  „ Seremby Church, Lincoln—8s. 9½d.

  „ Mitchel Dean Church, Gloucester—9s. 8d.

  „ Monmouth Church, Wales—9s. 1d.

1734. Collected upon a Brief for Ealing Church, Middx.,
May 26—13s. 0d.

  „ Monford Church, Salop, June 23—8s. 3d.

1734. Gressingham Chapel, Lancaster, July 28—13s. 3d.
„ Redmarley Church, Worcester, } Aug. 25—8s. 11½d.
„ Edengale Church, Stafford, }
„ Christleton Church, Chester, Sep. 2—11s. 0d.
„ All Saints' Church, Worcester, Dec. 8—9s. 2d.
1734. Guilden Morden, Cambridge, Oct. 27—9s. 5d.
„ Onniley, Staffords., Nov. 10—10s. 4d.
„ Barnwell, Cambridge, Jan. 23—£2 17s. 8d.
„ Epworth, Lincolns., Feb. 23—7s. 2d.
1735. June 8. Fire at Cottenham, Cambridge—8s. 10½d.
„ Apr. For Machyleth Church, Montgomery—12s. 0d.
„ May 11. North Meels Church, Lancashire—10s. 8d.

List of Vicars.

(Extracted by Rev. C. Coates from the Episcopal Registers
of Salisbury, with additions and corrections.)

PATRON.—*The Abbat and Convent.*

Register of Simon de Gandavo.

1299. 6to Id. Mar.—HUGO DE DREYTON.
1307. 5to Kal. Jan.—WILLIELMUS DE DEPEFORD.

Register Mortival.

1324. JOHN DE WYNCHEDON.
1325. 13. Cal. April.—JOHANNES DE LONGA SUTTON.

Register Wyvill.

1332. 3 Id. Maii.—WILLIELMUS DE BERTON.
1342. 3 Id. Oct.—WILLIELMUS DE APPLEFORD.
1344. Jan. 30.—ADAM ATT AUMERIE.
1349. 10 Kal. Jun.—WALTER DE HAREWELL.
„ Sep. 22.—JOHANNES DE NORTHLECH, by resignation of Harewell.

Register Waltham.

1360. 1 Aug.—HENRY LAMBYN, by the death of William, the last vicar.

1389. 9 Mar.—JOHANNES SCHIPPELAKE, by the death of Lambyn.

1397. WALTER BARTHOLOMEW.

1399. June 17.—JOHANNES SERNE.

Register Chandler.

1418. Dec. 11.—THOMAS BLOXAM.

„   Jan. 5.—LAURENCE HOREWODE, by the resignation of Bloxam.

1419. Feb. 5.—DAVID MICHELL, vicar of Tilehurst, of which the Abbat and Convent were also patrons, by the resignation of Horewode.

1420. Sep. 6.—JOHN ANDREWS, by the resignation of Michell. (See *Monuments.*)

Register Nevylle.

1428. Mar. 16.—JOHN MASON.

1434. Mar. 19.—HENRY COUPER, by the death of Mason (gave a donation to the church in 1440–1).

1434–5. Feb. 19.—WILLIAM GOLDORE, Rector of Lasham in Hampshire, by exchange with Couper . . . . ob. 1468. (See *Monuments.*)

1468. Oct. 14.—NICHOLAS MORE, M.A., by the death of Goldore. Ob. 31 Jan. 1477. (See *Monuments.*)

1477. Jan. 3.—THOMAS HILL, B.LL., by the death of More.

Register Audeley.

1502. Sep. 18.—THOMAS JUSTICE, by the death of Hill. (See *Monuments.*)

1518. Dec. 20.—RICHARD BEDOO, M.A., by the resignation of Justice.

(The will of Richard Bedoo or Bedoe is preserved at Somerset House—Reg. " Hogen," fo. 22. C.K.)

Register Campegio.

1534. Jan. 22.—JOHN MAYNSFORTH, by the death of Bedoo, reserving a pension of £12 to Thomas Justice. (Maynsforth died anno 3–4 Edward VI. 1550. C.K.)

PATRON.—*The Crown.*

1553. Sep. 12.—THOMAS GRENEWAY, canon of Christ Church.

> Between the presentation of Greneway and Radley there is a void: in 1560 is this entry—" To the preacher Mr Underwood v^s. To Richard Cam, our curate, for a fortnight xiij^s iiij^d." In an account of the vicarage given by Joel Stephens, Esq. of the Commons in 1744, to Mr. Boudry then vicar, it is stated from a record in the First Fruits Office, that in Q. Elizabeth's reign, the vicarage was in *arrears to the Crown* for the first-fruits and tenths for 13 years past.

Register Jewell.

1565. Nov. 29.—JOHN RADLEY, by the death of the last incumbent.

Register Geast.

1574. April 23.—JOHN SMITH, M.A., by the resignation of Radley. He was previously master of the Grammar School, being appointed thereto 1569.

> Anno 1589-90. "Joh^an Smithe vica. St. Laurētii." " The Queere or Chansell was lastye repaired at the Costes of the Quenes Matie, our vicar Mr Smith folowing the longe suite therof, and obteyned of the lord Treasurer through the reddye helpe and counsell of Mr Martin hir Maties Supvisor : And the L : Treasurer allotted xxix^ll x^s to be received of the Q. auditours towards the Reparations thereof, being comitted vnto Mr Ellys Burgesse, then Maior, and the sayd Vicar, to be bestowed theron: w^c was done according—1593."

1597. "Mr CHANDLER, vicar" occurs in the C.W. accounts of this year ; and the signature "Joh'an Smithe," in those of the year preceding.

1602. "Mr ABRAM CREY, vicar."

1603. Jan. 7.—JOHN DENNISON, by the death of Abraham Crey. In Hearne's "Antiquities of Glastonbury," p. 275, he gives this extract from the register of

Thatcham, in Berks—"1603, Abraham Gray,
preacher dwelling in Reading, came to
Thatcham, and died there and was buried
the 11ᵗʰ of September, 1603." (There is a
manifest discrepancy between "Crey" and
"Gray," but the name is spelt "Crey" in the
C. W. accounts of St. Lawrence's.)

Register Abbott.

1618. THEOPHILUS TAYLOR, M.A., by cession of the
last incumbent.

Register Davenant.

PATRON.—*The President and Fellows of St. John's College
in Oxford.*

1640. Aug. 5.—THOMAS LLOYD, LL.D., by the death of
Taylor.

Register Duppa.

1643. Sep. 30.—THOMAS TUER, M.A. He was admitted
of St. John's College, August 2, 1624. From
1645 to 1660 Bishop Duppa's register is
defective.

1645. DR. PORDAGE, son of Samuel Pordage, a citizen
of London. He afterwards became Rector of
Bradfield, Berks, from which he was ejected in
1654. He was reinstated after the Restoration,
and lived there several years. There is an
interesting account of him in Mr. Coates'
"Reading," p. 205.

In the second volume of Churchwardens'
Accts. p. 250, is the following :—
"12 July, 1646.
The day & yeare aboue written,
Mʳ George Wooldridge, Maior
Mʳ Peter Burningham
Mʳ Richard Holloway
Mʳ John Webb
Were chosen Ruling Elders of the pochiall &
Congregationall Eldershipp of St. Lawrence in
Reading, according to the directions of the
Lᵈˢ & Coṁons assembled in Parliamēt &c."
(57 parishioners present, including Dʳ Pordage.)

1647. THOMAS GILBERT, M.A. The son of William
Gilbert, of Priss, in Shropshire: admitted
Student of Edmund Hall in 1629. M.A. in
1638. Became an "Independent." Resigned
1650. Afterwards rector of Edgemond, Salop,
from which he was ejected in 1660. Died
July 15, 1694, & was buried in the church of
St. Aldate, Oxford.

1651. SYMON FORD, D.D. Resigned 1659. Son of
Rich. Ford, of East Ogwell, Devon. By the
Worths, his mother's family, he was descended
from the Founder of Wadham College, Oxford.
Joined the Puritan party 1641. He married
Mrs Anne Thackham, of St. Mary's, Reading.
He was accounted an able scholar, an elegant
Latin poet, and a preacher of great eminence.

Register Henchman.

1671. Dec. 4.—JOHN BRASIER, of St. John's College,
B.D., by the death of *Tuer*, according to the
Bishop's register. It appears by Archbishop
Laud's Book that Tuer was restored in 1660.
He was buried, according to the parish register,
Oct. 1, 1671.

Register Ward.

1678. Jan. 6.—SARGENT HUGHES, of St. Mary Hall,
M.A., by the death of Brasier.

Register Burnet.

1688. June 11.—PHANNEL BACON, by the death of
Hughes. He was admitted of St. John's College
in 1669; M.A. Mar. 23, 1677; B.D. July, 1684.
Buried in St. Lawrence's Jan. 16, 1731-2, aged
80 years.

Register Hoadley.

1732. March 29.—EDWARD OWEN, by the death of
Bacon. He was M.A. Mar. 9, 1720; B.D.
Apr. 23, 1725; D.D. Mar. 29, 1729. Afterwards Vicar of Great Stoughton, Huntingdon-
shire.

1733. Oct. 16.—WILLIAM BOUDRY, by the resignation of

Owen. Born Dec. 11, 1700. Elected Scholar of St. John's from Merchant Tailors' School 1719; M.A. Apr. 10, 1727; B.D. May 17, 1732. Afterwards Rector of Checkendon, Oxon.

1747. Mar. 3.—THOMES SHUTE, by the resignation of Boudry. D.D. Dec. 1, 1742. Died August 19, 1762. Buried in St. Lawrence's. His tablet was erected near one of the south windows of the chancel. The eight bells were recast under his auspices in 1748, and two trebles added to the original octave.

1763. Nov. 25.—JEREMIAH NICHOLSON, by the death of Shute. M.A. 1749; B.D. 1755; D.D. 1759. Died July 18, 1771.

There is a small tablet to his memory on the north side of the altar, under a recess in the east respond in the chancel.

1772. Jan. 16.—JOHN NICHOLLS, by the death of Nicholson. M.A. 1749; B.D. 1755; D.D. 1760. Died June 25, 1788. His broken memorial now lies on the step ascending into St. John's chapel.

1788. Dec. 2.—JOHN GREEN, B.D.

1812. WILLIAM WISE, D.D. Died Oct. 14, 1883, aged 64 years.

1833. JOHN BALL, B.D. Died Dec. 17, 1865. Presented by St. John's College, Oxford.

PATRON.—*The Lord Bishop of Oxford.*

1865. LEWIN GEORGE MAINE, M.A., Vicar of Sowerby, Yorks., 1874.

1874. JOHN MELVILLE GUILDING, by exchange with the Rev. Lewin Geo. Maine.

Priests and Chaplains, not Vicars, whose names are recorded in the Church-wardens' Accounts.

1498. " It. rec. of SIR WIHM SYMMYS pish p^r)st of his gyfte to the church, iij^s iiij^d."

He was one of the sponsors with Richard

Clech and Mistress Smyth at the consecration of the great Bell " Harry" the same year.

1501-2. " It. rec. of wast of torchis at the berying of Sr JOHN HIDE vicar of Sonyng ij^s vj^d."

1502-3. " It. rec. at the burying of SIR JOHN PYMBER ij^s iiij^d."

1503-4. " It. payed to SIR THOMAS pisshe preste of Seynt Maryes for his labo^r in ryding to Newbery for Thomas Edard the clerke."

1507-8. " It. rec. of John Puncer for the grete bel at the buryng of SIR JOHN STYRY xij^d."
" For removyng of a nop m'lble stone & for the leyng of þ^e same on Sir John Styrys g^ave —(part of) xx^d." (Orig. p. 37.)
" It. rec. of John Pownser ffor the grete bell at Sir John is meynd xij^d."

1510-11. " It. rec. of Sr JOHN TENDALL in money found in the church ij^d."

1512-3. " It. payd for caryage of Sr THOMAS grete antiphoner to & fro the church at all dyvyne ss'vice to Wittm Longe for the yer viij^d."

1517 (Inventory). " It. a Cope of red silke w^t signes of the Son (sun), of the gifte of DAN ROB^t REYDNG, Monke."

1517. " It. a chesible of whit Damaske, w^t braunches of gold : the orfrey blew velwett w^t thappell of the gifte of JOHN THORNE, abbott of Redyng." (Inventory).

1519-20. " It. Ryngyng the knyll for Sr JOHN RICHEMOND, xij^d."

1523. " It. to Sr JOHN SMYTH for a q^art wages endyd at Crystmas xxxiij^s iij^d."

1524. " It. payd to S^r. RIC. BAYNTON for mendyng the grett organs at ij tymes iiij^s."

1524-5. " Repacõns of Sr Bayntons Chamber."
" It. payd for q^arts eveslath & lyme, vj^s iiij^d ob."
" It. for vij^c (700) laths and ix^c lath naylls, iij^s viij^d."
" It. for bord naylls, laths naylls, q^art & bords iij^s ix^d."
" It to the carpent ij dayes, xij^d."
" It. to Troll & his man for workmanshypp vij^s vj^d."

1527. "It. for the grave of SYR WILLIAM WRYGHT, vj^s vij^d."

1531-2. "Payd for ryngyng of Sr GEORGE FFOSTER'S knyll vj^d."

1533-4. "Rec. for the grave of SIR ROB^t HETH vj^s viij^d."

1535-6. "Costs don apon S^r NIC' Chamber."
     "For ffewtryng the drowȝght there xvj^d."
     "A key for the shopp dore ij^d."
     "Bryks to pave the hall xvij^d."
     "Payd for bordyng the walls there & for naylls therto viij^d."
     "Payd for iij busshells of stone lyme vj^d."
     "Payd to the Carpen^t for workmanshypp & for tymb ij^s vj^d."

1537-8. "Rec. for a Surples of Sr Niclius sold iij^s."
     "Payd for horse hire for SIR RIC. DEAN, iiij^d."

1547. "Paid to Sr Richard Deane for wagis allowed hym by the pisshe x^s."

1549-50. "Paid to Sr Ric. A-Deane for his yer^s wag^s xx^s."

1540-1. "Payd to FFATHER REYNOLDS for di yeres waygcs ended then viij^s viij^d."

1541-2. "Rec. for grave of Sr WILLIZ^m, chapleyn to Sir Williz^m Penyson, Knyght, vj^s viij^d."

1547. "Paid to Sr HARPER for wag^s allowed hym by the pishe, x^s."

1548. Paid to Sr Harper for his yer^s wag^s xx^s."

1549-50. Paid to Sr Harper for his yer^s wag^s xx^s."

1548. "Paid to S^r WIłłM WEBBE for his yer^s wag^s xx^s.

1549-50. "Paid to S^r Wiłłm Webbe for makyng & prykkyng of Songs iij^s iiij^d.

1556. "Paid to Sir Willm Webbe for the prests noble, vj^s viij^d."

1558. "Syr Willyam Webbes knyll xx^d."

1552. "Paied to SIR FARYNGTON for his wag^s xiij^s. iiij^d."

1558-9. "It. to SYR JOHN OF CAU')SHAM for xiij week^s servyce vj^s." A French priest served for one day this year.

1559. "To SIR THOMAS SEARLE xij^s vj^d."
     "To Mr THACKHAM for ij wekes servyce, v^s."
     (succeeded Julius Palmer as master of the Grammar school. *Vide* Coates, p. 331).

1567. " ' The gret bel '—In p^{r}mis of Thomas **Kenryck**
for A PRIESTS knell xx^d."

" Of Thomas Kenryck for ye prestes grave
vij^s viij^d."

1563. " Itm. that I (Will Duddelsoll) and Master Tylby
dyd gather toward the fyndynge of the
mynister Mr CROFT for v weekes xvij^s iij^d."

1564. " SYR JOHN RADLYE held a stable in Gutter
Lane."

Q

Sports, Pastimes, Mysteries, &c.

Church Ale.

The ancient records of St. Lawrence abound with references to the sports and pastimes of our ancestors. The various games and exhibitions appear to have been under the special patronage of the Churchwardens as the chief parochial officers in those days, and were resorted to by them as a means of obtaining money for the discharge of their annual liabilities. The commonest of these sports was the Morris Dance, which seems to have accompanied all other diversions. It was frequently joined to processions and pageants, and especially figured in the festivities and gambols of May Day. The following extracts supply many graphic details of a performance which requires but little mental effort to reanimate :—

1513. "It. payed for a hope (hoop) for the joyaunt and for ale to the Moreys dawnc]s on the dedicacön day iij^d.

"It payed to the Mynstrells for iiij days xxij^d."

1529. "It. for bells for the Morece daunces iij^s vj^d.

("These bells were attached to the elbows and points of the dress and specially to garters for the legs & ankles. . . . They were of unequal sizes and differently denominated, as the fore-bell, the second bell, the treble, the tenor, &c., and mention is also made of double bells."—Strutt, 224.)

"It. for iij hatts for the Morece dauncers vj^d.

"It. for ffyve ells of Canves for a cote for made Maryon at iij^d ob. the ell, xvij^d ob.

"It. for iij yerds of bockerham for the morece dauncers xij^d.

1530. "It. for a grosse of bells for the morece dauncers iij^s.

1541-2. "Payd for lyverys & payntyng the mores cotes xj^d.

1553. Debts—"It. uppon John Saunders, th'appells of the mores dauncers. He saith he delyued them to Mr Buklond."

> This relates to an inquiry made in Q. Mary's time regarding the alienation of church goods.

From the mention of Maid Marian it will at once appear that the Robin Hood play accompanied the Morris dance. The principal characters were Robin Hood, Little John, Will Stukeley, Maid Marian, Friar Tuck and Much the Miller's son, who seems to have played the Fool. This performance was especially associated with the festivities of May Day.

1498–9. "It. rec. of the gaderyng of Robyn Hod xix^s."

1501–2. "It. rec. of the May play callyd Robȳ Hod on the fayre day vj^s.

> "It. payed to mynstrells at the chosyng of Robyn Hod vj^d."

> "It. payd to Willm Stayner for ij^c (200) lyuays viij^d.
>> (The liveries were badges, ribbons, or other tokens worn by the performers.)

> "It. payed for cc lyveryes & c pynnys ayenst maydaye vj^d.

1501–2. "It. payed to Willm Stayn^r) for makyng vp of the maydens ban^r) cloth, viij^d.

1503–4. "It. rec. of the gaderyng of Robin Hod x busshells malt p^r)c v^s. (for the brewing of the church ale).

> "It. rec. of the gaderyng of the same Robyn Hod 1 bȝ of whete p̄c, xij^d.

> "It. rec. of the gaderyng of the seid Robyn Hod in money, xlix^s.

> "It. payed to an harp on the church holy day, iiij^d.

> "It. payed for bred & ale to Robyn Hod & hys cōpany the 5 day, iiij^d.

> "It. payed for a cote to Robyn Hod, v^s iiij^d.

> "It. payed to a Taberer on Philips Day & Jacob (May Day) for his wagis mete & drynk & bed, viij^d.

> "It. for mete & drynk to Robyn Hod and his cōpany xvj^d.

1503-4. "It. payed for fellyng & bryngyng home of the bow set in þᵉ m') cat place for settyng vp of the same mete & drynk, viijᵈ.

1505. "It. payed for the Bachelors dyn') & sop on the Mayday xviijᵈ.

"It. payed to Maisᵗ Clech for Robin Hods cote & his hosyn vjˢ vijᵈ—payed for lyueryes, xjᵈ.

"It. rec. of the maydens gaderyng at Whitson-tyde at þᵉ *tre* (tree) at þᵉ church dore, clerly ijˢ xjᵈ.

(Was this a May bower?)

"It. payed to Crystyan Bryll by the honds of Wittm Stamford for wyne to Robyn Hod of Handley & his cōpany, vjˢ.

"It. payed to the Taberer, vjˢ.

1506. "It. payed to Thomas Taberer on the dedicacōn day for his wagis mete and drynke, xᵈ.

"It. payed for a supper to Robyn Hod & his company when he cam from ffynchamsted, xviijᵈ.

1507-8. "It. rec. of the gaderyng of Robin Hod pley xvijˢ x .

"Payed to Mors son the harper, iiijᵈ.

1510. "It. receyvyd on Seynt Phylypp & Jacob day (May Day) for ij° stondyngs at þᵉ church porch, vjᵈ.

(This was the old south porch mentioned on page 151. The standings were for the spectators of the May Games.)

1529. "It. to the carpynᵗ for ij dayes to make a laddar of the May poole & for hys mete & drynk, xiiijᵈ.

1557. "Itm. yᵉ gatheringe of yᵉ yonge folkes & maydens on Maydaye & at Whytsontyde—nichil (*i.e.*, nothing).

"Itm. for the yeough tree, iiijᵈ.

"Itm. for fetchinge the summar pole, ijᵈ.

"Itm. for a breakfast to the yonge men, xvjᵈ.

"Itm. for a quarter of veale & a qᵃrᵗ of lambe, iijˢ iijᵈ.

Note.—There is an almost exhaustive article on this game in Hone's "Every-Day Book," vol. i.

Corpus Christi.

The festival of Corpus Christi was instituted in honour of the Sacrament of the Holy Eucharist, and was commemorated on the Thursday next after Trinity Sunday. The ceremonies observed cannot be better described than by Googe, a hostile writer of the Reformation era :—

Then doth ensue the solemne feast
   of Corpus Christi Day,
Who then can shewe their wicked use
   and fond and foolish play.
The hallowed bread with worship great
   in silver pix they beare
About the churche or in the citie
   passing here and theare.
His armes that beares the same, two of
   the wealthiest men do holde:
And over him a canopey
   of silke and cloth of golde.
Christe's passion here derided is
   with sundrie maskes and playes.
Fair Ursley, with her maydens all
   doth passe amid the wayes.
And valiant George with speare thou killest
   the dreadfull dragon here,
The devil's house is drawne about
   wherein there doth appere
A wondrous sort of damned spirites
   with foule and fearfull looke.
Great Christopher doth wade and passe
   with Christ amid the brooke.
Sebastian full of feathered shaftes
   the dint of dart doth feele.
There walketh Kathren with hir sworde
   in hand, and cruel wheele.
The Challis and the singing Cake
   with Barbara is led,
And sundrie other pageants playde
   in worship of this bred. . . . .
The common ways with bowes are strawde
   and every streete beside,
And to the walles and windowes all
   are boughes and braunches tide.
The monkes in every place do roame,
   the nonnes abroad are sent,

The priestes and schoolmen lowd do rore,
   some use the instrument.
The straunger passing through the streete
   uppon his knees doth fall,
And earnestly uppon this brede
   as on his God, doth calle. . . . .
A number grete of armed men
   here all this while do stand,
To look that no disorder be
   nor any filching hand.
for all the church goodes out are brought
   which certainly would be
A bootie good, if every man
   might have his libertie.

HONE, i. 743.

The Religious Plays, termed "Mysteries," or dramatic representations of Scripture Histories, were celebrated on this festival. York, Coventry, and Chester were especially famous for these performances, which were enacted in sections by the various trade guilds of those places. The Coventry Mysteries abound in stories from the Apocryphal Gospels engrafted on the New Testament narrative. The Chester plays adhere in their plot more closely to the Scripture story.

Henry VII. was entertained one Sunday when at dinner at Winchester Castle by the play of "Christ's Descent into Hell," performed by the choir boys of Hyde Abbey and St. Swithun's Priory there.

Dugdale, in his "History of Warwickshire," published in 1656, writes, that "the Coventry pageants were acted with mighty state and reverence by the Grey Friars, who had theatres for the several scenes, very large and high placed upon wheels, and drawn to all the eminent parts of the city for the better advantage of spectators." The play contained the principal stories in the Old and New Testaments, composed in old English rhythm. The original may be seen in the British Museum (Cotton, Vest. D. viij.), entitled "Ludus Corporis Christi," or "Ludus Coventriæ."

The Chester Mysteries were performed by the trading companies of the city.

"Every company had its pagiante or parte consisting of a high scaffolde with two rowmes, a higher and a lower, upon four wheeles. In the lower they apparelled them-

selves, in the higher rowme they played, being all open on
the tope, that all behoulders might heare and see them.
The places where they played them was in euery streete.
They beganne first at the Abay gates, and when the
pagiante was played, it was wheeled to the High Crosse
before the, mayor, and so to euery streete; and so euery
streete had a pagiante playing before them till all the
pagiantes for the daye appointed were played, and when
one pagiant was neer ended, worde was brought from streete
to streete, that soe the might come in place therof exceding
orderlye, and all the streetes had their pagiant afore them
all at one tyme playing togeather, to se which playes was
greate resorte, and also scafolds, and stages m^{n}de in the
streetes in those places where they determined to playe
their pagiants." (Extract given by Hone, i. 757.)

Drake, in his " History of York" (vol. ii. edit. 1785), gives
out of the city registers many curious particulars of the
city pageants held there in the reign of Henry V.

In 1415 the Armourers represented Adam and Eve—an
angel with a spade and distaff assigning them labour.

The Fishmongers, Mariners, &c., set forth Noah in the
Ark, with his wife and three sons, with divers animals.

The Bookbinders—Abraham sacrificing his son Isaac—
with a ram, a bush, and an angel.

Vestment makers and skinners—The Triumphal Entry
—Jesus on an ass with its foal. The twelve Apostles following—six rich and six poor men—with eight boys bearing
branches of palm-trees, crying, "Blessed is He," &c.,
Zacchæus ascending a sycamore-tree.

The following is an extract, slightly modernized, from the
representation of Christ's appearance to His disciples in
the upper room after His resurrection—and the incredulity
of St. Thomas. (Corpus Christi Play, York. 1415.)

> *Peter.*—Welcome, Thomas! where hast thou been ?
> For wit thou well withouten ween
> Jesus our Lord then have we seen
> On ground here gone.
> *Thomas.*—What say ye ? Man ! alas for teyne (*sorrow*),
> I trow ye mang (*wander mentally*).
> *John.*—Thomas, truly that is not to layne (*conceal*),
> Jesus our Lord is risen again.
> *Thomas.*—Do-way ! your tales are but a train
> of fools unwise.

For he that was so fully slain
  how should he rise ?
James.—Thomas, really he is our Life,
  That tholed the Jews, his flesh rise ;
  He let us feel his wounds five
   That Lord, very.
Thomas.—That trow (*believe*) I not, so mote I thrive
   What ye so say.
 Peter.—Thomas, we saw his wounds wet,
  How he was nailed through hands and feet
  Honey and fish with no he ate,
   That body free.
Thomas.—I lay my life it was some spirit
   Ye wened was he.
 John.—Nay, Thomas, then he is misgone.
  For why ? he bade us everyone
  To grip him grathly, blood and bone,
  And flesh to feel.
  Such things, Thomas, have spirits none,
   That knowst thou well.
Thomas.—Now, fellows, let be your fare (*proceedings*)
  Till that I see that body bare,
  And syne my fingers put in there
  Within his hide,
  And feel the wound the spear shear (*cut* or *tore*)
  Right in his side.
  Ere I shall trow no tales between.
James.—Thomas, that wound then have we seen.
Thomas.—Yea, ye wot never what ye mean,
  Your wits ye want,
  Think no sin thus me to teyn (*vex*)
  And fill with traunts (*tricks*).
 Jesus.—Peace, and rest be unto you !
  And, Thomas, tente to me take you
  Put forth thy fingers to me now :
  My hands you see
  How I was nailed for man's prow
  Upon a tree.
  Behold my wounds are all bleds and
  Here in my side put in thy hand
  And feel this wound and understand
  That it is I.
  And be no more so mistroward (*unbelieving*),
  But trow truly.

Thomas.—My Lord! My God! full well is me!
    Ah, Blood of price! blest might thou be!
    Mankind in earth, behold and see
    This blessed blood!
    Mercy, Lord, now ask I thee
    With main and mood.
  Jesus.—Thomas, for thou hast seen this sight
    That I am risen, as I thee hight (*called*):
    Therefore trow that every like wight (*person*)
    Blest be they ever,
    That trows wholly in my rising right
    And saw it never.
    My "brethren," "friends," now forth in fere
      (*company*)
    Over all in every country sere (*many*).
    My rising both far and near
    Preached shall be,
    And my blessing I give you here
    And this menye (*company*).

With this introduction the following extracts from the Churchwardens' book will be more intelligible :—

1498. " It. rec. of the gaderyng of a stage play xvij^s.
1507. " It. rec. of the Sonday afore Bartylmastyde for the pley in the forbery xxiij^s viij^d. (S. Barthol. 24 August, about half-way through the Trinity Season.)
" It. paied for a lode of Aldren polls xij^d.
" It. paied a cart for carying off pypys & hogshedds in to the forbury ij^d.
" It. paied to the Laborers in the forbury for setting vp off the polls for the schaphold ix^d.
" It. paied to the Bere-man for ber for þ^e pley yn þ^e forbury x^d.
" It. paied to Roberd Lynacre for havyng awey off all man') of things owȝt off the Forbury.
" It. paied for brede ale & bere y^t longyd to ye pleye in the forbury ij^s vj^d.
" It. paied for j ell q^{a}rt of crescloth for Adam for to make j peyr of hosyn & j ell for a dowblett x^d.
" It. paied for course canvass to make xiij capps wth the makyng & wth the hers (ears) therto longyng, ij^s iiij^d.

1507. " It. paied for ij ells di of crescloth for to make
Eve a cote x^d.

> (The crescloth was a fine linen material—
> the garments of our first parents were pro-
> bably made very close-fitting, and stained
> flesh-colour.)

" It. paied for ij qweyer of pap for the pagentts v^d.

" It. paied for dyed flex iij^{li}—v^d (for wigs for the
performers.)

" It. paied for the makyng of a dublett of lethur
& j peyr off hosyn off lethur agaynst Corp⁹
Xpi day viij^d.

"It. paied to Henry Peynt for hys labo^r þ^e
Korp⁹ Xpi day xx^d."

1509. "It. payed for the tymber & naylis and the werke-
manschip of the fframe ffor the canopye and
ffor whyte lyre ffor the same canopye x^d.

" Itm. payed for xij thredyn poyntys for to
ffasten the same canopy to the fframe j^d.

" It. payed for iij new stavys and for the payntyng
of the hole (*whole*) iiij stavys ffor to bere the
seyd canopy xij^d.

1512. " It. payed to Robt Slan for wasting of the *Taylours
torchis* on Corpus X^t day iij^d.

1539. " Rec. of the *Shomakers* for wex to ther lights v^s."

> Here we find as usual the trade guilds taking
> their part in these performances. (See *Altars*
> of *St. Blaise, St. Thomas*, and *St. Clement*.)

The King Play.

This was a representation of the visit of the Eastern
sages (supposed to be *Kings*) to the infant Saviour. It
was clearly an " out-of-door" performance, usually terminating in a " church ale" and a supper. The names of these
monarchs are said to have been Gaspar, Melchior, and Bel-
thasar; but other traditions name them differently. Cressy
(quoted by Hone) tells us that the Empress Helena, who
died about the year 328, brought their bodies from the
East to Constantinople, from whence they were transferred
to Milan, and afterwards, in A.D. 1164, on the capture of
Milan by the Emperor Frederick, presented by him to the
Abp. of Cologne, who put them in the principal church of

that city, where (says Cressy) they are celebrated with great veneration."

W. Traheron, in his translation of Pedro Mexia's " History of the Roman Emperors," writes :—

" The reliques and bodies of saints which were in the citie (of Milan) and held in great account here (Fred. Barbarossa, Emperor) divided amongst the Bishops and prelates which were there with him ; of which the three Kings, which came out of the East to adore Christ in Bethlehem, were given to the Archbishop and Cathedrall Church of *Colen*, where (it is said) they are at this day." (1560).

James Philip, in his " Supplementum Chronicarum" (fol. 227, edit. 1486), writes :—" But a certain Rudolph, then Abp. of Cologne, being present with the Emperor, and assisting at this overthrow, seized the bodies of the three Magi which Eustorgius, Bp. of Milan, had a long time previously translated from Constantinople, and carried them with great joy to his own city, as is related by Vincentius."

There is a very ingenious note in Man's " History of Reading," in which he derives " Kings of *Colen*" from " *Coley*," a district of Reading ! ! ! In Hone's " Every-Day Book" (i. 46) there is an account from Du Cange of the Feast of the Star, or Office of the Three Kings, anciently performed by the clergy *within* the church on the Feast of the Epiphany.

1498–9. " Itm. payed for horse mete to the horssys for the Kyngs of Colen on May Day, vj^d.

" Itm. payed to mynstrells the same day, xij^d.

1502–3. " It. rec. of the Kyng play, xj^s.

1507–8. " It. payed for carying of a bough for the King play at Whitsontyde, iiij^d.

" It. payed to the taberer at Whyssontyde for his labo^r, iiij^s viij^d.

1514–5. " It. payd for a Kyltherkyn of bere ayēst Wytsontyde, xvj^d.

" It. payd for a dosen of good ale & iij galons of peny ale to Richard Turner, xx^d.

" It. payd for cariage of the tre at Witsontyde, vj^d.

1516–7. " It. of the yong men for the gatheryng at the Kyng play, xxiij^s.

" It. of the tree of the Kyng play late stondyng in the m ,catt place, xij^d.

1519.   " It. paid to Thomas Taberer for the Kyng pley at Whitsontide, x⁸.

"It. for his mete & drynk at Thom⁸s Barbors.

1539.   " Payd for watchyng the sepulcr & for Colen, x^d.

1540-1. " Rec. of the Kyng game this yere, iij^ll viij⁸.

1557.   " Itm. the saide churchwardens gatheringe at ye Kyngale in the Whytsontyde at the church ale suppars, xlviij⁸."

The following may perhaps illustrate the method in which this King Play was performed with reference to type and prophecy. One of the ancient painted windows of Canterbury Cathedral is divided into seven stages, each containing three pictures. The first illustrates the visit of the Magi.

1. Balaam riding on an ass. (*Type.*)

> Over his figure in the glass is inscribed the word 'BALAAM'. The surrounding inscription is "ORIETVR STELLA EX IACOB ET CONSVRGET VIRGO DE ISRAEL." Here are type and prophecy combined.

2. Three wise men riding. (*Antitype.*)

> They seem to be in doubt of the way. Over them is the *Star*—indicated in Balaam's prophecy.

3. The prophet Isaiah standing near a gate leading into the city.

> By his head is the word 'YSA'. The inscription is 'AMBVLABVNT GENTES IN LVMINE TVO ET REGES IN SPLENDORE ORTU VENIABANT.'

The subject is continued in the next three pictures.

> The first has Pharaoh, refusing to be convinced of the Divine Commission of Moses, in spite of the column of fire leading Israel.
>
> The second has the antitype—Herod refusing to be convinced by the star which led the Magi.
>
> The third has the conversion of the Heathen, and following Christ the light.
>
> STELLA MAGOS DVXIT ET AB EOS HERODE REDVXIT. Under this—
>
> SIC SATHANAM GENTES FVGIVNT TE CHRISTE SEQVENTES.

"Caymes Pageaunt.'

Fuller, in his "Church History" (vi. i. 14.) writes—" Wick-liffe constantly inveigheth against Friars under the name ' CAIM,' which he thus explains :—

C = 'C' armelites,
A = 'A' ugustinians,
I = 'I' acobins or Dominicans,
M = 'M' inorites or Franciscans."

This pageant probably derives its name from these four orders of Friars, who were the principal performers. If not, the Play of Kayme can only have been another name for that of ' Robin Hood,' whose grandfather, Ralph Fitz Ooth, was Earl of *Kyme*.

1512. " It. rec. in money at the play of Kayme, x^s vj^d.
1515. " It. payd for nayles to Caymes pageaunt in the m^t]cat place, iij^d."
These nails seem to imply the use of a scaffold.

The Passion Play.

This name sufficiently indicates its character. It was a representation of the trial, sufferings, and crucifixion of our Blessed Lord, performed apparently for the most part on the Rood Loft in the church.

1505. " It. payed to the clerks for syngyng of the passion on Palme Sonday in ale j^d."
1507. "It. paied to Sybel Darling for nayles for the Sepulcre & for rosyn to the *resurrecyon pley* ij^d ob." (The resin was undoubtedly for the burst of light or illumination at the moment of the Resurrection.)
1508. " It. payed to Willm Poo vnder sexton for carying & recarying of bords to the church for the *pageunt of the Passion* on Est^r] monday & for swepyng of the church at the same tyme viij^d." It is quite clear from this entry that the Resurrection Play must have followed that of the Passion Play.

1509. " Itm. payed ffor the caryage off the Burdys ffor the
      pageant on Estyr monday j^d.
      " Itm. payed for iij baner pollis v^s iiij^d.

1512. " Itm. for a q^arte of Malmesey to the clerks on
      Palme Sonday iiij^d.

1524. " It. for drynk *in the rood loft* vppon Palme
      Sonday.

1534. " Payd for a q^arte of basterd for the Passion apon
      Palme Sonday iij^d.

1533-4. " Payd to Mr Laborne for reformyng the Resur-
      recon Play viij^d iiij^d.

1535. " Payd to Sr Laborne for a boke of the resurrecon
      play—for a q^ure of paper & for byndyng
      therof ix^s x^d.

1540-1. " Payd for a quarte of Malmesey for the clerks
      vppon Palme Sonday iiij^d.

  „   " Payd to Loreman for playing the pphet on Palme
      Sonday. ij^d."

      (One great feature in these old Scripture
      plays was the arrangement of type and prophecy
      followed immediately by their antitype or
      fulfilment. Loreman performed the Old Tes-
      tament shadows as a prophetic intimation of
      the next scene taken from the New Testament.
      This is the plan still pursued in the Passion
      Play of Ober Ammergau. (*See under King Play.*)

1541. " Payd for bred, ale & beare apon Palme Sonday
      for syngyng the passion iiij^d.

1549. (2 Ed. VI.) " Paid for a q^arte of wyne on Palme
      Sonday at *Redyng* the Passion iiij^d." (This can
      only allude to the recitation of the Gospel set
      forth in the 1st Prayer Book of Ed. VI.—
      which for Palm Sunday included the whole of
      the xxvi. chap. of St. Matthew, and the xxvii.
      chapter to the 57th verse.)

" Ibock Ciſe" and " Ibock Moneẏ."

" Hock." A.S. Heah = high. High tide or festival, the
time of Easter.

On the Monday and Tuesday in Easter week was commemorated the massacre of the Danes on St. Brice's Day,
1002. Collections were then made by the churchwardens

in most parishes in England. Hock Monday was specially
set apart for the men, and Hock Tuesday (the principal
day) for the women. On both days the men and women
alternately with great merriment intercepted the public
roads with ropes impounding passengers in their folds, and
only releasing them on the payment of a fine. The ladies
always appear to have been more successful than the men
on these occasions.

It was also the custom in some parts of England for the
men to lift or hoist the women, either in their arms or in a
chair, between 9 and 12 on Monday morning, and on the
following day at the same time for the women to hoist the
men—a rude method of illustrating the Easter commemoration.

1498-9. "It. rec. of Hok money gaderyd of women xxˢ.
    "It. rec. of Hok money gaderyd of men iiijˢ."
In 1501 the women gathered 17ˢ 6ᵈ and the men 5ˢ 4₄.
In 1546-7 the women raised 31ˢ 3ᵈ and the men 8ˢ 4ᵈ.
29 H. VIII. "Rec. at the ffirst play in East weke
    xxiijˢ ijᵈ.
    "Rec. at the second play xjˢ ijᵈ."

Church Ale.

"For the church ale two young men of the parishe are
yerely chosen by their last foregoers to be Wardens, who,
devidingthe taske, make collection amongthe parishioners of
whatsoever provision it pleaseth them voluntarily to bestow.
This they employ in brewing, baking, & other acts against
Whitsuntide : vpon which holydayes the neighbours meet at
the Church House, and there merily feed on their own
victuals, contributing some petty portion to the stock which
by many smalls, groweth to a meetly greatness : for there
is entertayned a kinde of emulation between these wardens, who by his graciousnes in gathering, and good
husbandry in expending, can best advance the church's
profit.

"Besides, the neighbour parishes at those times lovingly
visit one another, and this way frankly spend their money
together. The afternoones are consumed in such exercises
as olde and yong folke (hauying leysure) doe accustomably
weare out the time withal.

"When the feaste is ended, the Wardens yeeld in their

account to the parishioners, and such money as exceedeth
the disbursements is layd up in store to defray any extra-
ordinary charges arising in the parish or imposed on them
for the good of the country, or the Prince's service, neither
of which commonly gripe so much, but that somewhat still
remaineth to couer the purses bottom." (Carew's " Survey
of Cornwall," 1602 ; repr. 1723.)

1506. " It. payed to the same Macrell for makyng clene
        of the Church agaynst the day of drynking in
        the seid Church iiij^d.

" It. payed for flessh spyce and bakyng of pasteys
agaynst the said drynkyng ij^s ix^d ob.

" It. payed for ale at the same drynking xviij^d.

" It. payed for mete & drynke to the Taberer ix^d."

General Index.

(The asterisk (*) indicates a recurrence on the same page.)

A

ABBEY, Charles I. at, 94
  ,,   Foundation of, 8
  ,,   GATEWAY, 2
  ,,   Queen at the, 93
  ,,   the, 192
Adam and Eve, 233, 234
Addams, 142
Adene, or "Dene," q. v., 11
Ades, 185
Adwell, 176
AGLOTTS, or Aylotts of silver, 112
Alcock, organist, 63
Aldworth, old pulpit at, 54
  ,,   family, 191, 193, 194, 197
ALE, for the clerks on Palm Sunday, 56
  ,, for the ringers, 92, 93
  ,, Church ale, 239
Aleward, 12
Alexander, 198, 191
Allesaunder, 191
ALL HALLOW TIDE, 56, 57
Alloway, 192
ALMSHOUSES of John a Larder, 172
ALTAR CLOTHS, list of, 106
ALTARS, 25–48
Alvyngton, 136
Aman, 187
AMIENS, great bell at, 127
Andrew, 101, 195, 176, 188, 189, 190, 191, 194
Andrews, 58, 167, 187, 218
ANGELUS, the, 33
Anne, St., 111
Annesley, 167
ANTHONY CROSSES, 106
Apledreham, 8
APOSTLES, figures of the twelve, 27
Appleford, 217
Appowell, 190
ARBORFIELD, 184
ARCHES, nave, 13, 70
  ,, new, 14

Aris, 156
Arlatt, 192 ·
ARMORIAL BEARINGS in nave, 14
   ,,   ,,   on tower, 17
   ,,   ,,   in Knolly's transept, 19
Arnold, 186
Ashendon, 172
ASSUMPTION OF OUR LADY, 111
ASTEN Church, 176
Athelard, 13
Atkinson, 179
AUMBRYES, 16, 27
Aumerie, 217
Austwick, 167
Avis, 191*
Awberry, 128, 155
AYLETTS, 112
Ayscough, Bishop of Salisbury, 17

B

Backbye, or Barkbye, organ-builder, 59, 60, 61
Bacon, 200, 221
Bagley, 80
Baigant, 158
Baker, 22
Bakestur, 85
Ball, 163, 222
BANGOR, Brief for, 213
Banister, 192
BANNERS, 109
BAPTIST, ST. JOHN, altar of, 36
   ,,   ,, chapel, 36, 175
   ,,   ,, stalls in, 39, 170
   ,,   ,, Hospital, 11, 39
   (see "St. John's Chapel")
Barber, 188, 191, 190
Barbour, 22, 105, 115
Barentyne, 138
Barfote, 34, 103, 174,* 189, 190
Barker, 30, 190

R

Bryssele, 12

Buck, 13, 189

Buckland, 30, 32, 40, 118, 190, 192, 227

BUCKS, *Briefs for*
,, Aylesbury, 216
,, Buckingham, 214
,, Colnbrook, 215
,, Chalfont St. Peter's, 207
,, Little Brickhill, 208
,, North Marston, 205
,, Orwood, 214
,, Stoney Stratford, 205
,, Wycombe, 210
,, Wyradisbury, 205

Buckworth, 188

Budd, 12, 192

Bull, 118

Bullinger, 62

Bun, 79

Bunting, 186

Burden, 199

Bureton, 27, 29, 135, 180, 181, 189, 191

Burges, or Burgeys, 80, 191, 192,* 198,* 199, 219

BURGHFIELD Church, 171

Burlei, or Burley, 187

Burningham, 144

BURTON-ON-TRENT, 163

Burwey, 180

BURY, THE, 6

Bush, 192

Butler, 30, 43,* 50, 118, 140-143, 162, 185, 189, 190, 191, 192, 194, 200

Buttell, 142

Button, 148

BUTTS, the parish, 68

Byfield, organ-builder, 63

Byggs (*see* Bigge), 46, 191, 200

Byrd, or Bird, q.v., 190

Byrcham, 193

C

Calcroft, 75

Calton, 80

Cam, 219

CAMBRIDGES., *Briefs for*
,, Barnwell, 217
,, Bottisham, 209
,, Conington, 216
,, Campshall, 214
,, Cherry Hinton, 214
,, Grantchester, 204
,, Guilden Morden, 217

CAMBRIDGES., *Briefs for (continued)*
,, Little St. Andrews, 211
,, Milbourn, 215
,, Swaresey, 212

CAMPANILE, 13

CANDLEMAS DAY, 52

CANDLESTICKS, 26, 34, 37, 42

CANOPY over high altar, 26, 108

CANTERBURY, a window at, 236

Capper, 77

Carden, 197

CARDIGAN, Wales, 207

Cardmaker, the, 192

Carpenter, 22, 32, 40, 77, 174, 185, 188,* 189

Carter, bellfounder, 77, 80, 86, 87, 193
,, Silvanus, a brief for, 209

Casse, 122

CASTLE, Reading, 3

Cater, 191

CATHARINE, ST., 125
,, play of, 37
,, guild of, 31, 45
,, lights of, 36, 53
,, WHEEL hotel, 37

Cave, 187

CAVERSHAM, 86, 171, 224

Cawarden, 44

Cawood, 22, 190

CAYME'S PAGEANT, 237

CENTRES for arches, 14

Cerne, vicar, 138, 157

Chamberlayn, 80, 190

CHANCEL arch, 15
,, roof, 22, 70
,, monuments in, 140

Chandler, vicar, 219

CHAPLAINS, list of, 222

Chapman, 185, 191

CHARDFORD, 136

Charlton, 197

CHARTER HOUSE, London, 135, 138

Chaundler, 12, 22

Chauntrell, 191

CHAUNTRY LANDS, 30, 31, 78, 118

CHECKENDON, Oxon, 222

CHEESE ROW, 174

CHELSEY Abbey, 8

Cheney, a mason from Hampton Court, 14, 24

CHESHIRE, *Briefs for*
,, Ashton-super-Merly, 207
,, Backford, 215
,, Barnston, 211
,, Bickley, 211
,, Burton, 212
,, Chester, 209, 212
,, Christleton, 217

DANISH INVASION, and the entrenchment, 2, 3
Darling, 42, 77, 186, 187, 188
Darlyngton, 30
DAVID'S, ST., **175**
Davy, 191
Dayne, 185
Dayntre, **77**
Deane, 20, 133, 136, **164**
,,   Ric. a-, 31, 33, **224**
,,   Alice, 111, 186
Deddlesall, or Duddlesale, 193*
DEDICATION of the original church, 5; festival of, 91
Delamere, 12
Dell, 198
DENBIGHS., *Briefs for*
,,   Denbigh, **215**
,,   Holt, **213**
,,   Llandulas, **215**
,,   Ruthin, 209
,,   Wrexham, 209, 210
Denison, or Dennison, 81, 120, **219**
Dennys, 192
Depeford, **217**
Derby, Wm., M.P., **22**
,,   Alderman of London, 105, 113
,,   Earl of, 182
DERBYS., *Briefs for*
,,   All Saints, Derby, 209
,,   Ashbourn, **211**
,,   Bakewell, **213**
,,   Chapel-in-le-Frith, **215**
,,   Harsto . . . . , **210**
,,   Ilkeston, **213**
,,   Mapleton, **211**
,,   Tibshelf, **215**
,,   Wirksworth, **214**
DEVONS., *Briefs for*
,,   Crediton, **214**
,,   Gt. Torrington, 205, **214**
,,   Heavitree, 206
,,   Ottery St. Mary, 210
,,   South Molton, **205**
,,   St. Mary's, 208
,,   Witheridge, 208
Dewbury, **79**
Deyer, 12
DISPENSARY, Reading, **113**
Dixon, a singer, 30
Dodgson, 117, 189, 190
Dodson, 186,* 187,* 188, 191, 200
DOMESDAY, account of, Reading, **6**
DORSETS., *Briefs for*
,,   Blandford, 209, **216**
,,   Dorchester, 209
,,   East Morden, **214** ;
,,   Frampton, 210

DORSETS., *Briefs for (continued)*
,,   Gillingham, 204
,,   Newton Castle, **216**
Douglas, 148
Downar, 192
Drayton, vicar, **217**
DRINK for ringers, 92
,,   on a Coronation Day, in 1612, 93
Drover, 12
Duddlesoll, 38, **46**, **58**, 192, 193 (*see* Deddlesal)
Dudley, R., Earl of Leicester, 75
,,   John, Earl of Warwick, 75
,,   William and Elizabeth, 145
Dukinfield, **165**
Dunsdale, **64**
Dunster, 29
DURHAM CO., *Briefs for*
,,   Darlington, 205
,,   Hartlepool, **211**
,,   Stockton, 207
,,   Sunderland, 210
Dwyght, **188**
Dyer, 12, 22, **77**

Œ

Eades, 83, 144
EARLY HISTORY of the parish, 1
,,   Manor, **7**
EDGMOND, Salop, **221**
EDINBURGH, *Brief for*, 206, 207
Edmonds, 34, 60, 68, 174, 193, 200
Edmund, 22, 90, 191
EDWARD, ST., **107**
Edwards of the Royal Stable, 187, 190
ELDERS, RULING, election of, 220
Elizabeth, Queen of Henry VII., 114
,,   Queen, her birth, 92
,,   at St. Lawrence's Church, 79, 92, 93
Elkins, 150
Elly, **164**
Ellys, 189, 190
ELY, ISLE OF, *Briefs for*
,,   Chatteris, 205
,,   Littleport, 206
,,   Wisbeach, 210
ENGLAND, arms of, 109
ENGLEFIELD, 3, 179
,,   Mr., **183**
Englefold, 189
EPITAPHS in the church, 128

Roys, 190
Rudge, 192
Russell, 87, 189
Ryder, 192, 197
Rysbye, 187, 189
Rythe, 22
Ryther, 192

S

Sacering, or Sacring, 26
Sadeler, 172, 175, 185, 188
Sales of church goods, 27, 53
Salmon, 167
Salter, 192
Sampford, Vicar of St. Giles', 145
160
Sanctus bell, 92
Saunders, 28, 29, 50, 53, 58, 121,
122, 124, 171, 190, 191, 194, 200,
227
Sawyer, 43, 193
Sayntmond, 178 (? Sentman), 191
Sayntmore, 30, 78, 200
Schyppelake, 218
Scochon, 29
Scots, King of, 92
Seakes, 148
Seale, Surrey, 44
Seamen, widows of, Brief for, after
the storm of 1703, 205
Searle, 224
Seats, 77-79
,, broken, 94
Sedilia, 16, 27
Segar, 192
Segesmund, organ-builder, 61
Semper, 187
Sentence, 155
Sepulchre altar, 41
,, ,, ornaments of, 42
,, the, 53, 107, 112
Sepulchre's, St., 137
Serne, 101, 218
Service books, 31, 32, 101
Sewdary, or maniple, 115
Sexton, the, 23
Sharpe, 186
Shaw, 190, 192*
Shefford, 177
Sheford, 184
Sheperege, 183
Shields in the nave, 14
Shinfield, 171
Shiplake, 171, 179, 180

Shropshire, Briefs for
,, Albrington, 214
,, Adderley, 208
,, Bowley, 214
,, Broseley, 206
,, Chelmarsh, 210
,, Condover, 210
,, Ensden, 211
,, Fitts Church, 212
,, St. Germains, 204
,, Hinstock, 212
,, Idsall, 210
,, Kemberton, 212
,, Leighton, 209
,, Monford, 216
,, Newport, 212, 213
,, Quatford, 209
,, Ryton, 210
,, Shrewsbury, 204
,, Stanton Lacy, 205
,, Stockton, 205
,, Shipwash, 209
,, Shrawardine, 212
,, Townjay, 211
,, Wilcott, 211
,, Whitechurch, 208
Shrouded figures, 126
Shute, 89, 147, 222
Side altar, 48
Silver, 100
Simeon, 83
Simonds, 64
Singers, 30, 65
Singing bread, 49
Sippell, 63, 64
Sitting in church, 33
Skinner, 190
Slade, 54
Slithurst, 61,* 115, 190
Smith, 15, 46, 53, 60, 77, 87, 115,
165, 219, 223
Smyth, Ric., Gent., 29, 30, 50, 51, 53,
57, 100, 104, 105, 106, 107, 114
Smyzt, 22
Somersetshire, Briefs for
,, Bristol, 207
,, Pensford, 208
,, Whitefield, 216
,, Wincanton, 206
Sonning, 50, 171, 185
Southampton, 168, 172*
Southey, 184
Southstoke, 181
Spakeman, 187
Spencer, 63, 64
Spicer, 22, 133
Sports and pastimes, 226
Stable, the King's, 187

Wilcox, 194 (*see* Wylcox)
Wild, 75
Wilder, 139
Williams, 177, 190
Willizm, Sr., 224
WILLS, 168
WILTSHIRE, *Briefs for*
,, Cricklade, 214
,, Damerham, 212
,, Downton, 214
,, Erchfoot, 216
,, Fiddleton, 204
,, Kingswood, 212
,, Market Lavington, 214
,, Netherhaven, 204
,, Waddington, 216
WINCHESTER, 158
WINDING SHEETS, 125
WINDSOR, Berks
Wise, 104, 222
Wod, or Wood, "My Lord," 186
Wodeman Court, 22
Wodenet, 28, 86
Wodham, 138
WODEWOSES, what, 170
WOKYNGHAM, 171, 178, 196
Wolsey, Cardinal, 14
Wood, 60
Woodhatch, 171
WOOLCOMBERS and staplers, 39
Worcester, Thos., Abbot of Reading, 188
WORCESTERS., *Briefs for*
,, Bewdley, 206
,, Dudley, 216
,, Pershore, 215
,, Redmarley, 217
,, Worcester, All Saints, 217
,, Worcester, St. Nich., 215
WORTHY, Hants, 158
Wray, 191
Wright, 33, 175, 187, 188,* 224

Wyar, 189, 191
Wye, 179
Wylcock, 159, 160, 187
Wylcox, 29, 103, 186, 187, 194
Wyld, 187
Wylmer, 143
Wynchedon, 217
Wynyet, 188

Y

Ydefisch, 22
YEOMEN of the King's crown, 115
,, ,, chamber, 115
Yerpe, 191
YEW in church at Easter, 94
YORK, Extract from a Mystery Play performed there, 231
YORKSHIRE, *Briefs for*
,, Austerfield, 216
,, Beverley, 205
,, Dunnington, 204
,, Halifax, 214
,, Healthwaite, 210
,, Howden, 208
,, Igmanthorpe, 212
,, Kingston-on-Hull, 212
,, Kirk Deighton, 214
,, Market Rayson, 208
,, Tadmore, 208
,, Weatherley, 213
,, York, St. Olave's, 212
Young, 13, 98
YRINGSMED, 8

Z

Zouch, arms of, 136

THE END.

PRINTED BY BALLANTYNE, HANSON AND CO.
LONDON AND EDINBURGH

www.ingramcontent.com/pod-product-compliance
Lightning Source LLC
Chambersburg PA
CBHW020503270326
41926CB00008B/721